Writing Logically, Thinking Critically

"Our <u>real</u> first line of defense, wouldn't you agree, is our capacity to reason."

Writing Logically, Thinking Critically

2nd Edition

SHEILA COOPER

ROSEMARY PATTON

 LONGMAN

An imprint of Addison Wesley Longman, Inc.

New York • Reading, Massachusetts • Menlo Park, California • Harlow, England
Don Mills, Ontario • Sydney • Mexico City • Madrid • Amsterdam

Acquisitions Editor: Anne Elizabeth Smith
Project Coordination and text design: Ruttle, Shaw & Wetherill, Inc.
Cover Designer: Kay Petronio
Cover Illustration: Mark Rothko, Yellow, Blue on Orange, 1955. Oil on canvas. The
Carnegie Museum of Art, Pittsburgh: Fellows of the Museum of Art Fund, Women's
Committee of the Museum of Art, and Patrons Art Fund, 74.55.
Electronic Production Manager: Angel Gonzalez, Jr
Manufacturing Manager: Willie Lane
Electronic Page Makeup: Ruttle, Shaw & Wetherill, Inc.
Printer and Binder: RR Donnelley & Sons Company
Cover Printer: The Lehigh Press, Inc.

For permission to use copyrighted material, grateful acknowledgment is made to the
copyright holders on pp. 213–216 , which are hereby made part of this copyright page.

Library of Congress Cataloging-in-Publication Data
Cooper, Sheila, 1946–
    Writing logically, thinking critically / Sheila Cooper, Rosemary
Patton. -- 2nd ed.
        p.   cm.
    Rev. ed. of: Ergo. c1993.
    Includes index.
    ISBN 0-673-98069-3
    1. English language--Rhetoric.   2. Critical thinking.   3. Logic.
I. Patton, Rosemary.   II. Cooper, Sheila, 1946–   Ergo.   III. Title.
PE1408.C5485   1996
808'.042--dc20   96-1470
                                                               CIP

ISBN 0-673-980693

345678910—DOC—999897

He who will not reason, is a bigot; he who cannot, is a fool; and he who dares not, is a slave.

—Lord Byron

A mind that is stretched to a new idea never returns to its original dimension.

—Oliver Wendell Holmes

The vital habits of democracy: the ability to follow an argument, grasp the point of view of another, expand the boundaries of understanding, debate the alternative purposes that might be pursued.

—John Dewey

Brief Contents

Contents

Writing Assignments

Preface

*Good Writing
is Good Thinking.*

The New York Times Magazine

We agree and embrace the corollary, good thinking is essential for good writing. More and more, experts admit that in this age of ever-expanding information, knowledge of facts alone will not serve. As futurist Heidi Toffler puts it, "Teach people how to think. There are no facts. Everything is open to interpretation." And long ago in 1914, Herbert Croly saw the importance of thinking critically when he described the purpose of his new magazine, *The New Republic,* as "less to inform or entertain its readers than to start little insurrections in the realm of their convictions."

With this second edition, we continue to promote such views. We have dropped the "Ergo" from the title, but *Writing Logically, Thinking Critically* is still designed as the central text in a course combining writing and critical thinking or in a course devoted to composition with an emphasis on argumentation. For independent readers interested in sharpening the logic and fluency of their prose, *Writing Logically* offers many practical strategies.

We expect instructors to change the sequence of chapters to suit the particular needs of a given class, to pick and choose as occasion demands. For some, the emphasis will fall on writing, for others, the exercises in logic will be valuable as well. We do not, as readers will notice, provide a reference of correct grammar and usage. Handbooks on these topics abound. As California writers, we still recognize a regional slant in some of our examples, but we feel that all the issues presented are sufficiently universal to interest readers in all parts of the country. To make the material more locally appealing, some may choose to supplement with additional selections or substitute other articles for the readings offered here.

CONTENT CHANGES

This new edition has given us the opportunity to update examples and exercises for relevancy and to add some fresh new cartoons. In response to helpful suggestions from those who have used the first edition, we have rearranged the sequence of some material to make what we think is a stronger, more accessible text. We offer a few words here to help you find old topics or identify additions.

We have reduced the original ten chapters to nine, with material from former Chapter 5, "Evaluating Arguments: Premises," distributed among earlier chapters. To improve the balance of critical thinking and writing instruction, we have moved the first section of Chapter 4, "Writing as a Process," to Chapter 1, where it provides immediate help to students as they embark on their first writing assignments. We have also addressed the importance of "world view" in the introductory discussion of critical thinking.

We have expanded Chapter 2, "Inference," to include a short introduction to writing about literature and added "The Story of an Hour" by early feminist Kate Chopin. Where literature is a major component of a composition class, this chapter can serve as a platform on which to build further readings.

In Chapter 3, "The Structure of Argument," we have added a discussion of the term "opinion" and included from other chapters the sections on argument and explanation and on writing summaries, where they can better relate to the analysis and reduction of arguments. Those of you familiar with the first edition will note that we have removed the section on diagramming arguments because of its technical features and apparently minimal carry-over to writing.

Chapter 4, with a major section moved to Chapter 1, is now in better balance with the rest of the text. Exercises and a sample essay have been brought up to date.

Chapters 5, 6, and 7, which cover informal deductive and inductive reasoning, have undergone only minor changes, with one assignment shifted and more relevant examples provided. While these chapters on reasoning are not essential for all writing classes, we and many other users of the text have found that the work on logic pays dividends for student writers. Chapter 8, "Logical Fallacies," reveals our efforts to update examples.

Chapter 9, previously Chapter 10, has a new title, "Language: Meaning and Style," which reflects the new emphasis on strategies for achieving a fluent, polished style in the overhauled "Application to Writing" section. We have also updated the appendix on research.

As before, we assume that *Writing Logically, Thinking Critically* will be most effective in classes where the students have already completed an introductory composition course. However, with more advanced writers or if supplemented with additional writing instruction, the text could serve in a freshman writing class. Some secondary school instructors have been enthusiastic about its success in their advanced composition classes.

PEDAGOGY

We include a number of collaborative activities to encourage an interactive aproach to learning. Most of the exercises and assignments can, in fact, be approached collaboratively. Writing assignments and exercises invite a broad range of responses that should cover the demands of writing across a diverse curriculum. In some exercises, to reassure students, we have starred selected examples and provided a list of possible answers at the end of the text.

ACKNOWLEDGMENTS

Once again, we owe many debts of gratitude. We continue to be grateful to our students, a few of whom are represented here and to whom we dedicate this text.

They too have helped us test, shape, and reflect upon the material of the first edition, and, with their enthusiasm and their questions, inspired us to grow with them in the rewarding enterprise of writing logically and thinking critically. We are now also indebted to those instructors who have commented on our book and helped us improve it. Our debt to colleague William Robinson remains. We are also grateful to Susan Bronstein and Richard Sammons for helpful suggestions.

Finally, we remain delighted and astonished that our friendship has flourished and grown through another round of critical collaboration.

Sheila Cooper

Rosemary Patton

Chapter
1

Thinking and Writing— A Critical Connection

It is doubtful whether a man [or woman?] ever brings his faculties to bear with their full force on a subject until he writes upon it.

—Cicero

*F*or more than 2000 years, thinkers and writers have commented on the close relationship between thinking and writing. It would hardly seem debatable that to write well we need to think clearly. And the evidence is strong for concluding that writing about our ideas can help to clarify them. Taking this notion a step further, many would argue that the act of writing can create ideas, can lead writers to discover what they think. Language, according to many scholars, gives birth to thought, and written language provides a way to refine our thoughts since, unlike speech, it can be manipulated until it accurately reflects our thinking.

THINKING MADE VISIBLE

Consider writing then as thinking made visible, as thinking in slow motion, a process whereby we can inspect and reflect on what we are thinking about. As novelist E. M. Forster put it, "How can I tell what I think till I see what I've said?" Roger Traynor, a former Chief Justice of the California Supreme Court, agreed when he spoke of writing and the law:

> I have not found a better test for the solution of a case than in its articulation in *writing*, which is *thinking at its hardest*.

Writing and thinking, when taken seriously, are not easy—a reality that led painter and critic Sir Joshua Reynolds to comment, "There is no expedient to which we will not resort to avoid the real labor of thinking." And many writers have groaned over the pain of writing. New York writer Fran Lebowitz takes an extreme position on the subject: "Writing is torture. It is very hard work. It's not coal mining, but it's work."

After visiting the Galapagos Islands in the 1830s, evolutionist Charles Darwin wrote to his sister from his ship, the *Beagle,* about the special challenge of reasoning on paper, the kind of writing we emphasize in this book.

> I am just now beginning to discover the difficulty of expressing one's ideas on paper. As long as it consists solely of description it is pretty easy; but where reasoning comes into play, to make a proper connection, a clearness and a moderate fluency, is to me a difficulty of which I had no idea.

THE POWER OF WRITING PERSUASIVELY

But, while writing and thinking may be difficult, mastery and success in both can be well worth the effort. We live in an increasingly complex society where clear writing is often essential. If we are not able to articulate a request, a complaint, or an endorsement in precise, forceful language, we may find ourselves settling for less than we need or deserve, or giving to others the right to impose their decisions on us. If we can't write a persuasive application, the job or graduate school position may go to someone else. Linguist Robin Lakoff, in her book, *Talking Power,* puts it this way:

> In a meritocracy such as ours, we believe that those who best demonstrate the ability to think and persuade should have the lion's share of power. Articulateness according to the rules goes a long way; and its possessors are assumed to possess intelligence and virtue as inseparable concomitants. People who say things right, who plead their cases well, will be listened to and their suggestions acted upon. They will make the money, win the offices, find love, get all the goodies their society has to give.

OUR MULTICULTURAL SOCIETY

It should be noted, however, that in a multicultural society such as ours, there are those who question our singular admiration for persuasive rhetoric, who look to less confrontational means of exploring issues and resolving differences. Seen through the eyes of a Japanese visitor, Yoshimi Ishikawa, who came here at age 18 and spent two years working and observing, the United States is a surprisingly violent nation. In his book, *Strawberry Road,* he claims that "the violent impression that America makes on foreigners is a result not just of its high crime rate but also of the one-sided nature of conversation here." But he too concludes that "the power to persuade and be eloquent are weapons one needs to survive in America." Whether a virtue or a weapon, the power of persuasion is seen as an asset in America today.

As you will discover in *Writing Logically,* we are inclined to share both Lakoff and Ishikawa's views and recognize that if we are to embrace the multiplicity of views represented in our culture we must avoid dogmatic, one-sided advocacy.

CRITICAL THINKING

If, as we maintain, there is a strong relationship between thinking clearly and writing well—if one skill strengthens the other—then integrating the two as a course of study makes sense. But what do we mean by "thinking clearly"? Poets and engineers, marketing experts and philosophers would find any number of differing applications for such a broad term. For our purposes we have found it helpful to narrow our focus and concentrate on the phrase *critical thinking.* This term has assumed a central position in both academic and public life and is variously defined today.

EXERCISE 1A

Defining Critical Thinking

Before you read further in this chapter, put this book aside, take a piece of paper and write a few sentences discussing what you think the phrase *critical thinking* means. If you do this in class, you may want to compare notes with other students.

Critical Thinking as Self-Defense

In most contexts today the term critical thinking means censorious or faultfinding, but it comes to us from the Greek *kriticos* and Latin *criticus,* meaning able to discern or separate. It is this sense of critical that we have in mind—discerning or discriminating; thought characterized by careful analysis and judgment. As student Denise Selleck once put it: "Thinking critically is the ability to understand a concept fully, taking in different sides of an issue or idea while not being swayed by the propaganda or other fraudulent methods used to promote it." She recognizes the importance of an open mind and and the element of self-defense implicit in critical thinking. In particular, the media and advertising, with which we are confronted daily, require the rigorous application of critical thinking if we want to be protected adequately from false claims, questionable judgments, and deceptive argument.

Take, for example, food packaging. Until recently, little scrutiny was given to extravagant and often deliberately misleading information about the fat content of many foods. Only the most discerning shopper could figure out where the truth lay when a frozen dinner was advertised on the front of the package as being 91 percent fat free (in weight), while the fine print on the back revealed it to be 20 percent fat free (in content). It took an act of Congress to protect us from this kind of duplicity. Similar deception has surrounded the word *light*, an undefined term used indiscriminately to suggest that a product is low in calories and healthy. (You will find more on definition and the precise use of language in Chapter 9.)

In the fall of 1989 and winter of 1990, the Philip Morris Companies, makers of cigarettes and other products, ran what were called by *Newsweek* the "Smokeless Cigarette" ads, a series showing celebrated public figures endorsing the Bill of Rights. Nowhere did the actual product—cigarettes—appear, either in print or image. These ads were designed for people like you—literate adults. The creators of such ads expect you to apply limited critical thinking at one level—to make the necessary connections—but to suspend such thinking at a crucial point. It's not surprising that the Philip Morris Company refused to grant permission for us to reprint these ads in this text.

We cannot be vigilant enough in our efforts to defend ourselves from those who would manipulate us, all too often for their personal gain.

An Open Mind

Another definition of critical thinking that also captures the spirit we hope to foster in this book comes from Richard Paul of Sonoma State University: "The disposition to think clearly and accurately in order to be fair." Like student Denise Selleck, Paul suggests the importance of developing an open mind, of listening attentively to the views of others.

But it is equally important to be aware of where your views come from. Cultures, subgroups within those cultures, and families within these groups tend to share what is called a *world view,* a set of assumptions about the world and the behavior of people in it. Without acknowledging that we hold such views, we may harbor prejudices about groups that cloud our thinking and restrict fair judgment. Many of these attitudes grow from the contexts of our lives that we take for granted—the opinions of parents and friends, our ethnic and religious backgrounds. Questioning our personal world view can be one of the most challenging steps in our growth as critical thinkers.

Where does the weakness in Jennifer's defense lie?

Profile of a Critical Thinker

If we examine the implications of Denise Selleck and Richard Paul's defin-itions, we can begin to formulate a profile of how a critical thinker might behave. Try a little self-analysis. Rate yourself according to the following checklist to discover how closely your critical thinking conforms to Paul's definition:

Do you automatically dismiss positions opposed to your own?

Do you take your own beliefs for granted without recognizing the need for support?

Do you deny that your beliefs could change?

Do you accept public information without question?

Do you recognize that some assumptions based on your world view need to be critically evaluated?

As this checklist implies, critical thinkers question their own beliefs and the sources of these beliefs as well as the beliefs of others, formulate well-reasoned arguments to support their beliefs, recognize the possibility of change in their beliefs, and express their beliefs in clear, coherent lan-guage. As a consequence, they stand a better chance of being both fair and reliable in the conclusions they reach and the actions they take and will find themselves better protected from those who seek to take advan-tage of them.

Sometimes a successful critical thinker must be able to hold two or more opposing views on an issue at once. For example, raising tuition at your college could be the only way to ensure current levels of instruction. But, paradoxically, doing so could mean that you and other students would be unable to stay in school. Reconciling such conflicts, thinking through the issues to discover alternatives, can represent a difficult but important accomplishment of critical thinking.

Reason, Intuition, and Imagination

The heart has its reasons which reason knows nothing of.

—*Blaise Pascal*

But there can be more to critical thinking than logical analysis. The creative imagination adds another dimension. We don't see sharp lines drawn between reason and imagination or rational analysis and intuition, but rather an interplay between them. A daydreamer may be just as capable of thinking critically as a rational pragmatist is. Intuition, imagination, and creativity as well as logic are ways of knowing. Poet John Ciardi, for example, found reason inadequate for explaining the natural world:

Who could believe an ant in theory?

A giraffe in blueprint?

Ten thousand doctors of what's possible.

Could reason half the jungle out of being.

Sometimes a *metaphor* (a figure of speech that imaginatively implies a comparison between one object and another) can carry, through images and associations, an understanding beyond what explicit reasoning can convey. Writer Zora Neale Hurston, in her autobiography, *Dust Tracks on a Road*, remembers the persuasive power of a mentor's argument for honesty: "Truth is a letter from courage." The image contributes to the point she is making.

Our theory of critical thinking welcomes originality, encourages personal opinion, and considers paradox and ambiguity to be central to thinking and writing well, reflecting the world as we know it.

AUDIENCE AND PURPOSE

A major distinction between writing outside the classroom and writing for a class lies in the audience to whom we write, what novelist and essayist Virginia Woolf refers to as "the face beneath the page." Job-related writing tasks, for example, include a designated audience and a real purpose. An employee may write to a superior requesting a raise or to another company proposing a cooperative venture. Readers of a newspaper often express their opinions in persuasive letters to the editor, and many a college student has depended on familiarity with the audience and careful manipulation of circumstance to explain a poor grade to parents. But in a class, students are asked to write papers for the teacher to critique and grade, usually with no specified purpose beyond successfully completing an assignment. Teachers cannot remove themselves from the role of ultimate audience, but for most of the major writing assignments in this text we have suggested an additional audience to lend some authenticity to each project. You will find that different academic disciplines require variations in format. The task of thinking through a potential audience and purpose for your writing will extend the critical thinking component of many assignments.

WRITING ASSIGNMENT 1

Considering Your Audience

Choose any public issue that disturbs you—be it small or large, campus, community, or cosmic—and write *two* short papers (one-and-a-half to two pages *each*) expressing your concern.

1. In the first version, direct your writing to someone connected to, perhaps responsible for, the problem you are concerned about. Your purpose here is to communicate your concern or displeasure and possibly persuade the person responsible to take appropriate action.
2. In the second version, address an individual who is in no way connected to the problem you are disturbed about. Your purpose here is to explain the situation, to inform your reader of something he may know nothing about and is not in a position to change.

Label the two papers at the top (1) and (2) and clearly identify each audience.

WRITING AS A PROCESS

Where do you begin when faced with a writing assignment? Many students turn to the five-paragraph essay format—introduction, three supporting paragraphs, and conclusion—and choose material that will easily fit into this preconceived mold. Writers rely on this formula because they fear that without it they will produce an incoherent essay. They assume that if they follow it, their writing will at least be organized. Student writers must learn to let go of this "safety net" because even though it may save them from anxiety and a disorganized essay, it can also determine the content of the essay; if an idea does not fit easily into the mold, the writer must discard it. This rigid structure prevents writers from exploring their topic, from following thoughts that may lead to interesting insights, and from allowing the material, the content, to find the shape that best suits it.

The most common misconception that student writers have is that a good writer is one who sits at his desk and produces in one sitting a polished, mechanically correct, cohesive piece of writing. If students are unable to do this, they conclude that they cannot write and approach all writing tasks with dread and apprehension. As a first step toward improving their writing, students must discard this myth and replace it with a realistic picture of how writers write. Hemingway, in Paris in the 1920s writing his first collection of short stories, *In Our Time,* spent whole mornings on single paragraphs. French novelist Gustave Flaubert, who wrote *Madame Bovary,* would spend a day finding "le mot juste," the right word. While no one expects students, whose goal is to produce a competent essay or report rather than a literary masterpiece, to spend this kind of time on their writing, students must realize that writing is a complex intellectual act, that it involves many separate tasks, and that the mind is simply not able to handle all of these tasks at once. It is unrealistic to expect that it should.

As writer Henry Miller saw it, "Writing, like life itself, is a voyage of discovery." Let's look at the distinct tasks involved in the act of writing a paper, in this voyage of discovery:

Generating ideas

Focusing a topic

Establishing a thesis

Organizing the essay

Organizing paragraphs

Providing transitions between sentences and paragraphs

Polishing sentences for fluency

Choosing appropriate diction (word choice)

Correcting grammar, usage, spelling, and punctuation

And of course each of these tasks could be broken down further. What is the solution to this problem, this mental overload that writing forces on us? The answer is that it must be done in stages.

Writing is a *process* that breaks down into roughly three stages—creating, shaping, and correcting. A common error students make is to focus their energy on what should be the last stage (correcting) at the beginning, when the focus should be on the creative stage of the writing process. The effect of this misplaced attention is to inhibit *creative thinking.* It is essential that the writer give ample time to the first stage, to generating ideas, to following impulsive thoughts even if they may initially appear unrelated or irrelevant. At this stage a writer must allow himself to experience confusion, to be comfortable with chaos; he must learn to trust the writing process, to realize that out of this chaos a logical train of thought will gradually emerge. Most important of all, writers must learn to suspend all criticism as they explore their topic and their thinking.

Strategies for Generating Ideas

Two concrete methods for beginning this exploration are brainstorming and freewriting, one or both of which you may already be familiar with.

To *brainstorm,* simply put the topic of the writing assignment at the top of a blank piece of paper or your screen. Then jot down words or phrases that come to mind as you think about this topic—as many words as possible even if you are not sure they relate directly to the topic. After brainstorming, look at your list, circling ideas that you want to develop, drawing lines through those that are decidedly unrelated or uninteresting, and drawing arrows or making lists of ideas that are connected to one another. At this point you should be able to go on to the next stage, organizing your essay either by writing an outline or by simply listing main points that you want to develop into paragraphs. Brainstorming is particularly effective with two or more people.

In *freewriting,* you once again begin by writing your topic on a blank sheet, but instead of jotting down words and phrases, you write continuously, using sentences. These sentences do not have to be mechanically correct, nor do they have to be connected. The only rule of freewriting is that you may not stop writing; you may not put down your pen or leave the keyboard for a set length of time. After freewriting for five to ten minutes if writing by hand, or longer if using a computer, read over your freewriting, circling ideas that you find interesting or insightful. Now you may do another freewriting on the idea or ideas you have circled, or you may try to formulate a thesis or list ideas you want to develop.

Both of these methods have two things in common. They are relatively painless ways to begin the writing process, and they allow you to circumvent your own worst enemy, your self-criticism, the voice that says, "That's not right," "That's not what I mean," "This doesn't make sense." Critical evaluation of your writing is necessary but inappropriate and self-defeating if you are critical at the beginning. In addition, freewriting may offer surprising access to ideas you never knew you had.

The First Draft

After exploring your topic in this way, and examining your data if you have done research, you will have a sense of what you want to say and will be ready for a first draft. When you complete this draft, you can reshape it, adding and deleting ideas, refining your thesis, polishing sentences for fluency, and finally writing another draft. Writer Zora Neale Hurston described the process as "rubbing your paragraphs with a soft cloth."

The Time To Be Critical

The time to be critical arrives when you have a complete draft. Now is the time to read with a critical mind, trusting your instinct that if a word, a sentence, or a passage seems unclear or awkward to you, your reader will most likely stumble over the same word, sentence, or passage. Finally, you will be ready to check your spelling (in the dictionary or with a computer spell check) and your punctuation (in an English handbook) and to read your essay aloud to yourself or to a friend, always ready to write another draft if it becomes necessary.

Teacher and writer Donald Murray in an essay on revision entitled "The Maker's Eye," points out a key difference between student writers and professional writers:

> When students complete a first draft, they consider the job of writing done—and their teachers too often agree. When professional writers complete a first draft, they usually feel that they are at the start of the writing process. When a draft is completed, the job of writing can begin.

Every stage in the writing process is important, and each must be given its due. To slight one is to limit the success of the final product. There are exceptions of course. Some writers, for example, are able to compress some of these steps, to generate and organize ideas before ever putting pen to paper. But for most of us, successful writing results from an extended writing process that is continually recursive.

A caution: The danger in the way we have described the writing process is that we make it seem as though it progresses in three neat steps, that it proceeds, in a linear fashion from prewriting to writing to rewriting and correction. In fact, this process is messy. You may be editing the final draft when you decide to add a completely new paragraph, an idea that didn't exist in any of the previous drafts. Nevertheless, if you realize that writing involves many separate tasks, that it is chaotic and unpredictable, you will not be defeated before you begin by criticizing yourself for having to do what all writers do—struggle to find your way, to express your thoughts so that you and your reader understand them.

In the following poem, Richard Wilbur describes this struggle.

THE WRITER

In her room at the prow of the house
Where light breaks, and the windows are tossed with linden,
My daughter is writing a story.

I pause in the stairwell, hearing
From her shut door a commotion of typewriter-keys
Like a chain hauled over a gunwale.

Young as she is, the stuff
Of her life is a great cargo, and some of it heavy:
I wish her a lucky passage.

But now it is she who pauses,
As if to reject my thought and its easy figure.
A stillness greatens, in which

The whole house seems to be thinking,
And then she is at it again with a bunched clamor
Of strokes, and again is silent.

I remember the dazed starling
Which was trapped in that very room, two years ago;
How we stole in, lifted a sash

And retreated, not to affright it;
And how for a helpless hour, through the crack of the door,
We watched the sleek, wild, dark

And iridescent creature
Batter against the brilliance, drop like a glove
To the hard floor, or the desk-top,

And wait then, humped and bloody,
For the wits to try it again; and how our spirits
Rose when, suddenly sure,

It lifted off from a chair-back,
Beating a smooth course for the right window
And clearing the sill of the world

It is always a matter, my darling,
Of life or death, as I had forgotten. I wish
What I wished you before, but harder.

EXERCISE 1B

Describing Your Writing Process

Consider this poem for a few minutes. What two things does Wilbur compare the writing process to? What do these metaphors say about his view of the writing process? Identify and explain a metaphor that describes your own writing process.

Metaphors can provide a vivid means of probing and revealing ideas. The creative thinking we do when we compare one thing to another can lead to new understanding. When we think creatively about our writing process, we are likely to *see* our writing in fresh and instructive ways.

"I was on the cutting edge. I pushed the envelope. I did the heavy lifting. I was the rainmaker. Then I ran out of metaphors."

The New Yorker

One Writer's Process

Let us add to Wilbur's poem a description of the writing process that produced this section of chapter one.

Day 1:
I spent two hours at the computer writing on the topic, "Writing as a process." During this freewriting, my goal was to say everything I could think of on this subject that was important for students to know. Most of the paragraphs were focused on one point, but there were no transitions between sentences and paragraphs, and most of the sentences were only an approximation of the ideas I was trying to express. As I typed, I jotted down ideas which I wanted to include but which at the moment were interrupting the idea I was currently working on. I gave no thought to punctuation or spelling. Getting ideas on paper was my top priority.

Day 2:
I printed a copy of the three pages of freewriting I h
vious day, and spent three hours revising: eliminat
moving passages; providing transitions; and rephras
sentences.

Day 3:
I spent one hour polishing my sentences but made no major additions
or deletions in the content.

Day 4:
I spent one last hour on a final review of my sentences, revising only a
few of them. I checked my spelling with the help of a computer program, which indeed turned up several misspellings.

As you can see, it took a total of seven hours to write three single-
spaced, typed pages which will take most readers ten minutes to read.
And still I was not finished. The next step was to give this draft to my
coauthor, who made further revisions. As Donald Murray notes in his essay on revision, "Most readers underestimate the amount of rewriting it
usually takes to produce spontaneous reading." But we can take heart
from novelist Kurt Vonnegut: "This is what I find most encouraging about
the writing trades: They allow mediocre people who are patient and in-
dustrious to revise their stupidity, to edit themselves into something like
intelligence."

 ## WRITING ASSIGNMENT 2

Your Writing

Write an essay in which you discuss your writing experiences, in school and
out—how you feel about writing, what you consider your strengths and
weaknesses as a writer, your ideas on the value of learning to write well,
and any other thoughts you have about yourself as a writer.

Audience
Your primary audience for this assignment is your instructor, but you as the
writer will also be an audience as you write your way to an understanding
of your attitude toward writing.

Purpose
To inform your instructor about your writing experiences and to gain insight into your individual writing process.

WHAT YOU CAN EXPECT FROM THIS BOOK

In this book we explore a variety of strategies for expanding both writing
and thinking skills, emphasizing the symbiotic relationship between them.

propose no formulas, no quick solutions. Rather, we view the development of each as a process that can take different turns for different people. Reflecting our views on this diversity, the writing assignments throughout this book aim to avoid rigid adherence to form. Contrary to the advice of many writing texts, assignments in real life are not limited to prescribed numbers of paragraphs or a required sequence of parts. Essays or reports, whether explanatory or persuasive, should be designed to communicate a writer's ideas in such a way that the writer's purpose is clear and logical and satisfies the needs of a particular audience. And obviously, while there may be advantages in one approach to thinking over another, there is no one right way to think.

The Sequence

We begin, in Chapter 2, with reading critically and making inferences, essential tasks for the analysis and construction of arguments to come. You will start writing immediately, in this first chapter, but before we ask you to build your own fully developed arguments in Chapter 4, you will practice recognizing and analyzing argument structure in Chapter 3. As you cover the rhetoric of argument and prepare the longer writing assignments in Chapter 4, you will reinforce reasoning by continuing to look to logic—both formal and informal—in Chapters 5 through 8. Logic, from the Greek word *logos*, which means both "word" and "reason" (no accident, perhaps), can be defined as the branch of philosophy that studies the consistency of arguments. And in Chapter 9, "Language: Meaning and Style," we fine-tune style and writing strategies.

Collaborative Approaches

With your instructor, you can work out collaborative approaches to many exercises and writing assignments. You will find that the more opportunities you have to work with classmates the clearer your thinking is likely to become, and the more likely it will be that the assignments will reflect the writing and problem solving you will encounter in all academic disciplines and in the working world, where we must often work on projects in collaboration with others. (This text, written by two authors, represents an example of such a collaboration.)

Sharpening Sentence Skills

Throughout many of the chapters, you will find practice in sentence-building skills, simple review for some of you, new strategies for others. Ideas tend to travel in sentences, and the greater the fluency of your sentences, the better equipped you will be to express complex reasoning in cohesive, logical prose. This is not a handbook of grammar and usage, but rather, a carefully sequenced selection of rhetorical strategies selected to complement particular topics and issues. The logical relationships between ideas in a sentence come early, in Chapters 2, 3, and 4. Some refinements come later: parallelism, particularly important in persuasive writing, in Chapter 6; sentence development with appositives and verbal modifiers, and sentence focus with concrete subjects and active verbs, in Chapter 9. These sentence skills may also be addressed on an individual basis, not necessarily in the sequence given here.

He or She?

You will notice that in our references to a writer or a student in this text, we alternate between female and male designations. This reflects not arbitrary choice but one of the ways writers today resolve the problem posed by the lack of a gender neutral pronoun for the third person singular. Refer to Appendix II for further discussion of this problem and for solutions to it in your own writing.

"You'll just love the way he handles."

ENJOYING THE CHALLENGE OF THINKING AND WRITING

In his poem "The Four Quartets," T. S. Eliot writes of the "intolerable wrestle / With words and meaning." But before you conclude that this whole enterprise is to be a bleak struggle, let us assure you that our goal is quite the contrary. Systematic thinking can be an exciting adventure. Polishing your prose to convey your ideas precisely and logically can be enormously satisfying. Writer Isaac Asimov expresses such an outlook well:

> Thinking is the activity I love best, and writing to me is simply thinking through my fingers.

Our expectations are broad and flexible. What we ask is that you reflect on your ideas, support your opinions, and practice writing about them with care. We hope to foster fair and independent thinking, a capacity for empathy, and the ability to advocate your own ideas logically and fluently.

Chapter
2

Inference

THE FAR SIDE   By GARY LARSON

Question
What do you infer from this cartoon?

Answer
As the evidence suggests, the joke is on the snake whose attempt to bite the man is thwarted by the man's wooden leg. Though we do not see the snake strike the wooden leg, we see its crumpled fangs and the man's footprints. On the basis of these observations we infer what must have happened. But it is important to note that we do not see the snake strike; instead, we see evidence indicating that this is the case. We make an inference.

WHAT IS AN INFERENCE?

An inference is a conclusion about the unknown made on the basis of the known. We see a car beside us on the freeway with several old and new dents; we infer that the driver must be a very bad one. A close friend hasn't called in several weeks and doesn't return our calls when we leave messages;

we infer that she is angry with us. Much of our thinking, whether about casual observations or personal relationships, involves making inferences. Indeed, entire careers are based on the ability to make logical inferences. In *Snow Falling On Cedars*, a contemporary novel by David Guterson, a coroner describes his job.

> It's my job to infer. Look, if a night watchman is struck over the head with a crowbar during the course of a robbery, the wounds you're going to see in his head will look like they were made with a crowbar. If they were made by a ball-peen hammer you can seen that, too—a ball-peen leaves behind a crescent-shaped injury, a crowbar leaves, well, linear wounds with V-shaped ends. You get hit with a pistol butt, that's one thing; somebody hits you with a bottle, that's another. You fall off a motorcycle at 40 miles an hour and hit your head on gravel, the gravel will leave behind patterned abrasions that don't look like anything else. So yes, I **infer** from the deceased's wound that something narrow and flat caused his injury. To infer—it's what coroners **do.**

How Reliable Is an Inference?

There is an enormous range in the reliability of inferences; some inferences are quite credible, but inferences based on very little evidence or on evidence which may support many different interpretations should be treated with skepticism. In fact, the strength of an inference can be tested by the number of different explanations we can draw from the same set of facts. The greater the number of possible interpretations, the less reliable the inference.

In the cartoon, given the footprints and the snake's extended fangs, we cannot arrive at any other inferences but that the snake bit the wooden leg and that by extension, the usual pattern of pain inflicted is reversed. But the inferences drawn in the other two cases are not as reliable. The driver of the dented car may not be the owner: she may have borrowed the car from a friend, or she may own the car but have recently bought it "as is." Our friend may not have called us for a number of reasons: a heavy work schedule, three term papers, a family crisis. She may not have received our messages. These alternate explanations weaken the reliability of the original inferences. Clearly, the more evidence we have to support our inferences and the fewer interpretations possible, the more we can trust in their accuracy.

The language of inference

The verbs *to infer* and *to imply* are often confused, but they can be readily distinguished.

to imply: To suggest, indicate indirectly, hint, intimate. What a writer, speaker, action, or object conveys.

to infer: To arrive at a conclusion by reasoning from facts or evidence. What a reader, listener, or observer determines or concludes.

A writer, speaker, action, or object implies something, and readers, listeners, or observers infer what that something is. A final distinction: Only *people* can make inferences; *anything* can imply meaning.

EXERCISE 2A

Interpreting a Cartoon

Quickly determine the message the following cartoon implies. What inferences do you draw from the evidence given? After writing a short response, compare your interpretation with others in the class. Are they the same?

WHAT IS A FACT?

We make inferences based on our own observations or on the observations of others as they are presented to us through speech or print. These observations often consist of facts, information that can be verified. There are footprints in the sand. There are dents in the car. You have not spoken to your friend in several weeks. "A crowbar leaves linear wounds with V-shaped ends." Our own observations attest to the truth of these claims. But often we are dependent on others' observations about people, places, and events which we cannot directly observe. Take, for example, the claim that the last Americans left Vietnam in 1975. Few of us observed this action firsthand, but those who did reported it, and we trust the veracity of their reports. Books, newspapers, magazines, and television programs are filled with reports—facts—giving us information about the world that we are unable to gain from direct observation. If we doubt the truth of these claims, we usually can turn to other sources to verify or discredit them.

Facts come in a vast array of forms—statistics, names, events—and are distinguished by their ability to be verified. Confusions tend to grow less from the facts themselves, more from the inferences we make based on a given set of facts. It is important, however, to think critically about our sources, including our own observations, in order to understand possible biases. Eyewitness reports and individual experiences, your own or those of others, can serve as valuable factual evidence. But whether or not this evidence will be accepted will depend on how your audience views you as a witness or on their evaluation of a witness you cite and the circumstances under which a report was made. The celebrated Japanese movie, "Roshomon," in which four witnesses give different reports of the same crime, and numerous other tales, such as Lawrence Durrell's *Alexandria Quartets* or Ford Maddox Ford's *The Good Soldier,* illustrate how perceptions of the same event can vary.

WHAT IS A JUDGMENT?

When we infer that the snake struck the wooden leg, we laugh but are unlikely to express approval or disapproval of the snake's action. On the other hand, when we infer that the woman in the car in front of us is a poor driver, we express disapproval of her driving skills; we make a judgment, in this case, a statement of disapproval. Or, when we infer from a friend's volunteer work with the homeless that she is an admirable person, we express our approval, make a favorable judgment. A judgment is also an inference, but although many inferences are free of positive or negative connotation, such as "I think it's going to rain," a judgment will always express the writer's or speaker's approval or disapproval.

Certain judgments are taken for granted, become a part of a culture's shared belief system, and are unlikely to be challenged under most circumstances. For example, most of us would accept the following statements: "Taking the property of others is wrong"; or "People who physically abuse children should be punished." But many judgments will not be universally accepted without considerable well-reasoned support, or may be rejected regardless of additional support and cogent reasoning. Frequently, a judgment is further complicated by potentially ambiguous language and even punctuation. Take for example the highly controversial wording of the Second Amendment to the Constitution:

AMENDMENT II

A well-regulated militia, being necessary to the security of a free State, the right of the people to keep and bear arms, shall not be infringed.

Those in favor of gun control interpret this to mean that only "a well-regulated militia," not every individual, is guaranteed the right to bear arms. "Well-regulated" implies an official militia, not a private one free of government regulations. But those against gun control believe that the Second Amendment guarantees "the people," meaning all individuals, the right to bear arms.

To merit the right to be heard on this volatile issue, a person must provide considerable factual evidence and cogent reasoning.

EXERCISE 2B

Distinguishing Between Facts, Inferences, and Judgments

Determine whether the following statements are *facts* (reports), *inferences,* or *judgments* and explain your reasoning. Note that some may include more than one, and some may be open to interpretation.

Example: I heard on the morning news that the city subway system has ground to a halt this morning; many students will arrive late for class.

"I heard on the morning news that the city subway system has ground to a halt this morning": *fact.* I did hear it and the information can be verified.

"Many students will arrive late for class": *inference.* This is a conclusion drawn from the information about the breakdown of the subway.

*1. The death penalty should be abolished.
2. For sale: lovely three-bedroom house in forest setting, easy commute, a bargain at $325,000.
3. The largest source of man-made carbon dioxide is the combustion of fossil fuel: oil, coal, and gas.
4. Arnold has a drinking problem.
5. Walter Clemmons, reviewing *You Must Remember This,* states that "Joyce Carol Oates' 17th novel is one of her most powerful."
6. After I took Richard Simmons' Vitamin Pills, the boss gave me a raise. Those pills sure did the trick.
7. Commuter—one who spends his life
   In riding to and from his wife;
   A man who shaves and takes a train
   And then rides back to shave again.

—E. B. White

THE FAR SIDE   By GARY LARSON

9-17   © 1985 Universal Press Syndicate

"Oh, what a cute little Siamese. ... Is he friendly?"

Failure to draw logical inferences can sometimes be dangerous.

EXERCISE 2C

Drawing Logical Inferences

Draw inferences from the following statements and evaluate the relative reliability of your inferences. [The first three statements are taken from a survey comparing the college freshmen of today to the college freshmen of the sixties.]

1. This year's college freshmen smoke less than previous classes (down from 17 to 9 percent).
2. College students today consider being "very well off" a top personal goal (up from 44 to 71 percent).
3. The college freshmen of today have higher high school grades than their predecessors of 30 years ago, but need more remedial help, according to a study done for the American Council on Education by the Higher Education Research Institute of UCLA.

4. In 1990, 36 percent of high school athletes were girls, compared with only 7 percent in 1972. Similarly, women accounted for one-third of all college athletes in 1990, according to the NCAA.

5.

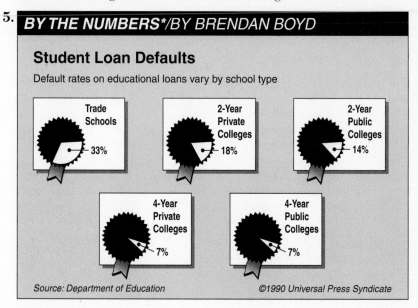

BY THE NUMBERS/BY BRENDAN BOYD*

Student Loan Defaults

Default rates on educational loans vary by school type

Trade Schools — 33%

2-Year Private Colleges — 18%

2-Year Public Colleges — 14%

4-Year Private Colleges — 7%

4-Year Public Colleges — 7%

Source: Department of Education   ©1990 Universal Press Syndicate

---

EXERCISE 2D

Solving Riddles

Use your inferential skills to solve these riddles by English poet John Cotton.

1.
Insubstantial I can fill lives,
Cathedrals, worlds.
I can haunt islands,
Raise passions
Or calm the madness of kings.
I've even fed the affectionate.
I can't be touched or seen,
But I can be noted.

2.
We are a crystal zoo,
Wielders of fortunes,
The top of our professions.
Like hard silver nails
Hammered into the dark
We make charts for mariners.

3.

I reveal your secrets.
I am your morning enemy,
Though I give reassurance of presence.
I can be magic,
or the judge in beauty contests.
Count Dracula has no use for me.
When you leave
I am left to my own reflections.

4.

My tensions and pressures
Are precise if transitory.
Iridescent, I can float
And catch small rainbows.
Beauties luxuriate in me.
I can inhabit ovens
Or sparkle in bottles.
I am filled with that
Which surrounds me.

5.

Containing nothing
I can bind people forever,
Or just hold a finger.
Without end or beginning
I go on to appear in fields,
Ensnare enemies,
Or in another guise
Carry in the air
Messages from tower to tower.

6.

Silent I invade cities,
Blur edges, confuse travellers,
My thumb smudging the light.
I drift from rivers
To loiter in early morning fields,
Until Constable Sun
Moves me on.

—John Cotton, *Times Literary Supplement*

Now apply the same skills to these two poems by Sylvia Plath (1933–1963).
What does each describe?

7.

I am silver and exact. I have no preconceptions.
Whatever I see I swallow immediately

Just as it is, unmisted by love or dislike.
I am not cruel, only truthful—
The eye of a little god, four-cornered.
Most of the time I meditate on the opposite wall.
It is pink, with speckles. I have looked at it so long
I think it is a part of my heart. But it flickers.
Faces and darkness separate us over and over.

Now I am a lake. A woman bends over me,
Searching my reaches for what she really is.
Then she turns to those liars, the candles or the moon.
I see her back, and reflect it faithfully.
She rewards me with tears and an agitation of hands.
I am important to her. She comes and goes.
Each morning it is her face that replaces the darkness.
In me she has drowned a young girl, and in me an old woman
Rises toward her day after day, like a terrible fish.

8.
I'm a riddle in nine syllables,
An elephant, a ponderous house,
A melon strolling on two tendrils.
O red fruit, ivory, fine timbers.
This loaf's big with its yeasty rising.
Money's new-minted in this fat purse.
I'm a means, a stage, a cow in calf.
I've eaten a bag of green apples,
Boarded the train there's no getting off.

APPLICATION TO WRITING

ACHIEVING A BALANCE BETWEEN INFERENCE AND FACTS

We need to distinguish inferences, facts, and judgments from one another in order to evaluate as fairly as possible the events in our world. Whether these events are personal or global, we need to be able to distinguish between facts, verifiable information that we can rely on, and inferences and judgments, which may or may not be reliable.

We also need to evaluate the reliability of our own inferences. Are there other interpretations of the facts? Have we considered all other possible interpretations? Do we need more information before drawing a conclusion? These are useful thinking skills which we need to practice, but how do these skills relate to writing? To answer that question, read the following paragraph and distinguish between statements of fact and inference.

A white player's life in the National Basketball Association is a reverse-image experience all but unique in American culture. Although fewer than 13 percent of United States citizens are African-American, about 80 percent of the N.B.A.'s players are. Of the 357 players on N.B.A. rosters, 290 were African-American, including several of mixed descent. Every one of the league's 20 leading scorers was black, and all but 2 of its leading rebounders. Not one N.B.A. team has as many whites as blacks.

—adapted from "The Loneliness of Being White" by Bruce Schoenfeld

This paragraph contains one inference while the remaining statements are factual, capable of verification. Notice that the facts support and convince us of the inference.

INFERENCE	FACTS
A white player's life in the National Basketball Association is a reverse-image experience all but unique in American culture.	Although fewer than 13 percent of United States citizens are African-American, about 80 percent of the N.B.A.'s players are.
	Of the 357 players on N.B.A. rosters, 290 were African-American, including several of mixed descent.
	Every one of the league's 20 leading scorers was black, and all but 2 of its 20 leading rebounders.
	Not one N.B.A. team has as many whites as blacks.

Facts Only

'"Now, what I want is Facts. Teach these boys and girls nothing but Facts. Facts alone are wanted in life. Plant nothing else, and root out everything else. You can only form the minds of reasoning animals upon Facts: nothing else will ever be of any service to them. This is the principle on which I bring up my own children, and this is the principle on which I bring up these children. Stick to Facts, sir!'"

So says Thomas Gradgrind in Charles Dickens' novel *Hard Times*, an indictment against Victorian industrial society. Dickens knew that facts alone do not make for a good education, nor for good writing. Expository writing will frequently consist of a blend of inference and fact with the one supporting the other. If you were to write a paper consisting only of facts, it would be of no interest to the reader because reading facts that lead nowhere, that fail to support a conclusion, is like reading the telephone book. Jeff Jarvis, a book reviewer for *The New York Times Book Review,* comments on the dangers of this kind of writing:

> Objectivity, in some quarters, means just the facts, ma'am—names, dates, and quotations dumped from a notebook onto the page. But facts alone, without perspective, do not tell a story. Facts alone, without a conclusion to hold them together, seem unglued. Facts alone force writers to use awkward transitions, unbending formats or simple chronologies to fend off disorganization.

A facts-only approach can also have serious consequences in our schools' textbooks. A recent report on public education cites such facts-only textbooks as one of the causes of students' lack of interest and poor achievement.

> Elementary school children are stuck with insipid books that "belabor what is obvious" even to first graders. At the high school level, history—or "social studies"—texts are crammed with facts but omit human motivations or any sense of what events really meant.
>
> Deputy chairman John Agresto of the National Endowment for the Humanities said that "at the end of each chapter, I could imagine any student saying, 'So what?'"

Keep the danger of a facts-only approach in mind when you are assigned a research paper. Do not assume that teachers are looking exclusively for well-documented facts; they also want to see what you make of the data, what conclusions you draw, what criticisms and recommendations you offer. Do not fall into the trap of one eager young college freshman, Charles Renfrew, who, proud of his photographic memory, expected high praise from a distinguished philosophy professor for a paper on Descartes. He suffered disappointment but learned a lasting lesson when he read the comment: "Too much Descartes, not enough Renfrew." A photographic memory for factual information can be an asset, but your own inferences and judgments fully explained are also important.

Selecting Facts

Equally important when considering the facts you use in your papers is your selection of which facts to include and which to omit. When we omit relevant facts we may be reflecting personal, political, or cultural biases, and in the process distorting "reality." The omission of certain facts from accounts of historical events can have serious consequences, in small ways and large. Audre Lorde in her book, *Zami: A New Spelling of My Name,* illustrates this point eloquently.

> I had spent four years at Hunter High School, with the most academically advanced and intellectually accurate education available for "preparing young women for college and career." I had been taught by some of the most highly considered historians in the country. Yet, I had never once heard the name mentioned of the first man to fall in the American revolution [Crispus Attucks], nor even been told that he was a Negro. What did that mean about the history I had learned?

Lorde is illustrating what others in recent decades have been noting. For example, Harvey Wasserman's *History of the United States* and

Frances Fitzgerald's *America Revised: History School Books in the Twentieth Century* explore the ways in which historians, through a systematic selection process, have distorted history. (Some would say Wasserman also distorts history in his efforts to right past wrongs.)

Inferences Only

It is possible to err in another direction as well; a paper consisting only of inferences and judgments would bore and antagonize readers as they search for the basis of our claims, the facts to support our opinions. If our writing is to be logical, convincing, and interesting, we must draw inferences and support them with relevant facts.

WRITING ASSIGNMENT 3

Analyzing a Recent Inference

Write a paragraph or two about a recent inference you've made. Include what facts the inference was based on and why you made it. Discuss with your classmates whether the inference was logical given the facts that led to it, whether others might have made a different inference from the same data, and why they might have done so.

Audience
Yourself and other members of the class.

Purpose
To think critically about your own thinking.

WRITING ASSIGNMENT 4

Reconstructing the Lost Tribe

> Every language is also a special way of looking at the world and interpreting experience. Concealed in the structure of language are a whole set of unconscious assumptions about the world and the life in it.
>
> —*Clyde Kluckhohn*

With the above quotation in mind, imagine that a previously unknown civilization has been discovered and that linguistic anthropologists, after observing the civilization for a while, have delineated the following characteristics about the society's language:

Three words for terrain, designating "absolutely flat," "rolling," and "slightly hilly."

No word for ocean.

Dozens of terms for grains, including eight for wheat alone.

Several words for children, some of which translate as "wise small one," "innocent leader," and "little stargazer."

Seven terms to describe the stages of life up to puberty, only one term to describe life from puberty to death.

The word for sex translates as "to plant a wise one."

Terms for woman are synonymous with "wife and mother."

Terms for man are synonymous with "husband and father."

Twenty words for book.

No words for violent conflict or war.

Nine words for artist.

Terms for praise translate as "peacemaker" and "conciliator."

Words designating cow, pig, calf, and sheep, but no terms for beef, pork, veal, leather, or mutton.

Several words for precipitation, most translating as "rain," only one meaning "snow."

Several words for leader but all are plural.

Four words meaning theater.

The topic
Write an essay in which you characterize the society that uses this language.

As you analyze the characteristics of the language, you will be reconstructing a culture. Obviously, because the data are very limited, you will have to make a few educated guesses and qualify conclusions carefully. ("Perhaps," "possibly," "one might conclude," "the evidence suggests," and similar hedges will be useful.)

The approach
Examine and group the data; look for patterns.

Draw inferences, depending only on the data given.

Cite evidence to support these inferences—be sure to base all your conclusions on the linguistic evidence provided. Do not draw inferences that you don't support with specific examples. Be sure to use all the data. Explain your line of reasoning—how and why the data lead to the inferences you have made.

Don't simply write a narration or description based on the information. A narrative or story will only *imply* the conclusions you have arrived at from examining the data. This can be enjoyable to write and entertaining to read, and certainly requires critical thinking, as does all good fiction. But your purpose here is *to explain* why you have made the inferences you have and to back up your inferences with facts drawn from the language list.

Consider giving a name to this tribe to help focus your sentences.

Audience and Purpose

You have a wide range of possibilities here; we leave the choice to you. Your paper may assume the form of a report, scholarly or simply informative, directed to any audience you choose. It may be a letter to a personal friend or fictional colleague. It may be a traditional essay for an audience unfamiliar with the assignment, explaining what the language tells us about the people who use or used it. What is crucial for success is that you, as the reporter-writer, assume that *you have not seen this tribe and have no first-hand evidence of it. You will also assume that your reader does not have a copy of this assignment;* it is up to you to cite all the specific evidence (the terms given in the list) to justify your inferences.

Writing About Fiction

Many students are intimidated by assignments which ask them to write about a poem, play, short story, or novel. What can they say about a piece of literature? Isn't there a right answer known to the author and the teacher but not to them?

Fiction is implicit. Writers of fiction—through character, plot, setting, theme, point of view, symbolism, irony, and imagery—imply meaning. Fiction is oblique. The work implies meaning; you infer what that meaning is. As you can see, interpreting literature requires critical thinking; it requires you to make inferences about the meaning of the work and to support these inferences with details from it.

Reading is the making of meaning and the meaning we make will depend on who we are—our sex, age, ethnicity, culture, and experience will all influence our reading. Given the multiple interpretations possible, there is not a single right answer but only well-supported inferences that add up to a logical interpretation.

A final point. A critical essay is not a continuation of class discussion but a formal piece of writing that can stand on its own apart from the class. To accomplish this, you may think of your audience as one who is not familiar with the work you are writing about. This does not require you to retell every detail of the piece, but it ensures that you will include the relevant details, the facts, on which your inferences are based rather than assume your reader knows them.

EXERCISE 2E

Making Inferences About Fiction

Read "The Story of an Hour" by Kate Chopin [1850–1904], and answer the following question: Does Louise die "of joy" as her doctors suggest? Support your answer, your inference, with facts from the story.

The Story of an Hour

Knowing that Mrs. Mallard was afflicted with a heart trouble, great care was taken to break to her as gently as possible the news of her husband's death.

It was her sister Josephine who told her, in broken sentences; veiled hints that revealed in half concealing. Her husband's friend Richards was there, too, near her. It was he who had been in the newspaper office when intelligence of the railroad disaster was received, with Brently Mallard's name leading the list of "killed." He had only taken the time to assure himself of its truth by a second telegram, and had hastened to forestall any less careful, less tender friend in bearing the sad message.

She did not hear the story as many women have heard the same, with a paralyzed inability to accept its significance. She wept at once, with sudden, wild abandonment, in her sister's arms. When the storm of grief had spent itself she went away to her room alone. She would have no one follow her.

There stood, facing the open window, a comfortable, roomy armchair. Into this she sank, pressed down by a physical exhaustion that haunted her body and seemed to reach into her soul.

She could see in the open square before her house the tops of trees that were all aquiver with the new spring life. The delicious breath of rain was in the air. In the street below a peddler was crying his wares. The notes of a distant song which some one was singing reached her faintly, and countless sparrows were twittering in the eaves.

There were patches of blue sky showing here and there through the clouds that had met and piled one above the other in the west facing her window.

She sat with her head thrown back upon the cushion of the chair, quite motionless, except when a sob came up into her throat and shook her, as a child who has cried itself to sleep continues to sob in its dreams.

She was young, with a fair, calm face, whose lines bespoke repression and even a certain strength. But now there was a dull stare in her eyes, whose gaze was fixed away off yonder on one of those patches of blue sky. It was not a glance of reflection, but rather indicated a suspension of intelligent thought.

There was something coming to her and she was waiting for it, fearfully. What was it? She did not know; it was too subtle and elusive to name. But she felt it, creeping out of the sky, reaching toward her through the sounds, the scents, the color that filled the air.

Now her bosom rose and fell tumultuously. She was beginning to recognize this thing that was approaching to possess her, and she was striving to beat it back with her will—as powerless as her two white slender hands would have been.

When she abandoned herself a little whispered word escaped her slightly parted lips. She said it over and over under her breath: "free, free, free!" The vacant stare and the look of terror that had followed it went from her eyes. They stayed keen and bright. Her pulses beat fast, and the coursing blood warmed and relaxed every inch of her body.

She did not stop to ask if it were or were not a monstrous joy that held her. A clear and exalted perception enabled her to dismiss the suggestion as trivial.

She knew that she would weep again when she saw the kind, tender hands folded in death; the face that had never looked save with love upon her, fixed and gray and dead. But she saw beyond that bitter moment a long procession of years to come that would belong to her absolutely. And she opened and spread her arms out to them in welcome.

There would be no one to live for her during those coming years; she would live for herself. There would be no powerful will bending hers in that blind persistence with which men and women believe they have a right to impose a private will upon a fellow-creature. A kind intention or a cruel intention made the act seem no less a crime as she looked upon it in that brief moment of illumination.

And yet she had loved him—sometimes. Often she had not. What did it matter! What could love, the unsolved mystery, count for in face of this possession of self-assertion which she suddenly recognized as the strongest impulse of her being!

"Free! Body and soul free!" she kept whispering.

Josephine was kneeling before the closed door with her lips to the keyhole, imploring for admission. "Louise, open the door! I beg; open the door—you will make yourself ill. What are you doing, Louise? For heaven's sake open the door."

"Go away. I am not making myself ill." No; she was drinking in a very elixir of life through that open window.

Her fancy was running riot along those days ahead of her. Spring days, and summer days, and all sorts of days that would be her own. She breathed a quick prayer that life might be long. It was only yesterday she had thought with a shudder that life might be long.

She rose at length and opened the door to her sister's importunities. There was a feverish triumph in her eyes, and she carried herself unwittingly like a goddess of Victory. She clasped her sister's waist, and together they descended the stairs. Richards stood waiting for them at the bottom.

Some one was opening the front door with a latchkey. It was Brently Mallard who entered, a little travel-stained, composedly carrying his grip-sack and umbrella. He had been far from the scene of the accident, and did not even know there had been one. He stood amazed at Josephine's piercing cry; at Richards' quick motion to screen him from the view of his wife.

But Richards was too late.

When the doctors came they said she had died of heart disease—of joy that kills.

1894

 ## WRITING ASSIGNMENT 5

Interpreting Fiction

Read the short story, *Hostess,* by Donald Mangum, and write an essay based on the inferences you make about the narrator. Include the facts on which these inferences are based and an explanation of why you made such inferences.

Audience
Someone who has not read the story.

Purpose
To characterize the hostess—what kind of woman is she?

Hostess

My husband was promoted to crew chief, and with the raise we moved into a double-wide, just up the drive. Half the park came to the house-warming. Well, Meg drank herself to tears and holed up in the toilet, poor thing. "Meg? Hon?" I said from the hall. "You going to live?" She groaned something. It was seeing R.L. with that tramp down in 18 that made her do this to herself. Now there was a whole line of beer drinkers doing the rain dance out in the hall, this being a single-bath unit. I was the hostess, and I had to do something. "Sweetheart," I said, knocking. "I'm going to put you a bowl on the floor in the utility room." The rest of the trailer was carpeted.

Dale, my husband, was in the kitchen with an egg in his hand, squeezing it for all he was worth. Veins stuck out everywhere on his arm. Paul and Eric were laughing. "What's going on in here?" I said.

Dale stopped squeezing and breathed. "I got to admit," he said, "I never knew that about eggs." I could have kicked him when he handed Paul five dollars. I found the bowl I was after, plus a blanket, and took care of Meg.

Then Hank and Boyce almost got into a fight over a remark Hank made about somebody named Linda. They had already squared off outside when it came out that Hank was talking about a Linda *Stillman,* when Boyce thought he meant a Linda *Faye.* Well, by that time everybody was ready for something, so the guys agreed to arm-wrestle. Hank won, but only because Boyce started laughing when Kathy Sueanne sat in Jason's supper and Jason got madder than Kathy Sueanne did because there wasn't any more potato salad left.

You won't believe who showed up then. R.L.! Said he was looking for Meg. "You think she wants to see you, R.L.?" I said. "After what you did to her with that trash Elaine?" So he said he'd only kissed Elaine a couple of times. "Or not even that," he said. "She was the one kissed *me.*"

"You know what you can kiss," I said. He stood there looking like some dog you'd just hauled off and kicked for no good reason. "Well, come on," I said, taking him by the shirt. I led him to the utility room to show him the condition he'd driven his darling to. I'm here to say, when R.L. saw that precious thing curled up in front of the hot-water heater he sank to his knees in shame. I just closed the door.

Back in the den, there was this Australian kangaroo giving birth on the television. The little baby kangaroo, which looked sort of like an anchovy with legs, had just made it out of its mama and was crawling around looking for her pouch. The man on the show said it had about ten minutes to get in there and find a teat or it would die. He said a lot of them don't make it. I got so wrought up watching that trembly little fellow that I started cheering him on. So did everyone else. Well, to everyone's relief, the little thing made it. Then Gus wanted to know why everyone over there always called each other Mike. Nobody had any idea.

Eric ate a whole bunch of dried cat food before figuring out what it was and that somebody had put it in the party dish as a joke. He tried to act like it didn't bother him, but he didn't stay too long after that. Melinda went out to her car for cigarettes, and a yellow jacket stung her behind the knee, so when she came in howling, Rod slapped this big wad of chewed tobacco on the spot to draw out the poison, which made her howl even louder, till I washed it off and applied meat tenderizer and let her go lie in the guest bed for awhile.

That's when something strange happened. The phone started ringing, and I ran back to get it in Dale's and my bedroom, which was the closest to quiet in the trailer. I answered and just got this hollow sound at first, like you get with a bad connection over long-distance.

There was a mumble, then a woman's voice said, "She's gone." I didn't recognize the voice, but I was sure what "gone" meant by the way she said it. It meant someone had died. Then she said—and she almost screamed it—"Someone should have been here. Why weren't you and Clarence here?"

Now, I don't know a soul in this world named Clarence, and this was clearly a case of the wrong number. "Ma'am," I said as gently as I knew how.

"You'll have to talk louder," she said. "I can hardly hear you."

I curled my hand around my lips and the mouthpiece and said, "Ma'am, you have dialled the wrong number."

"Oh, God, I'm sorry," she said. "Oh dear God." And here is the strange thing. The woman did not hang up. She just kept saying, "Dear God" and crying.

I sat there listening to that woman and to all the happy noise coming from everywhere in the trailer and through the window from outside, and when she finally brought it down to a sniffle I said, "Honey, who was it that passed away?"

"My sister," she said. "My sister, Beatrice." And it was like saying the name started her to sobbing again.

"And none of your people are there?" I said.

"Just me," she said.

"Sweetheart, you listen to me," I said, trying to close the window for more quiet. Sweet Christ, I thought. Dear sweet Christ in Heaven. "Are you listening, angel? You should not be alone right now. You understand what I'm telling you?" I said, "Now, I am right here."

—Donald Mangum

SUMMARY

In order to interpret the world around us and write effectively about it, we need to be able to distinguish facts, inferences, and judgments from one another and to evaluate the reliability of our inferences.

In written exposition and argument, and in the interpretation of literature, it is important to achieve a balance between fact and inference, to support our inferences with facts and reasoning.

The way a community uses language can both reflect and shape its culture and social organization.

KEY TERMS

Facts information that can be verified.
Inference a conclusion about something we don't know based on what we do know.
Judgment an inference that expresses either approval or disapproval.

Chapter
3

The Structure of
Argument

You always hurt the one you love!

When we offer our own views on an issue we are expressing an **opinion.** We all have them. We all should have them. But we should also recognize the difference between voicing an opinion and developing an argument. Someone might insist that using animals for medical research is wrong; a research physician might respond that this attitude is misguided. Both are expressing opinions. If they both stick to their guns but refuse to elaborate their positions, then each may simply dismiss the opponent's statement as "mere opinion," as nothing more than an emotional reaction. If, on the other hand, they start to offer reasons in support of their opinions, then they have moved the discussion to an argument. The critic might add that animals suffer pain in much the same way that humans do, and thus experiments inflict cruel suffering on the animals. The physician might respond that modern techniques have greatly reduced animal suffering and that such experiments are necessary for medical breakthroughs. They are now offering support for their opinions. Don't be afraid of your opinions. Just be prepared to defend them with good reasoning. Think of opinions as starting points for arguments.

In logic, an argument is not a fight but a rational piece of discourse, written or spoken, which attempts to persuade the reader or listener to believe something. For instance, we can attempt to persuade others to believe that cutting old timber will harm the environment or that a vote for a particular candidate will ensure a better city government. Though many arguments are concerned with political issues, arguments are not limited to such topics. We can argue about books, movies, restaurants, and cars, to name just a few of the possibilities. Whenever we want to convince someone else of the "rightness" of our position by offering reasons for that position, we are presenting an argument.

PREMISES AND CONCLUSIONS

The structure of all arguments, no matter what the subject, consists of two components: **premises** and **conclusions.** The **conclusion** is the key assertion which the other assertions support. These other assertions are the **premises,** reasons that support the conclusion.* For example:

> Because a child born with anencephaly (a developmental disorder that prevents the brain from forming) has no capacity for mental functioning, and because there are infants in desperate need of organ transplants, the organs of such a child should be harvested.

In this example, the conclusion—that the anencephalic child's organs should be harvested—is supported by two premises: that such a child has no capacity for mental functioning and that there are infants in desperate need of organ transplants. For a group of assertions to be an argument, the passage must contain both these elements—a conclusion and at least one premise.

Look at the following letter to the editor of a news magazine:

> I was horrified to read "Corporate Mind Control" and learn that some companies are training employees in New Age thinking, which is a blend of the occult, Eastern religions, and a smattering of Christianity. What they're dealing with is dangerous— Krone Training will be disastrous to the company and the employee.

This writer thinks that she has written an argument against Krone Training, but her letter consists of a conclusion only, which is in essence that Krone Training is not a good idea. Because she fails to include any premises in support of her conclusion, she fails to present an argument and fails to convince anyone who did not already share her belief that

---

*Throughout this book, we use the term *premise* in its contemporary, general sense, meaning a claim (or statement) that leads to a conclusion. We do not restrict its meaning to the classical definition—either one of the two propositions of a syllogism from which the conclusion is drawn. See syllogisms in Chapter 6.

Krone Training is "dangerous" and "disastrous." A conclusion repeated in different words may look like an argument but shouldn't deceive a careful reader. (See Chapter 8 for more on deceptive arguments.) Can you formulate a premise that would transform the letter into an argument?

DISTINGUISHING BETWEEN PREMISES AND CONCLUSIONS

In order to evaluate the strength of an argument, we need to understand its structure, to distinguish between its premises and conclusion. Joining words—conjunctions and transitional words and phrases—indicate logical relationships between ideas, and therefore often help us to make this distinction. Notice the radical change in meaning that results from the reversal of two clauses joined by the conjunction "because":

> I didn't drink because I had problems. I had problems because I drank.
> —*Writer Barnaby Conrad*

The use of joining words in argument is especially important because they indicate which assertions are being offered as premises and which are offered as conclusions. For example:

> Our government's decision to apply a similar tariff on luxury Japanese cars sold here was a just one *because* Japan imposed a prohibitive tariff on the sale of new American cars in their country.

or

> Japan imposed a prohibitive tariff on the sale of new American cars in their country, *so* our government's decision to apply a similar tariff on luxury Japanese cars sold here was a just one.

In the first example, "because" indicates a premise, a reason in support of the conclusion that the decision to impose a tariff on Japanese cars was a just one. In the second example, "so" indicates the conclusion.

"Because" and "since" frequently introduce premises whereas "so," "therefore," "thus," "hence," and "consequently" often introduce conclusions.

> *conclusion* because *premise*
> *premise* therefore *conclusion*

Special note: "and" as well as "but" often connect premises.

STANDARD FORM

With the help of joining words and transitional phrases, we can analyze the structure of an argument and then put it into **standard form.** An argument in standard form is an argument reduced to its essence, its premises and conclusion. In other words, it is an outline of the argument. In the previous argument on infant organ transplants, each premise is indicated

THE STRUCTURE OF ARGUMENT **39**

by the "because" that introduces it, the conclusion then following from these two premises. In standard form, the argument looks like this:

Premise 1 A child born with anencephaly has no capacity for mental functioning.
Premise 2 There are infants in desperate need of organ transplants.
∴ The organs of such a child should be harvested.
Note: ∴ is a symbol in logic meaning "therefore."

Read this argument about college grading policies taken from a *New York Times* editorial by Clifford Adelman, a senior research analyst with the Department of Education.

If there are 50 ways to leave your lover, there are almost as many ways to walk away from a college course without penalty. What are prospective employers to make of the following "grades" that I have seen on transcripts: W, WP, WI, WX, WM, WW, K, L, Q, X and Z. What does "Z" mean? "The student 'zeed out,'" one registrar told me. At another institution, I was told that it stood for "zapped." Despite the zap, I was informed, there was no penalty.

But there is a penalty. The time students lose by withdrawing is time they must recoup. All they have done is increase the cost of school to themselves, their families and, if at a public institution, to taxpayers.

This increasing volume of withdrawals and repeats does not bode well for students' future behavior in the workplace, where repeating tasks is costly. Many employers agree that work habits and time-management skills are as important as the knowledge new employees bring. It wouldn't take much for schools to change their grading policies so that students would have to finish what they start.

Though this argument is three paragraphs long, in standard form it can be reduced to four sentences:

Premise 1 The time students lose by withdrawing is time they must recoup.
Premise 2 They increase the cost of school to themselves, their families and, if at a public institution, to taxpayers.
Premise 3 Work habits and time-management skills are as important as the knowledge new employees bring.
∴ Schools should change their grading policies so that students would have to finish what they start.

The first paragraph provides the reader with necessary background information since the writer can't assume that his readers will know the specifics of current college grading policies. The second paragraph contains two of his three premises while the final paragraph contains his third premise (and development of that premise) and his conclusion.

The conclusion of this argument—that schools should change their grading policy—is an inference, a judgment. Indeed, all conclusions are inferences. If they were facts we would not need to supply premises to support them; we would simply verify them by checking the source. In this argument, the first two premises are factual and the third is an inference, one which, on the basis of experience, most of us would be inclined to accept.

Examine this argument:

San Francisco Giants fans have long argued that the city should build a downtown baseball stadium. If the city doesn't build a new stadium the team may leave, and a major city deserves a major league team. Furthermore, the summer weather in downtown San Francisco is superior to that at Candlestick Park, the present site, and access for San Franciscans would be greatly improved.

In this example, four separate premises are offered for the conclusion.

Premise 1 If the City doesn't build a new stadium, the team may leave.

Premise 2 A major city deserves a major league team.

Premise 3 Summer weather in downtown San Francisco is superior to that at Candlestick Park.

Premise 4 Access for San Franciscans would be greatly improved.
∴ The city should build a downtown baseball stadium.

EXERCISE 3A

Reducing Simple Arguments to Standard Form

Put each of the following arguments into standard form by first circling the joining words and transitional phrases, then identifying the conclusion, and finally identifying the premises. List the premises, numbering each separate statement, and write the conclusion using the symbol ∴. Leave out the joining words and phrases, since standard form identifies premises and conclusions, but write each premise and the conclusion as a complete sentence.

Example: All politicians make promises they can't keep, and Jerry is nothing if not a politician. He will, therefore, make promises he can't keep.

1. All politicians make promises they can't keep.
2. Jerry is a politician.
∴ He will make promises he can't keep.

1. Because technical jobs are increasing more rapidly than other jobs, American high schools need to collaborate with industry in apprenticeship programs for those students who do not plan to attend college.
2. Because school vouchers would undermine public schools, permit discrimination, and transfer taxpayer money to those who need it least, private school parents, voters should not pass such legislation.
3. The student union building is ugly and uncomfortable. The preponderance of cement makes the building appear cold and gray both inside and out. Many of the rooms lack windows so that one is left staring at the cement wall. The chairs are generally cheap and uncomfortable while the poor lighting makes studying diffi-

cult, and the terrible acoustics make conversations almost impossible.

*4. Abortion raises important moral questions, for abortion involves both a woman's right to privacy and the question of when life begins, and anything that involves personal rights and the onset of life raises serious moral questions.

5. Many biologists and gynecologists argue that life does not begin at conception. And the Supreme Court ruled in 1973 that to restrict a woman's right to have an abortion violates her right to privacy. These two facts lead us to believe that abortion should remain a woman's choice.

6. Capital punishment is not justified since with capital punishment, an innocent person might be executed, and no practice that might kill innocent people is justified.

7. Because some killers are beyond rehabilitation, society should have the right to execute those convicted of first-degree murder. More uniform implementation of the death penalty may serve as a deterrent, and victims' families are entitled to appropriate vengeance. Furthermore, the costs of maintaining a prisoner for life are too great, and no state guarantees that life imprisonment means no parole.

8. In his celebrated work "On Liberty," a defense of freedom of speech, John Stuart Mill argues that "power can be rightfully exercised over any member of a civilized community" only in order to "prevent harm to others." Because he maintains that no opinion, no matter how disagreeable, can inflict harm, it follows that we don't have the right to suppress opinion.

9. Despite the controversy, we didn't need the movie rating NC–17 as we did not need the X rating before it. The R rating already protects children, and any further restriction of choice violates our freedom of expression guaranteed under the First Amendment. And as critics have pointed out, there are several R-rated films that are more sexually explicit than some rated NC–17, making the distinction between the two ratings unclear as well as unnecessary.

10. S. Frederick Starr, President of Oberlin College, argues in a controversial *New York Times* column that "colleges and universities should explore the possibility of a three-year baccalaureate." He claims that "higher education, private and public, is too expensive" with costs having risen 4.4 percent faster than inflation over a decade. He believes that a three-year degree would automatically reduce the cost to families and taxpayers by one quarter, and would provide several concrete educational benefits as well.

EXERCISE 3B

Reducing an Editorial to Standard Form

Put the argument presented in the following editorial into standard form.

Solves Surplus Problem

To the Editor:
At last, someone else—Elizabeth Joseph (Op-Ed, May 23)—has put into words what I have been silently thinking for some time: Polygamy makes good sense.

Nurit Karlin

Ms. Joseph writes from the perspective of a wife. I write from the perspective of a divorced working mother. How much more advantageous it would be for me to be part of a household such as Ms. Joseph describes, rather than to be juggling my many roles alone.

If polygamy were legal, the problem—and I see it as a problem—of the surplus of extra women would disappear rapidly. No matter how many polemics there may be in favor of the free and single lifestyle, a divorced woman can feel extra in today's society, more so if she has children, which can isolate her from a full social life. How much easier to share the burdens—and the jobs.

When more women can rediscover the joys of sisterhood and co-wifehood (which are as old as the Bible), and overcome residual jealousy as a response to this type of situation, I think our society will have advanced considerably.

Frieda Brodsky
Brooklyn, New York

AMBIGUOUS ARGUMENT STRUCTURE

Sometimes, the precise direction of an argument seems ambiguous; what is offered as conclusion and what is meant as supporting premise can be unclear. In such cases, it is important to look for what is most reasonable to believe, to give *the benefit of the doubt*. Try each assertion as the conclusion and see if the premises provide logical support for it, beginning with what seems most likely to be the intended conclusion.

Closely allied with the benefit of the doubt is the ancient methodological principle known as *Occam's razor*. Named for William of Occam, the most influential philosopher of fourteenth-century Europe (immortalized a few years ago as William of Baskerville in Umberto Ecco's novel, *The Name of the Rose*), this principle advocates economy in argument. As William of Occam put it, "What can be done with fewer assumptions is done in vain with more." In other words, the simplest line of reasoning is usually the best. Newspaper columnist Jon Carroll invoked Occam's razor when commenting on the O.J. Simpson trial: "I am not a juror; I am not required to maintain the presumption of innocence. I used Occam's razor, a tool that has served me well before. The simplest explanation is usually the true one; if a wife is killed, look to the husband."

Convoluted arguments, often those that sound the most impressive, can be difficult to unravel and rarely advance good reasoning. The ultimate question, however, when constructing an argument is always: What is enough? In the words of Toni Morrison, in her novel *Beloved*, "Everything depends on knowing how much, and good is knowing when to stop." But in most cases, our readers require more detailed support than we, as the advocates of a position, are likely to think necessary.

ARGUMENT AND EXPLANATION—DISTINCTIONS

As you elaborate support for premises in written argument, you will often rely on explanation—of terminology, of background, of your reasoning—but you must not lose sight of your purpose, which is to persuade your reader of the wisdom of your position.

An **argument** is an attempt to establish a basis for belief, for the acceptability of your conclusion. In argument, you present reasons for your conclusion in order to convince someone of your point of view.

In **explanation,** on the other hand, you are clarifying why something has happened or why you hold a given opinion. Look at these examples:

> I'm convinced he committed the crime because his fingerprints were on the murder weapon.

We are given a reason for believing that he committed the crime. We have an *argument*.

> He committed the crime because he needed money.

We are given a reason why he committed the crime. We have an *explanation*.
What about these? Which illustrates argument, which explanation?

> Don't go to that market because it's closed for renovation.
> Don't go to that market because the prices are higher than anywhere else and the checkout lines are slow.

EXERCISE 3C

Distinguishing Arguments from Explanations

Read the following editorials carefully and identify arguments and explanations. How do they differ in purpose? Explain your answers with references to specific passages in the columns.

They're Getting Older on Campus

The average age of college students went up a couple of years after 1
World War II when millions of servicemen used their GI Bill benefits to return to school. The age also climbed during the Vietnam war for an opposite reason: people could beat the draft by staying in school. Now, a state survey of the composition of the 1.68 million people enrolled for credit in California's public colleges and universities shows that the trend toward an aging student population is continuing—for a number of unrelated reasons.

The average age of all freshmen enrolled in the state's commu- 2
nity colleges, for instance, is 21.9 years. And the average age of part-time community college freshmen is 30.8 years. The average age of state university full-time graduate students is 30.8 years, but this average age stretches from 28.2 years at San Luis Obispo to 36.9 years at Cal State Bakersfield. The average age of women master's degree candidates is 33.7 years, almost two and a half years older than that of males. At one state university, Dominguez Hills, which has heavy minority enrollment, the average age of senior students was 28.9 years.

Dr. Horace Crandell of the staff of the California Postsecondary *3* Education Commission compiled the study and terms the results "startling." He speculates that some delay occurs because many students study only part-time before amassing enough units to transfer to U.C. or a state university.

Financial pressures force people to take longer to attain degrees. *4* Many of these students are also delayed, he believes, because they must first complete remedial courses. Many minority students are simply poorly prepared for the demands of higher education. Some of the older student population results, Crandell believes, because of decisions to change careers or life goals. And some of the increase in age may be because of unexpected unemployment and the need to prepare for a different occupation.

The students are also showing a marked interest in their pocket- *5* books. Huge increases have taken place over the past decade in mathematics and computer enrollments; environmental majors have declined by almost one-half.

It was not all that long ago that student activists warned their *6* peers not to trust anyone over 30. Now an awful lot of people over 30 seem to be right there on campus hitting the books. The change is astonishing.

Ethnic Restriction at Lowell High

A patently unfair policy that needs adjustment has been applied to *1* academically elite Lowell High School, ordered to deny admission to superbly qualified students because they just happen to fall within an ethnic quota.

Under a court-ordered desegregation plan, alternative schools *2* such as Lowell must limit the enrollment of any one ethnic group to 40 percent of the student body and must admit members of at least four ethnic groups. Chinese students at Lowell have reached 44.1 percent of a student population of 2807. The percentage of Chinese students throughout the entire San Francisco public school district of 65,000 students is 22.3 percent.

Lowell High School features a disciplined, academic regimen, *3* with emphasis on college-preparatory courses. Its admission standards are high, requiring an almost straight-A average and test scores above the ninety-seventh percentile.

Strict enforcement of the integration decree, made at the behest *4* of several groups that participated in the plan, means that half a hundred outstanding students of Chinese origin who have already qualified for Lowell will have to go elsewhere. Some observers believe this is a welcome development that tends to diffuse academic skills throughout the district, with bright students serving as lightning rods for their dull fellows. The Superintendent feels, to, that other public high schools offer equivalent educational opportunities.

A well-balanced school population is a desirable concept, but   *5*
Lowell has long attracted a citywide selection of scholars that has
made it one of the most prestigious secondary schools in the country.
Its enrollment should not be confined to a strict ethnic percentage.

APPLICATION TO WRITING

Argument Structure and Logical Essay Organization

When we put arguments into standard form, we ask critical questions: Is
this assertion the conclusion we are being led to believe? Or is it a premise
supporting the conclusion? Or does it support another premise? Asking
and answering questions such as these sharpens our analytical skills. But
analyzing argument structure also has specific application to writing.

Standard form can provide an outline of the argument, an excellent aid
in essay organization, one you can use either to plan your essay or to revise
it. Such an outline states the thesis of the essay—the conclusion of the argument—and each premise signals a new point to be developed.

If you have thought out your argument very carefully before you start
writing, you will find that putting it in standard form can lead to a good
working outline from which to proceed. Or you may find that you can impose standard form on your argument only when you have done some
writing. (Remember writing's power to actually generate ideas.) This kind
of outlining is particularly helpful in the revision stage of your paper.

Summaries

One way to explore an argument and reveal the important premises leading to a conclusion is to write a summary. Educator Mike Rose sees summary as an essential writing skill: "I [can't] imagine a more crucial skill
than summarizing; we can't manage information, make crisp connections,
or rebut arguments without it. The great syntheses and refutations are
built on it."

Summaries come in many lengths, from one sentence to several pages,
depending on the purpose of the summary and the length of the piece to
be summarized. Note, for example, the brief summaries at the conclusion
of each chapter in this text.

A good summary will be both complete and concise. To meet these
conflicting goals, you must convey the essence of the whole piece without
copying whole passages verbatim or emphasizing inappropriate features of
the argument. Background information, detailed premise support, and
narrative illustrations are usually omitted from summaries. Paraphrases of
ideas—the author's meaning expressed in your own words—rather than direct quotations, except for a critically important phrase or two, are pre-

ferred. A summary should also be objective, excluding inferences and opinions. These are reserved for argument analysis.

Strategies for Writing a Summary

Read the piece you want to summarize carefully, identify the question at issue, and mark off the conclusion and important premises. A short summary sentence written in the margin beside each important premise and the conclusion(s) can be helpful. Now you are ready to write a first draft based on this outline. To ensure a smoothly written, coherent summary, in your second draft provide appropriate conjunctions and transitional phrases to join sentences and connect ideas (look ahead in this chapter for joining strategies). And to ensure the conciseness that a summary demands, eliminate all "deadwood" from your sentences.

SUMMARIES SHOULD BE OBJECTIVE, CONCISE, COMPLETE, COHERENT, AND WRITTEN IN YOUR OWN WORDS.

 WRITING ASSIGNMENT 6

Constructing a Summary and Response

A. Read the following newspaper essay carefully, identify the question at issue, and sort out the various arguments offered.

B. Identify the conclusion to the argument Charlton Heston presents and supply the key premises in its support. Standard form can help you here.

C. Now write a summary of the article (approximately 150–200 words). You may want to compare summaries with classmates.

D. Having read the article critically and organized your interpretation in writing, write a letter to the editor of *the newspaper* in which you express your opinion of Heston's article and your position on the issues he raises. Discuss the premises he presents, and if you think of others not mentioned in the article, include them. Letters to newspapers, like summaries, are usually compressed, so you will need to be economical and selective with words here, limiting yourself to between 300 and 400 words.

Audience

Readers of *the daily newspaper* who will need the key points of the original argument before they move on to your response.

Purpose

To present an insightful analysis of a complex argument in order to illuminate the issue for your readers.

Why U.S. Must Support the Arts

By Charlton Heston[*]

Congress faces difficult issues this year in considering appropriations for the endowments for the arts and humanities. Cultural funding has never been easy or free of controversy.

The endowments have made mistakes. Some of the claims of politics in the humanities and lack of quality in the arts have been accurate. Some of the grants have been indefensible: a crucifix in a pot of urine, a self-portrait of a photographer with a bull-whip up his butt almost toppled the National Endowment for the Arts by themselves. The Smithsonian's original plans for the Enola Gay exhibit were equally appalling. It's crucial to prevent such blunders in the future.

But this does not, in my view, lead to the conclusion that the endowments should be defunded. I join with many other conservatives in supporting their continuation.

Similar issues were raised in 1981 when Ronald Reagan asked me to cochair—along with Hanna Gray, then president of the University of Chicago—a task force on the arts and humanities.

The task force found "a clear public purpose in supporting the arts and humanities: preservation and advancement of America's cultural and intellectual heritage, the encouragement of creativity, the stimulation of quality in American education and the enhancement of our general well-being."

We also found that these public purposes are well-served by a diversity of sources of support, from the private, voluntary and governmental sectors. We found that endowments have helped stimulate private support, set standards and spur innovation—both in large and small institutions and in aiding individual scholars and artists.

Let me speak of my own experience. When I came back from overseas after World War II, my wife and I went to New York to make our livings. The American theater was then entirely concentrated in 50-some blocks of Manhattan. All the theaters were there, as were all the offices of agents, producers and designers. Most of the actors, directors, writers and producers lived there, too. All the plays done in America were conceived, cast and rehearsed there. If their Broadway runs were successful, they then toured the country in a dozen or so large cities, but the American theater was centered in Manhattan. I remember my wife did a national tour while I was on the West Coast making a movie. They played five weeks in Los Ange-

[*]Actor Charlton Heston is an actor and political activist.

les in the only professional theater in the city. It was considered a phenomenal run.

Now, due in some part to the National Endowment for the Arts, there are major theaters in San Francisco, Chicago, Houston, Dallas, Seattle and many other cities, often with indigenous companies. The decentralization of the American theater is the most significant development since the death of vaudeville. The NEA deserves credit for that.

The NEA also created the American Film Institute, which I chaired for some years. Basically it serves film, generally recognized not only as the art form of the 20th Century, but the American art form. Its activities in many areas, perhaps most importantly in the archival preservation of American films, may in the long run prove to be their most important contribution.

The arts endowment's effort, seeded by federal tax dollars, helped to stimulate a vast opening up of America's heritage to its people. Conservatives generally agree that such a result is a "public good."

When we wrote our task force report in 1981, we had serious economic problems as a nation and major budgetary constraints. While the policies of those years essentially licked the high inflation of the '70s, I recognize we now have an even more serious problem in the federal budget deficit. I particularly sympathize with the very hard choices Congress faces. Let me be clearer; I fully understand that the endowments will have to share in budget cuts made in other areas.

Having said that, I also believe that the federal presence in supporting the arts and humanities can help with educating our young people in art, history, literature and the social sciences, just as the National Science Foundation helps with education in math and science. The arts and humanities are no less important than math and science. The national investment must not be abandoned. To do so would declare that these things so essential to our understanding of who we are as Americans don't really count. I know former Education Secretary Bill Bennet and former Labor Secretary Lynne Cheney don't believe that. They are correct to criticize endowment mistakes. These must be acknowledged and corrected. But it would be hurtful to the American tradition, and sharply out of the national character to repudiate the arts and the humanities. The United States would then be the only industrialized democracy that does not provide support for its culture.

This, we submit, is not what the American people want.

A great democracy like ours must neither abandon nor retreat from the world of ideas and culture. I urge Congress not to do this. The arts, the humanities, libraries and museums are part of the fabric of American life.

It has been said that the creation of the United States was the single most important political act in the history of mankind. I believe that. But for 40 years we've been wandering in the wilderness, in search of the promised land, as the Israelites followed Moses. I remember it well.

Now, even as they did, we have built a Golden Cow of entitlements in every area of our society. I know it is the job of Congress to dismantle this greedy creature; I applaud that undertaking. However, I beg Congress not to sweep away at the same time the immense good that's been done, at a very small cost, by these endowments. The humanities enrich the life of the American mind; art is the bread of our soul.

Logical Relationships Between Ideas—Joining Words

Joining words and transitional phrases are especially important in written argument because the strength of an argument is in part dependent on the clarity of the relationships between the premises and the conclusion. But their use is not limited to argument. Whether we are describing our Aunt Frances or telling of our narrow escape from an avalanche, these words are essential to conveying a logical sequence of thought. If logical connections are missing, the reader cannot follow the line of reasoning and will either stop reading or supply his own connections which may not be the ones intended.

As an example of the kind of "choppy" or disjointed writing that results from the omission of logical connections, look at the following excerpt from President Clinton's Inaugural Address.

> (1) When our Founders boldly declared America's independence to the world and our purpose to the Almighty, they knew that America to endure would have to change. (2) Not change for change sake but change to preserve America's ideals—life, liberty, the pursuit of happiness. (3) Though we march to the music of our time, our mission is timeless. (4) Each generation of Americans must define what it means to be an American.

Although sentence 1 relates to sentence 2, sentences 3 and 4 fail to relate to these first two sentences or to each other. The result: a correct but incoherent paragraph. Joining words may not "fix" this paragraph—incoherence is sometimes the result of problems in organization that can't be remedied by the mere addition of joining words. But their use promotes coherence, showing your reader the logical connections between your ideas.

Joining words fall into three categories: coordinating conjunctions, subordinating conjunctions, and transition words.

Note that, while the list of coordinating conjunctions is complete, the other two lists are partial, featuring only the most commonly used words from both categories.

Many of these words mean almost the same thing; they express the same logical connections between the ideas they join. For example, "but," "although," and "however" all express contrast, so we can join the following two ideas with any one of the three, and arrive at a similar, if not identical, meaning.

JOINING CHART

Logical relationship	Coordinating conjunctions	Subordinating conjunctions	Major transitions
Addition	and		also moreover
Contrast and Concession	but yet	while whereas although though even though	however on the other hand
Cause	for	because since as	
Result Effect	so and so	so that in that in order that	therefore thus hence consequently
Condition		if unless provided that	

I love foreign films, *but* I have difficulty with subtitles.

I love foreign films *although* I have difficulty with subtitles.

I love foreign films; *however,* I have difficulty with subtitles.

Choice of Joining Words

So what determines our choice? Notice that the two sentences joined by "but" and "although" are less formal in tone than the sentences joined by "however." We often find transition words such as "however," "moreover," "hence," and "consequently" in formal documents—legal briefs and contracts. In less formal writing, these words can be distracting, and so the best writers use them sparingly. Try an "And" or a "But" instead of "Moreover" or "However" to open a sentence and save the transition words for major transitions.

On those occasions when we use transition words, it can often be effective for fluency to embed them within the clause rather than begin with them. For example:

Zoe loves foreign films and rarely sees American made movies; *however,* her roommate prefers American gangster films. ["However" begins the clause.]

Zoe loves foreign films and rarely sees American made movies; her roommate, *however*, prefers American gangster films. ["However" is embedded within the clause.]

A REVIEW: PUNCTUATION OF JOINING WORDS

Coordinating conjunctions—put a comma before the conjunction when it joins two independent clauses unless the clauses are quite short.

> The homeless are creating and living in unsanitary conditions all over America, so cities must provide housing for them.

Subordinating conjunctions—introductory subordinate clauses [clauses which begin with a subordinating conjunction] are usually followed by a comma.

> *Although* the homeless are creating and living in unsanitary conditions all over America, cities are not providing needed housing.

When a subordinate clause follows the main clause, the comma is usually omitted.

> Cities are not providing needed housing *even though* the homeless are creating and living in unsanitary conditions all over America.

Transition words—transitional words and phrases, because they do not join sentences but only connect ideas, should be preceded by a semicolon or a period when they come between two clauses.

> The homeless are creating and living in unsanitary conditions all over America; *therefore,* cities must provide adequate housing for them.

If in the example above a comma rather than the semicolon preceded "therefore," many readers would consider it a run-together sentence or comma splice.

When a transition word is embedded within a clause, it is usually set off with commas.

> The homeless are creating and living in unsanitary conditions all over America; cities, *therefore,* must provide adequate housing for them.

EXERCISE 3D

Joining Sentences for Logic and Fluency

Make this disjointed argument cohesive and logical by joining sentences with appropriate joining words. You don't need to change the sequence of sentences.

Obstetricians perform too many caesareans. They can schedule deliveries for their own convenience. They can avoid sleepless nights and canceled parties. They resort to caesareans in any difficult delivery to protect themselves against malpractice suits. Caesareans involve larger fees and hospital bills than normal deliveries. Caesarean patients spend about twice as many days in the hospital as other mothers.

The National Institutes of Health confirmed that doctors were performing many unnecessary caesarean sections. They suggested ways to reduce their use. The recommendation was widely publicized. The obstetricians apparently failed to take note. In 1985, the operation was performed in 16.5 percent of United States' births. In 1992, 24.7 percent of the births were Caesareans.

HIDDEN ASSUMPTIONS IN ARGUMENT

Even when arguments appear to be well supported with premises, and where necessary, logical relationships are signaled with joining words, many real life arguments come to us incomplete, depending on **hidden assumptions,** unstated premises, and conclusions. Sometimes a missing premise or conclusion will be so obvious that we don't even recognize that it is unstated.

The burglar had dark hair, so Tracey certainly wasn't the burglar. [Missing premise: Tracey does not have dark hair.]

Ken is lazy and lazy people don't last long around here. [Missing conclusion: Ken won't last long around here.]

Since I've sworn to put up with my tired VW until I can afford a BMW, I must resign myself to the bug for a while longer. [Missing premise: I can't afford a BMW now.]

Filling in the omitted assumptions here would seem unnecessarily pedantic or even insulting to our intelligence.

Literature, by its nature elliptical, depends on the reader to make plausible assumptions:

> Yon Cassius has a lean and hungry look; such men are dangerous.
> —Shakespeare, Julius Caesar

Shakespeare assumes his audience will automatically make the connection—Cassius is a dangerous man. But not all missing assumptions are as obvious or as acceptable. At the heart of critical thinking lies the ability to discern what a writer or speaker leaves **implicit**—unsaid—between the lines of what he has made **explicit**—what he has clearly stated.

Dear Abby's readers took her to task for a response she made to a man who complained that because he shared an apartment with a man, people thought he was gay. Abigail Van Buren called this rumor an "ugly accusation." The implicit assumption here is that homosexuality is ugly, an assumption many of her readers—both gay and straight—objected to. One reader asked, "If someone thought this man was Jewish, Catholic or African American—would you call that an 'ugly accusation?'" Van Buren apologized.

Law professor Patricia J. Williams in *The Alchemy of Race and Rights* examines the implicit assumptions which led to the death of a young black man in New York in the late eighties. In this incident, three young black men left their stalled car in Queens and walked to Howard Beach looking for help, where they were surrounded by eight white teenagers who taunted them with racial epithets and chased them for approximately three miles, beating them severely along the way. One of the black men died, struck by a car as he tried to flee across a highway; another suffered permanent blindness in one eye.

During the course of the resultant trial, the community of Howard Beach supported the white teenagers, asking "What were they [the three black teenagers] doing here in the first place?" Examining this question, Williams finds six underlying assumptions:

Everyone who lives here is white.

No black could live here.

No one here has a black friend.

No white would employ a black here.

No black is permitted to shop here.

No black is ever up to any good.

These assumptions reveal the racism that led the white teenagers to behave as they did and the community to defend their brutality.

Dangers of Hidden Assumptions

Examine this seemingly straightforward argument:

John is Lisa's father, so clearly he is obligated to support her.

What's missing here? All fathers are obligated to support their daughters (or their children). But would everyone find this premise acceptable under all conditions? Probably not. What about the age factor? What about special circumstances: Lisa's mother has ample means while John is penniless and terminally ill? Or Lisa was legally adopted by another family, John being her birth father?

The danger with such incomplete arguments lies in more than one direction. A writer may leave his readers to supply their own assumptions, which may or may not coincide with those of the writer. If the issue is controversial, the risks of distorting an argument increase. Or, writers may deliberately conceal assumptions to hide an unsound, often misleading argument. Watch for these in advertising and politics. If you are on the alert for such deceptions, you are better able to evaluate what you read and hear and thus protect your own interests.

An example of a misleading argument:

Echoing the arguments of the National Physicians for Social Responsibility and some public school districts, the Board of Education of a prominent Archdiocese refused to participate in a federal civil defense program that taught ways of preparing for nuclear war. They objected to instructions for teachers and students which recommended that "if there should be a nuclear flash, especially if you feel the warmth from it, take cover instantly in the best place you can find. If no cover is available, simply lie down on the ground and curl up." Their objections were leveled not at the specific suggestions but at the underlying un-stated assumption: that nuclear war is survivable. In the words of the Board: "To teach children that nuclear war is a survivable disaster is to teach them that nuclear war is an acceptable political or moral option."

Hidden Assumptions and Standard Form

To help sort out the stated and unstated assertions in an argument, it can be illuminating to write out the argument in standard form. This means in-cluding the important hidden assumptions so the complete argument is before you and putting brackets around these assumptions to distinguish them from stated premises and conclusions.

Examples:

1. Harold is a politician so he's looking out for himself.
   a. [All politicians look out for themselves.]
   b. Harold is a politician.
      ∴ Harold is looking out for himself.

2. Products made from natural ingredients promote good health, so you should buy Brand X breads.
   a. Products made from natural ingredients promote good health.
   b. [Brand X breads are made from natural ingredients.]
      ∴ You should buy Brand X breads.

3. Products made from natural ingredients promote good health, and Brand X breads are made from natural ingredients.
   a. Products made from natural ingredients promote good health.
   b. Brand X breads are made from natural ingredients.
      ∴ [You should buy Brand X breads.]

EXERCISE 3E

Identifying Hidden Assumptions

A. The following arguments are missing either a premise or a conclusion. Put them into standard form, adding the implicit premise or conclusion; then place brackets around the missing assumptions you have inserted. A word to the wise: As with all argument analysis, find the conclusion first and then look for what is offered in its support.

   *1. Maggie is a musician, so she won't understand the business end of the partnership.
   2. Those who exercise regularly increase their chances of living into old age, so we can expect to see Anna around for a very long time.

3. I never see Loretta without a book; she must be highly intelligent.

4. As part of a wide-ranging statement on human sexuality, the U.S. Catholic bishops declared yesterday that homosexuality "is not freely chosen" and, therefore, "is not sinful."

5. Having become so central a part of our culture, television cannot be without its redeeming features.

6. Who shall give this woman in marriage?

7. CONVICTED: U.S. Petty Officer 3/c **Mitchell T. Garraway, Jr.,** of premeditated murder in the stabbing of a superior officer; in Newport, Rhode Island, January 30, 1986. The military court must now decide his sentence; its options include the death penalty. The last execution carried out by the Navy took place in 1849. (*Newsweek*)

8. From a letter to the *Sacramento Bee* after an article reporting that a nursing mother had been evicted from a downtown department store cafeteria (Thanks to Perry Weddle of Sacramento State University for this one.):

It was inhumane to deny this woman the right to nurse her baby in the cafeteria because she was simply performing a natural bodily function. (Where will this argument take you once you supply the suppressed assumption?)

B. The following article appeared in the news section of several major newspapers. Read it carefully and supply the hidden assumption it seems to be leading us to. Why would the writer choose to make this assumption implicit?

ROBERT REDFORD'S DAUGHTER RESCUED

SALT LAKE CITY—Shauna Redford, daughter of actor Robert Redford, was rescued when her car plunged into a river, authorities said yesterday.

They said Redford was wearing a seatbelt and suffered only minor injuries in the accident Friday.

Redford, 23, of Boulder, was rescued from her partially submerged auto by three other motorists, who saw her vehicle crash through a guardrail into the Jordan River, eight miles south of Salt Lake City.

The Utah Highway Patrol said the three rescuers released Redford's seatbelt, pulled her from the car and carried her to the riverbank.

She was held at a hospital overnight for observation and released.

Last summer, Sidney Wells, 22, a Colorado University student who had dated Shauna Redford, was shot and killed in Boulder. Police said the killing may have been drug related.

C. In June 1989, the Republican National Committee, referring to the then newly elected Democratic Speaker of the House, issued a three-page memorandum titled "Tom Foley: Out of the Liberal Closet." The memo went on to compare Foley's voting record with that of Representative Barney Frank, Democrat of Massachusetts, openly homosexual, who was described in the memo as "the ultra-liberal representative from Massachusetts."

What **innuendo** (an indirect derogatory remark which is implicit rather than explicit) is the Republican National Committee making about former speaker of the house, Tom Foley?

D. Find one advertisement or political cartoon in print journalism that clearly depends for its message on one or more unstated assumptions. Clip or photocopy the ad, write out the principal argument including the missing assertions, and bring it to class to discuss with classmates.

APPLICATION TO WRITING

Hidden Assumptions—Audience Awareness

As stated above, politicians and advertisers may deliberately suppress assumptions in order to manipulate the public. We will assume that we, as careful writers, do not share this goal and would not deliberately leave important assumptions unstated. At the same time, we don't want to bore our readers by spelling out unnecessary details. How do we determine what material to include, what to leave out?

George Lakoff and Mark Johnson, in their book *Metaphors We Live By,* point out that meaning is often dependent on context. They offer the following sentence as an example.

We need new sources of energy.

This assertion means one thing to a group of oil executives and quite another to an environmental group. The executives may assume the writer is referring to more offshore drilling, while the environmentalists may think the writer is referring to greater development of solar or other alternate sources of energy.

As writers we must consider our audience very carefully and understand the purpose for which we are writing. We will make choices about which assumptions must be made explicit according to our knowledge of the reader. Are we writing for an audience predisposed to agree with us, or one that is opposed to our point of view? Are we writing for readers who are knowledgeable about the subject or ignorant? The answers to these questions help us to determine what material to include and what to omit.

A critic reviewing *Murderers and Other Friends* by British writer John Mortimer comments on this relationship between a writer and his audience.

> Mortimer doesn't for a moment seem to believe that his new book will be read by anyone but old friends. He assumes we know Horace Rumpole and She Who Must Be Obeyed and that we've seen the television adaptations he has written of Evelyn Waugh's novel "Brideshead Revisited" and his own "Summer's Lease." He knows that we know about his father, the blind divorce lawyer, and the play he wrote about him, just as we know about his own years as a Queen's Counsel defending colorful riffraff in

the Old Bailey. In short, he assumes we have not only read his autobiography but also have been paying close attention to "Mystery!" and "Masterpiece Theater."

EXERCISE 3F

Identifying Your Reader

A common feature of many publications today is a section called "Personals." *The Nation* and *The New York Review of Books* (both probably in your library), and many local periodicals, including some campus papers, carry "Personals." What follows are four such ads, two from women who advertised in *Focus,* a public television magazine; and two from men who advertised in *The Daily Californian,* the University of California at Berkeley student newspaper.

Form four groups and choose one of the following ads to analyze and respond to together.

From *The Daily Californian*

MALE UCB student, 25, 6'1", interested in music, religion, literature, psychedelics, nature etc. seeks Lithuanian woman with beautiful soul—witty, pretty, intellectual, virtuous—for fun, friendship, maybe more.

ENGLISH/MUSIC major, 25, would like to meet witty, intellectual, attractive female (pref. math/physics/other science major) for concerts, foreign films & after dinner activities.

From *Focus*

Sensual Blue-eyed Blonde, successful entrepreneur, 30, 5'4" who is attractive, well travelled, well read, and has a great sense of humor, seeks a spiritual, self aware single white male, 30–45, 5'10" or taller, who is worldly but grounded, successful but sensitive, healthy but not fanatical and open to pursuing a long-term commitment. Note and photo appreciated.

Pretty Woman, International travel, Ivy education, health career, would like to meet professional man, 35–50, for tennis, dancing, bear hugs and possible first-time family. Photo appreciated.

Your aim is to understand the writer of the ad who will then become the audience for your response. Read the ad of your choice carefully. What kind of person is the writer? What can you infer about his or her character, personality, and values? What does the publication he or she chose to advertise in reveal about the writer? Read between the lines; what hidden assumptions are buried there?

After completing your analysis, as a group write a brief response informed by your knowledge of the writer of the ad. If time permits, reading these responses to the class might be entertaining.

WRITING ASSIGNMENT 7

A Letter of Application

Now, turn to the classified ads in any newspaper, select a job, and write a letter of application (a one-page cover letter). You will need to consider your audience very carefully in order to create a profile of your reader and a response that will appeal to him. Instead of a job in the classifieds, you may prefer to select an internship or a job on campus for this application.

Audience

A person who will be evaluating you for a position you particularly want.

Purpose

To present yourself as a desirable and qualified applicant for the position.

This writer has certainly considered his audience very carefully.

SUMMARY

In logic, the word argument has a special meaning, referring to rational discourse composed of premises and a conclusion rather than to a fight. It is useful to be able to recognize premises and conclusions in order to fully understand what an argument is proposing. Expressing arguments in standard form is a helpful strategy for understanding arguments.

Understanding the structure of arguments can be useful to writers when considering the organization of their written arguments.

The logical connections between assertions in argument can be signaled by conjunctions and traditional phrases to promote a logical flow of prose and ideas.

Arguments are frequently presented with some of the premises or the conclusion implied rather than stated. Sometimes such hidden assumptions are obvious, but in some instances they can be misleading and need to be made explicit. Recognizing hidden assumptions in argument is an important part of critical thinking.

KEY TERMS

Opinion a provisional judgment or belief, requiring proof or support. A first step in developing an argument.

Argument a rational piece of discourse, written or spoken, which attempts to persuade the reader or listener to believe something. Composed of at least one premise in support of a conclusion.

Conclusion the key assertion in an argument, the statement which the other assertions support; the point one hopes to make when presenting an argument.

Premise a reason that supports the conclusion in an argument.

Joining words words or phrases that indicate, or signal, the logical relationship between assertions in an argument. "Therefore" and its synonyms signal a conclusion; "because" and its synonyms signal a premise.

Standard form an argument reduced to its essence, its principal premises, and conclusion listed in simple outline form with premises numbered and conclusion stated at the end.

Hidden assumptions missing, unstated premises and conclusions in arguments; assertions that are necessary to recognize in order to fully understand an argument.

Explanation an attempt to clarify why something has happened or why you hold a given opinion.

Explicit clearly stated, distinctly expressed.

Implicit suggested so as to be understood but not plainly expressed.

Innuendo an indirect remark or reference, usually implying something derogatory.

Chapter
4

Written Argument

If the cultivation of understanding consists in one thing more than in another, it is surely in learning the grounds of one's own opinions.

—John Stuart Mill

*I*n the previous chapter, we focused on the structure of argument, distinguishing between premises and conclusions and reducing arguments to these two basic components. But how do we begin to write an argument?

FOCUSING YOUR TOPIC

A first critical step is to focus and refine the topic. At one time or another, we have all been part of heated political discussions between friends or family members. Grandfather states that taxes are too high under the current administration. Cousin Susan points out that corporations do not pay their fair share, while Dad shouts that the government funds too many social programs and allows too many foreigners to immigrate to this country. These discussions are often discursive and unsatisfying because they are not focused on one clear and precise **question at issue.**

For an argument to be successful, one person does not necessarily have to defeat another; one point of view does not have to be proven superior to another. An argument can also be considered successful if it opens a line of communication between people and allows them to consider—with respect—points of view other than their own. But if an argument is to establish such a worthwhile exchange, it must focus first on a single issue and then on a particular **question at issue.**

The issue
An **issue** is any topic of concern and controversy. Not all topics are issues since many topics are not controversial. Pet care, for instance, is a topic but not an issue; laboratory testing of animals, on the other hand, is an issue. In the hypothetical family discussion above, four issues are raised: taxes, the current administration, immigration, and government-funded

social programs. No wonder such a discussion is fragmented and deteriorates into people shouting unsupported claims at one another.

The question at issue

Whether we choose our own issue or are assigned one, the next step is to choose one **question at issue**—a particular aspect of the issue under consideration. Affirmative action, for instance, is an issue that contains many distinct questions at issue.

Should affirmative action play a role in university admissions?

Should affirmative action play a role in the work place?

Should affirmative action play a role in government contracts?

Has affirmative action led to discrimination against white males?

Should affirmative action based on gender be separated from affirmative action based on ethnic origin?

A writer who does not focus on one and only one question at issue risks producing a disorganized essay, one that will be difficult to follow since the readers will not be sure they understand the point the writer is arguing. Writing on the issue of how affirmative action has benefitted women, one student kept drifting away from that question at issue to another: should affirmative action play a role in university admissions? Since both her questions at issue were part of the same issue, affirmative action, and hence related, she was unaware that her paper was going in two different directions. The result was a disorganized, disjointed essay.

The following diagram illustrates that a single issue may contain any number of separate and distinct questions as issue. Your task as a writer is to isolate a particular question at issue and stay focused on it.

AFFIRMATIVE ACTION

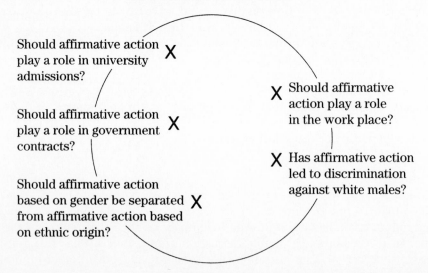

The thesis

The final step in establishing the focus of an essay is determining the **thesis.** While the issue and question at issue state, respectively, the subject and focus of the paper, they are neutral statements; they do not reveal the writer's opinion nor should they. To encourage objective analysis, the question at issue should be expressed in neutral rather than biased or emotionally charged language. The thesis, however, states the writer's position, her response to the question at issue, the conclusion of her argument.

When we begin a paper we may not know our position. We may need to learn more about the question at issue through research before arriving at a conclusion. But if our question at issue is clear and precise, we can proceed without a definite thesis or with only a tentative one since the writing process itself will help us to arrive at one. (Refer to chapter 1.)

And we don't necessarily have to arrive at a "yes" or "no" response to the question at issue. For example, if the question at issue is whether or not school administrators should have the right to censor student newspapers, our response may not be an unequivocal yes or no but a qualified response:

> School administrators should not have the right to censor student newspapers unless an article is libelous.

After completing the necessary research and examining various points of view, we may still be unable to reach a final conclusion. In this case, the thesis of the paper may be an evaluation of these various points of view with a tentative stand based on the unfolding of future events. [See Writing Assignment 10 on page 85.]

In essays by professional writers, the thesis is sometimes indirectly stated; it may be implicit rather than explicit. For instance, writer Sheila Koran argues in an essay that gay and lesbian couples should have the same legal spousal rights as married couples. She never directly states this thesis as she describes the life she lives with her mate, a life like any other family's, but the point is clearly made; the reader is never confused about the purpose of the essay. In general, the more experienced the writer, the more she is able to write a focused essay without an explicit thesis.

Another option we have when writing a thesis is to decide whether or not it should be "complete" or "open." An open thesis states the writer's opinion but not the reasons for her opinion. A complete thesis includes both the writer's opinion and all of the reasons or premises that support this conclusion. For example:

> An "open" thesis:
> Access to the Internet should be controlled.

> A "complete" thesis:
> Because children need protection from pornography, our right to privacy is threatened, and "intellectual property" can be too easily pirated, access to the Internet should be controlled.

A compromise:

Access to the Internet raises serious moral, legal, and even constitutional questions, the nature of which suggests that such access should be controlled.

Which thesis statement is preferable? It is a matter of choice, the writer's choice. Some writers fear that the complete thesis will not capture the reader's interest, believing that if all the reasons for the conclusion are given in the thesis, the reader's curiosity will not be aroused. On the other hand, a writer may prefer the greater clarity of the "complete" thesis, for herself and her readers. In any case, even if a writer chooses the open thesis approach, at some point in the process she should be just as clear about the reasons for her position as the writer who chooses the complete thesis.

As a general guideline to assist you in deciding the most suitable thesis approach to take, keep in mind the complexity of the topic, the length of the paper, the needs of your audience, and the purpose of your project. In a long paper on a complex topic, the reader may welcome the clarity of the complete thesis or at least a modified one, but in a short essay on a simple topic, the complete thesis is probably not necessary and may be too mechanical.

Keep in mind that a thesis is not necessarily restricted to one sentence as in the examples above. In fact, it's not unusual for a complete thesis to require a paragraph. And remember too, that a well-thought-out and clearly expressed thesis will guide writer and reader, keeping both focused on the question at issue and the writer's position.

EXERCISE 4A

Identifying the Issue, Question at Issue, and Thesis

Complete the following sets by supplying the missing element.

1. *Issue:*
   Question at Issue: Should universities put a cap on fee increases?
   Thesis: To ensure an economically diverse student population, universities should put a cap on fee increases.
2. *Issue:* Private militias
   Question at Issue: Should the government have the right to control the public speech of private militias?
   Thesis:
3. *Issue:* Affirmative action
   Question at Issue:
   Thesis: Because affirmative action offers the only sure way of addressing the documented discrimination of the past, it should play a role in college admissions.

SHAPING A WRITTEN ARGUMENT—RHETORICAL STRATEGIES

What do we mean by *rhetorical*? The term **rhetoric** has various shades of meaning, but the following definition adapted from Aristotle provides the most useful approach for our purposes: "The art of using language to good effect, to prove, to convince, to persuade."

And thus to argue. The structure of written argument as we know it today dates back to the orations of Greece and Rome. The following features of classical argument, modified by contemporary rhetoric, can serve us well as long as we recognize that they are options, not requisite components. We write to communicate, not to fit a formula or fulfill a set of narrow expectations.

The Introduction

How you begin your argument will depend on the issue, the audience, and your own style. The key question is: how much can you expect your readers to know about your question at issue? If your subject has received a great deal of recent media attention, you will probably not need to supply very much background. If, on the other hand, your subject is rather obscure or quite technical, then you will most likely have to supply your readers with the necessary background information—the history of the case or the specific circumstances that gave rise to the present problem—so that they can understand the argument to follow.

If not much background is required, you may want to begin your essay with a relevant narrative, either actual or fictional, which illustrates your question at issue. For example, if your subject is euthanasia, you may want to describe a day in the life of a terminally ill patient. Such a scene will capture the reader's interest—not a necessity but sometimes a valuable rhetorical strategy. A relevant quotation can also provide an interesting way into your argument. Or you may choose to open with an opposing view and build your argument on a refutation of what is often the prevailing wisdom on an issue.

No matter what approach you choose, you have considerable flexibility. Your introduction may be a single paragraph or run to three or four paragraphs depending on the strategies you choose and the amount of background required. Usually, although not always, you will state your position (your thesis, the conclusion of your argument) somewhere in the introductory paragraphs so that your reader is clear about the purpose of the essay.

For a variety of introductory strategies, examine the three sample essays in Exercise 4D, page 74. In "Capital Punishment," you will find an introduction composed of two paragraphs, the first making a concession, the second moving toward the writer's thesis at the end. The author of "Rap Takes a Bum Rap" includes an analogy and a statement of what Rap is not before stating his thesis. Randy Shilts, in a professional newspaper essay on a politically complex topic, provides considerable background information before arriving at his thesis.

The Development of Your Argument

Once again, the possibilities, while not infinite, are numerous. You will need to present as many strong premises in support of your position as necessary. These in turn will have to be elaborated, explained, and defended with as much specific detail, example, and illustration as you can provide. You may draw on personal experience, research, and respected authorities to support your position. Called, in classical rhetoric, the *confirmation* of your position, this support should be connected explicitly to your thesis unless the logical ties are self-evident. As Plato said in the *Phaedras*, "What is stated outright will be clearer than what is not."

Sometimes one premise will require a whole paragraph or more. Others may need only a few sentences and can be effectively grouped with additional premises. Audience and purpose as well as your topic will play a role in your choices. Here are two examples of paragraphs lifted from the middle of student essays, one that develops a single premise in some detail, another that groups a series of premises together in one paragraph.

A single premise paragraph:

Since the NCAA (National Collegiate Athletic Association) policy of random drug testing was begun some years ago, public debate on this issue has increased, and the idea of drug testing for college athletes has been challenged for a variety of reasons. The strongest argument against drug testing of college athletes is that it is unconstitutional. An athlete should be entitled to the same constitutional rights as other citizens, and drug testing violates both the Fourth Amendment's provisions against unreasonable search and seizure, and the Fifth Amendment's provision of the right to refuse to furnish potentially incriminating evidence about one's self?[*] As various forms of drug testing were subjected to legal challenges, the courts tended to rule that drug testing is, indeed, unconstitutional. *Time* magazine reported that " . . . a number of judges have already ruled that mass testing violates workers' constitutional rights to privacy and protection from self-incrimination," and quoted Federal Judge Robert Collins, who called a U.S. Customs Service drug testing program "unreasonable and wholly unconstitutional." In the late eighties, the Appellate Division of the New York State Supreme Court ruled that probationary teachers in a Long Island school district could not be compelled to submit to urinalysis because the tests would be an unconstitutional invasion of privacy (Kaufman, 19). In the case of Simone LeVant, the Stanford diver who has so far been the only athlete to challenge the NCAA drug tests in court, *The New York Times* reported that Judge Peter G. Stone of the Santa Clara county Superior Court agreed with the athlete and her attorney that mandatory urine tests were an obtrusive, unreasonable, and unconstitutional invasion of privacy.

A Multipremise Paragraph:

Although it is a controversial proposition, legalizing drugs has many advantages. First of all, it will free the now overburdened legal system to do its job dispensing justice.

---

[*]Given the length of this paragraph, some writers might choose to divide it in two, starting a new paragraph here where the examples begin. Paragraphing, while certainly not arbitrary, can be flexible and should serve the needs of the reader as well as the logic of the argument.

Cases will be processed with greater speed since the system won't be overwhelmed with drug cases. With the legalization of drugs, violent drug related crimes will decrease. As a result, prisons will be less crowded, which in turn will allow serious offenders to serve longer terms. Legalizing drugs will free law enforcement officials to combat other serious crimes more effectively. With the money saved from law enforcement and legal procedures, a more effective campaign of educating the public on the maladies of drugs can be mounted, and more money will be available for rehabilitation of drug addicts. Finally, by legalizing drugs, we can slow down the spread of AIDS among IV drug users, who will be able to get clean needles and not have to share with other drug addicts, many of whom are infected with AIDS. The positive results of legalizing drugs definitely outweigh the negative consequences.

In the case of the second paragraph, the writer has only just begun with such a summary approach to a broad subject. Each individual premise will have to be given specific support in subsequent paragraphs.

How Many Premises Should an Argument Have?

It would seem that the greater the number of premises, the stronger the argument, but this quest for quantity should not be at the expense of quality; in other words, weak or questionable premises should not be included just to increase the number of premises. It's possible to have a very strong argument with only one or two premises if those premises are extremely convincing and are developed in detail.

The Conclusion

We have no simple rule of thumb here other than to suggest you conclude your essay rather than simply stop. If your paper is long and complex, you need to help your reader by briefly summarizing where you have been and what you propose. If you present only a tentative or partial thesis in the introduction, then you need to be sure that your final position is clear in the conclusion. If you think that further investigation is still needed before you can arrive at a responsible "conclusion" on the issue, then recommend what direction you think such investigation should take. If, as a result of your argument, you have definite recommendations for action, your conclusion can carry such suggestions.

You and your readers should feel satisfied at the close of your paper. This does not mean that every paper needs a long and redundant formulaic conclusion. Once again we refer you to the sample essays in Exercise 4D for models.

And so your argument assumes its shape. Commenting on effective rhetoric, Plato, quoting Socrates, summed it up this way in *Phaedrus:*

> Every discourse, like a living creature, should be so put together that it has its own body and lacks neither head nor feet, middle nor extremities, all composed in such a way that they suit both each other and the whole.

A DIALECTICAL APPROACH TO ARGUMENT

Effective argument is more than the straightforward presentation of a thesis, premises, and their support. Most issues worth arguing today are complex, with evidence sometimes contradictory or ambiguous. Arguments on such issues should reflect a flexible mind, one capable of thinking *dialectically*. From this term's various meanings, we can extract a definition of **dialectic** appropriate for written argument:

> a process of examining an issue by looking at it from opposing points of view

or to elaborate a little:

> a method of argument that systematically weighs contradictory ideas with a view to resolution of their contradictions

It is this interplay of conflict among seeming opposites that can help us arrive at some form of "truth" or resolution. Through logical disputation we test and explore our ideas as we search for a viable position. As German philosopher Georg Hegel saw it, the dialectic is a *process* of change whereby an idea, a *thesis*, is transformed into its opposite, *antithesis*. The combination of the two is then resolved in a form of truth, *synthesis*. Aristotle described this final common ground as *stasis*.

English philosopher John Stuart Mill was trained by his father to argue both sides of every question and was taught that you had no right to a belief unless you understood the arguments for its opposite.

Eleanor Roosevelt advised women in politics to "argue the other side with a friend until you have found the answer to every point which might be brought up against you." We would second her advice.

And cognitive psychologist Piaget maintained that one mark of a maturing mind is the ability to take another's point of view and thus be capable of considering two conflicting views on the same issue.

A book reviewer takes Camille Paglia and her book *Sex, Art, and American Culture* to task for not having this capability:

> . . . she is constitutionally incapable of splitting a difference. She is one of the least dialectical minds that ever claimed to be critical. Her style is a style of pure assertion. It has no philosophical shading or depth.

Dialectical thinking moves us to a richer form of argument in which the process of interweaving premises and counterarguments leads us to a new, stronger position on the issue.

Addressing Counterarguments

To take this dialectical approach to argument, you as a writer must pay careful attention to opposing views, acknowledging within your paper important **counterarguments** and thus those members of your audience who might hold them.

But, one might ask, why aid and abet the opposition by calling attention to their arguments? For a number of good reasons such strategies can actually strengthen your own position.

- By *anticipating* your opponent's reasoning, you can often disarm the opposition. The "I recognize that. . . ." approach can be very effective, showing the writer's knowledge of the opposition's viewpoint.

- You can make your own position stronger when you state and then *refute* opposing premises by demonstrating their weakness or falseness. You must handle refutation tactfully, however, if you hope to convince those opposed to your position. If you treat them with contempt, as though they are shortsighted and thickheaded for holding the position they do, you will only alienate them and defeat your own purpose, which is to have your views heard.

- By addressing counterarguments to your position, you also appear more reasonable, more fair. You are seen not as narrow-minded, dogmatic, or unheedful of others' views, but as broad-minded and aware of complexity and so ultimately as more intelligent, reliable, and thus credible.

- And when you *acknowledge* the possibility of merit in some of your opponents' reasoning, you have taken the ultimate step in establishing yourself as a "generous" thinker. Arguments are rarely truly one-sided, no matter how strong your convictions. When you can *concede* a point, you move closer to a middle ground, opening a line of communication and thus increasing your chances of winning your final point.

- You may even discover weaknesses and contradictions in your own thinking as you sort through the reasoning of your opponents. It is not easy to abandon cherished beliefs, but clear thinkers often must.

How Much Counterargument?

How much counterargument should writers include in their papers? There is no precise answer to this question. If the writer has strong refutations for every one of the opposition's premises, then she may want to address all these premises. If, on the other hand, a writer thinks the premises she has to support her conclusion are stronger than her refutation, she may want to include only a minimum of counterargument. In any case, a writer cannot ignore the most compelling opposing premises even if they provide the greatest challenge to the writer's own view. For example, in a paper in favor of euthanasia, the writer would have to deal with the widely held belief that euthanasia is a form of murder or suicide.

Refutation and Concession

As you can see from this discussion, there is more than one way to address counterarguments. But address them you must, since to present a contradictory position and then leave it alone would confuse your reader. Here are two possible responses:

1. **Refutation:** Present a counterargument and then explain why this position is false, misleading, irrelevant, or weak; discredit it in some well-reasoned way.

   From a student essay in support of a law sanctioning active euthanasia:

   Some say death and suffering are in keeping with God's universal plan for humanity. Functioning to educate, to prepare people for the painless eternity of heaven, the dying process, no matter how long or how agonizing, has both spiritual and moral purpose. **To believe this argument though, one must believe there is life after death and many do not. So why can't people live and die in accordance with their own value system? Let both the religious and secular have some control of their own destiny; give those who choose to die that alternative, while honoring the belief of those who do not.** [emphasis added]

2. **Concession:** Recognize the merit of a counterargument and so concede that point or (as in our example below) a feature of it. If, for example, you are arguing in favor of euthanasia and want to refute the counterargument that euthanasia is a form of murder, you might begin this way:

   Although I also believe that life is sacred and murder is wrong, I don't think that ending the life of a brain-dead patient is equivalent to murder since in the true sense of the word "life," this patient is not living.

Visually, the relationship between Counterargument and Refutation and Concession looks something like this:

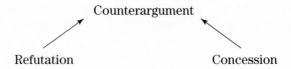

Counterargument

Refutation   Concession

Rogerian Strategy

For a deeper appreciation of concession we turn to the psychology of communication, particularly the work of Carl R. Rogers, a psychotherapist and communication theorist.

Carl Rogers recognized that people tend to establish barriers, grow more rigid in their beliefs when threatened, and are thus less open to alternatives. If we view argument, whether spoken or written, not as a hostile contest between adversaries but as a dialogue, as an open exchange of ideas directed toward mutual understanding, we may find a more responsive audience and thus have greater success with changing people's opinions. If we are genuinely concerned with communicating our ideas to others, we must cultivate the audience to whom we direct these ideas. To achieve this end, we must develop *empathy*—the ability, in Roger's words, "to see the expressed idea and attitude from the other person's point of view, to sense how it feels to him, to achieve his frame of reference in regard to the thing he is talking about." ("Communication: Its Blocking and Its Facilitation," *Et cetera,* vol. IX, no. 2.) It is through empathy that we can most successfully understand another's position and so concede appropriate points, often gaining rather than losing ground in the process.

Take, for example, the issue of the death penalty. If a writer can understand why someone believes the death penalty serves as a deterrent and can acknowledge that understanding, a reader who favors the death penalty will be more inclined to consider the writer's arguments opposing the death penalty. The reader will feel less threatened as the writer reduces the gap between them and replaces hostile judgment with "mutual communication," helping a defensive opponent to see alternatives to her beliefs. Such a commitment can, as Rogers points out, carry risks. As a writer begins to "really understand" another person's point of view, she runs "the risk of being changed" herself. This spirit of conciliation and cooperation can sometimes be painful. But the gain in understanding can pay off handsomely as rigidity and defensiveness evolve into problem solving.

These ideas are not entirely new. Well over two thousand years ago, Aristotle spoke of an essential triad in argument, *logos, ethos,* and *pathos:*

logos the argument itself (derived from the Greek, meaning both "word" and "reason")

ethos the disposition of the writer (speaker) to present herself well

pathos empathy with the audience

MACHLIS

Carl Rogers and Aristotle both suggest that effective argument depends not only on a well-informed writer but also on a writer who is acutely aware of her audience and well disposed toward them.

The alternatives for organizing Rogerian concessions within an essay are the same as those discussed above under refutation and concession and as illustrated in the sample essays in Exercise 4D.

Can you identify the Rogerian strategy in this cartoon?

"He says his ballads sing of the brotherhood of man, with due regard for the stabilizing influence of the nobility."

When There Is No Other Side

What makes an issue worth arguing? While there are no fast rules, issues inappropriate for argument fall into three general categories. Some positions are simply too offensive to the majority of writers or readers. Arguments advocating racial bigotry, for example, fall into this category. Others are so personal or so self-evident that they don't lend themselves to intelligent debate. Take for example the following claims:

Chocolate ice cream is far superior to strawberry.

or

Free, quality education should be provided for all children in America.

Neither proposition lends itself to the kind of exploration we have been discussing in this chapter, in the first instance because it concerns a personal and insignificant preference, and in the second because no one could in all seriousness argue against it.

For an effective argument

support your own position as thoroughly as possible

present relevant opposing views

provide appropriate concessions and refutations

develop empathy with your audience

APPLICATION TO WRITING

Logical Joining of Contrasting and Concessive Ideas

To express contrast and concession, so necessary for effective written argument, you need to manipulate your sentences to convey logical relationships. We introduced principles of logical joining with the discussion of conjunctions in Chapter 3 and continue that discussion here.

EXERCISE 4B

Expressing Contrast and Concession

Below are three different attitudes on smoking in the workplace. Read the passages carefully, examine the logical relationship between ideas, then state the position of each writer and explain how you reached your decision.

1. The battle rages on. Whereas some contend that smoking, as a direct threat to health, should be banned in the workplace, others maintain that forbidding smoking is too extreme a measure. Recent medical evidence demonstrates that cigarette smoke is harmful to nonsmoking bystanders as well as smokers, but smokers argue their emotional health is at stake. They point out that such discrimination threatens their constitutional civil rights, while executives and nonsmoking employees claim that medical costs from health problems and time lost from work justify such restrictions of personal choice.

2. Although most people recognize that smoking is a direct threat to health, making nonsmoking a condition of employment constitutes a new form of discrimination.

3. While banning smoking on the job can create serious personnel problems for a company, current medical evidence strongly supports those who argue for a completely smoke-free work environment.

As you have no doubt noticed, it is through the different choices of joining words that these writers established their slant on the issue here. Let's review these distinctions:

COORDINATING CONJUNCTIONS	SUBORDINATING CONJUNCTIONS	MAJOR TRANSITIONS
contrast:	contrast & concession:	contrast & concession:
but yet	while whereas although though	however on the other hand

The Concessive Sentence

The degree to which subordinating conjunctions express concession can vary according to the content of the sentence. In sentence 3 above, the writer recognizes the merit of a counterargument. But in some cases you may simply acknowledge your opponent's position without really conceding it, as in the following example:

> *Although* smokers defend their constitutional rights, the health of a nonsmoker should come first.

EXERCISE 4C

Making Rhetorical Choices

Try joining the following pair of sentences in three different ways: from the perspective of a film buff, a responsible financial planner, and someone genuinely uncommitted.

1. I desperately want to see the new Tarantino movie.
2. I know I need to save money for books, not to mention groceries.

EXERCISE 4D

Identifying Rhetorical Features of Argument

Three well-developed arguments follow, two written by students and one by the late Randy Shilts (Pulitzer Prize winner for *And the Band Played*

On, an examination of the AIDS crisis). They all use the rhetoric of argument effectively. In the first student essay, we identify the elements presented in this chapter:

thesis

premises

counterarguments

concessions and refutations used to address opposing views

Rogerian strategy

We ask you to identify these same features in the second student essay and the Shilts piece (or one of these if your class has time constraints).

Capital Punishment: Help or Hindrance to American Society

The newspaper headlines are appalling: a young man is brutally murdered by a gang of thugs when he attempts to defend his parents from attack; a woman jogger is abducted, raped, and killed, her mutilated body dumped like garbage in a ditch by the side of the road; a small child dies from the multiple broken bones and internal injuries received at the hands of his abusive parents. How is it possible to remain calm and rational when confronted with such senseless violence and cruelty directed by human beings against one another, especially when the result is disability or death for the victim? Perhaps it is not surprising to see members of our society, angry and afraid, attempting to deal with increasing criminal violence by supporting the use of capital punishment. *1*

More and more, our society relies on capital punishment to protect citizens by preventing and deterring violent crime: to avenge through retributive justice the pain and suffering inflicted by criminals on victims and their families, and to provide a kind of "collective relief" to its members by disposing of people who are aberrant, offensive, and unmanageable. However, I believe capital punishment should be abolished within the United States because I am convinced *2* that imposition of the death penalty is not the only effective way to decrease the incidence of violent crimes; the execution of criminals does not necessarily bring about justice; and the "sigh of relief" afforded society through the use of capital punishment actually results in the dehumanization of our society as a whole.

Obviously, the execution of convicted criminals can be viewed as a means of protecting society, since a dead person is unable to commit further crimes, violent or otherwise. However, because there is no way to predict accurately whether or not a criminal would break *3*

Rogerian Strategy

Counterargument

Thesis

Concession

the law again, two problems arise. First, it is impossible to know exactly how well capital punishment succeeds in preventing crimes of violence because the number of crimes prevented by execution cannot be accurately known. Second, in order to provide society with maximum protection, *every* criminal convicted of violent crime must be executed to ensure he will not repeat his crime. Given these problems, the continued use of capital punishment as a crime prevention measure seems unjustifiable and brutal, especially when long-term imprisonment can provide virtually the same amount of protection to society without taking human life.

Similarly, the deterrent effects commonly attributed by society to use of the death penalty cannot be demonstrated because they cannot be measured. Social scientists have no way of computing the number of violent crimes *not* committed, nor can they know the motivation of each violent criminal when he makes the decision whether or not to break the law. However, if capital punishment works to deter violent criminals, as its use increases the incidence of crimes of violence in our nation should show a correspondent decrease, which is unfortunately not the case. In this instance as well, the use of long-term imprisonment appears to have the same deterrent effect as imposition of the death penalty, without unnecessary loss of life. In light of these facts, clearly the use of capital punishment is not the best way of either preventing or deterring violent crime in our society.

When a murder has been committed, it is easy to view imposition of the death penalty as a good way to "even the score." Recently, I read a magazine article documenting an interview with a man whose only son had been murdered. The father kept repeating his wish to attend the execution of his son's convicted killer so he would know the boy's death has been avenged and "justice" done. Although I sympathize with the father's grief, several questions keep running through my mind: Is it really possible to "get even"? Will executing the murderer bring the son back to life? Will it obliterate the pain and terror the boy felt at the time of his death? How is "justice" served by trying to erase the death of one person by killing another? Perhaps my math is faulty, but I do not understand how one dead body added to another dead body can equal anything but two dead bodies. And I have another question: What happens if the wrong person is arrested, tried, convicted, and executed? To make an all-too-possible mistake and execute the wrong person in the name of justice would be the ultimate *injustice*. In order for the use of the death penalty to be viable, its application must be foolproof. Since the possibility of error exists, the use of capital punishment can never guarantee that justice will be carried out.

Last of all—and most of all—I am concerned about what happens to a society whose members condone capital punishment. I believe few of us would be willing to witness an execution, much less participate by shooting the gun, throwing the electrical switch, or

4

5

6

dropping the cyanide pellet to kill another person, even someone convicted of a heinous crime. Yet we seem to be perfectly willing to tell the government to do our dirty work for us, somehow believing personal responsibility can be eluded if the killing is delegated to an invisible civil servant paid to do the job. However, whether we like it or not, each member of our society becomes individually responsible when group approval is given for the taking of human life. Capital punishment involves the killing of a human being in the attempt to justify one murder by the commission of another, and human life is devalued when we succeed in distancing ourselves from that knowledge. Instead of strengthening our society, the use of capital punishment weakens it by allowing us to ignore the inherent humanity of *every* person.

Dependence on the execution of criminals is one way of attempting to deal with the increase of violent crime plaguing American society; yet it is not the only way of handling the problem, nor is it the best way. The use of capital punishment does not stop crimes or violence and it does not assure justice will be done. It does, however, damage our society by causing it to resort to violence in an attempt to control violence. Therefore, because use of the death penalty does not help society but actually hinders it, I suggest capital punishment no longer be allowed within the United States. 7

Mickie Lee Christensen

Rap Takes a Bum Rap

Even the president and vice president have gotten into the act, posturing about Ice-T's "Cop Killer" (as if boycotting Time Warner would reduce the national debt).

—Sherley Anne Williams[1]

Since its birth, Rap music has taken the blame for many of the problems plaguing America's inner cities—violence, drugs, AIDS, you name it. But Rap music cannot take the blame for these problems any more than, say, soap operas can shoulder the blame for infidelity in America. Rap is an art form, a medium which expresses, enrages and educates like most other art forms. As Guru says in the introduction to his album *Jazzmataz,* Rap is "musical, cultural expression based on reality." It does not cause problems but, instead, expresses them just as some movies, television shows and other forms of music do. However, unlike most of the mindless violence depicted in today's 1

---

[1]Williams, Sherley Anne. "Two Words on Music: Black Community." *Constellations: A Contextual Reader for Writers.* 2nd ed. Ed. John Schlib, Elizabeth Flynn & John Clifford. New York: Harper Collins, 1995. 611–617.

popular movies—*True Lies, Killing Zoe, Pulp Fiction*—Rap is a constructive outlet which brings attention to our country's problems in a creative, innovative and sometimes positive fashion.

In fact, the roots of rap are based in creativity and innovation. *2* With its humble beginnings in the black ghettos as filler between songs at parties, Rap has become a multi-million dollar business and one of the most established forms of new music in the past decade. The original idea was simple: two turntables and a microphone. The DJ, in command of the turntables, manipulates the records in order to form a beat or provide snippets of musical accompaniment. The "MC" then "busts out" in a fit of rhyme based stories, usually about the DJ's ability to "spin" or the MC's ability to "rap." However, as rap became more and more popular, the rappers began focusing their attention on the larger issues of life in the ghetto—violence, drugs, and oppression—forming two separate branches of Rap.

The first, and currently the most popular, is known as "gangsta" *3* rap, a rough mix of extreme violence and heavy rhythms, sounding something like broken glass on an inner city basketball court. The second, which is quickly gaining momentum, is known as hip-hop, a jazz based, dance mix which is much more complex and layered than gangster. The music of hip-hop evokes the feel of a smoky, Soho jazz club in the 1950s while the words relate stories of ghetto life in the 1990s. The message of hip-hop is upbeat, oftentimes offering solutions or alternatives to the problems rather than focusing solely on them. Although gangsta and hip-hop differ in their style and message, both forms are important for their ability to educate and to offer a creative outlet.

In fact, Rap's ability to educate its listeners is an often overlooked *4* but crucial element of the music. Several groups envision the music as their way to speak directly to kids. Groups such as the Bay Area's Disposable Heroes of Hiphoprisy believe that they, as Rap artists, are the only role models the children may have and therefore work to fill their music with thoughts on politics, environmentalism and other social issues in hopes of raising the consciousness of their listeners. Many of their songs are like quick morality plays. For instance, on the Disposable Heroes' latest album, *Hypocrisy is the Greatest Luxury,* they have a song entitled "The Language of Violence" about a boy who goes to jail for killing another boy. In the song, the killer is caught and sent to jail where he is raped by the inmates. Michael Franti, the lyricist of the group writes, "He had never questioned his own sexuality but this group of men didn't hesitate their reality, with an awful powerful showerful an hour full of violence." In the end, the song takes a more philosophical vein and asks: "is this a tale of rough justice in a land where there's no justice at all. Who is really the victim? Or are we all the cause, and victim of it all." Franti's aim is to get the kids who might commit acts of violence to think not only of the immediate physical consequences of their actions, but of the larger picture of violence and victimization. He says that "death is the silence in this circle of violence." The same is true of other rap artists such as the Digable Planets, The Pharcyde and Guru. These groups fill their albums with a smoky coolness of life on the streets and the choices available to the kids. They tell stories of street life with a more positive and hopeful edge, working to expand the vision of the listener, to help them see beyond the ghetto. Their music doesn't seek to exploit or cause violence but rather paint a picture of reality and offer alternatives.

But not all Rap music offers such positive alternatives. In fact, a   5
good portion of Rap, particularly gangsta, offers little or no alternatives. It simply paints a picture of a bleak world where the gun is king. And it is here where Rap foes focus their efforts and here where I would agree with them. They say that Rap glamorizes the violence on the streets. They say that kids look to these groups as heroes and follow their lyrics as a zealot Christian might follow the Bible. In fact, a recent *Newsweek* article entitled *A Gangster Wake-Up Call*, questions whether kids will "change their attitudes about money, sex, and violence now that gangster rap appears to be doing a drive-by on itself?"[2] In essence, the article is assuming that Rap is the only place that kids get these ideas. The article is about the death (due to AIDS) of Eazy-E, one of the first major Rap stars, and the jailing of three other Rap superstars because of their violent ways. It seems that the Rap foes are making an important point: Rap stars live the life they sing about. But all this is presupposing the fact that the listeners of Rap are motivated by the lyrics to take action in the streets. In fact, it completely bypasses the notion that violence has existed in our streets before Rap and that the musicians, particularly the ones indicated in the *Newsweek* article, are victims of these streets.

Rather than say that Rap lyrics are a cause of street violence, I   6
would like to offer the idea that violence is the cause of Rap lyrics, and that our society seems to have a double standard when it comes to judging the violence of Rap music versus the violence of popular cinema and television. If we are to isolate Rap for its violence what, then, do we make of movies like *Killing Zoe, Pulp Fiction, Reservoir Dogs* or *The Bad Lieutenant.* Or while we're on the subject, what about such popular TV shows as *Cops, Rescue 911* and *Real Stories of the California Highway Patrol*? It seems that violence is an obsession with Americans and still we don't indict these shows as being the cause of it. They are accepted and even called "artistic," and works of genius. For instance, in Francis Davis' article "Vox Populi" which appeared in the October 1993 issue of *The Atlantic,* he credits Quentin Tarantino for his subtle handling of an extremely violent scene in *Reservoir Dogs.* In the scene, a captive cop is bound to a chair while

---

[2]Marriott, Michel. "A Gangster Wake-Up Call." *Newsweek* April 10 1995: 74–76.

Mr. Blonde, played by Michael Madsen, dances around with a razor in his hand, eventually cutting off the cop's ear and dousing him in gasoline. Davis is impressed with the scene because it takes our emotions for a ride. He writes about the scene, saying that Madsen:

> does a series of graceful little dance steps to Stealers Wheel's "Stuck in the Middle with You," and closes in on his defenseless, screaming captive. "Was that as good for you as it was for me?" Madsen asks the cop afterward. . . . Madsen might also be asking those of us who sat through the scene without averting our eyes.[3]

Davis feels that this form of violence is more acceptable because it is complex and plays with the audience's emotions. Conversely, Rap artist Ice-T was forced, due to heavy protest from Police organizations, to remove the song *Cop Killer* from an album with the same name. The police groups, who felt that the album encouraged kids to kill police officers, won their argument and Ice-T had to pull the song and change the name of the album. Interestingly enough, Tarantino did not meet the same criticism and was praised by many for his "genius" in handling the violence of the police scene. A double standard? To say that one form of violence is better or more acceptable than another is ridiculous. The hard edges of gangsta Rap are no different than Tarantino's violence. By stating that the violence of movies and TV shows does not cause acts of aggression while at the same time indicting Rap music as a reason for aggression, we set an absurd double standard.

Rap music is violent because it reflects the real life struggles of   *7* life on the inner city streets. And although this is not an appealing vision for many, it is still a telling story, one that deserves attention. Of course many songs are often blown out of proportion, but the kernel of struggle is still discernible. When groups sing about drive-bys, drugs and beer drinking, it's because the singers grew up with these realities. These are not imaginary issues that are drummed up to sell records; they are the incidents of real life for many kids in America. Rap music is a window to real life, an expression of frustration and a way for Americans to understand what is going on in our streets. This is not to validate the violence, but to say that the expression is a positive release for both listener and singer, something that should not be so readily ignored and dismissed.

We look to expression—music, literature, cinema—as a way of   *8* release. Indeed, it is powerful; it can change hearts and minds. But expression is ultimately a product of experience. It is an interpretation of life and all the emotions that go along with it—fear, love, anger, happiness—feelings as old as our ability to express them. Rap, as a member of this community, cannot and should not be singled out as the cause of violence. It is an expression of life in our inner cities, a

---

[3]Davis, Francis. "Vox Populi." *Constellations: A Contextual Reader for Writers.* 2nd ed. Ed. John Schilb, Elizabeth Flynn & John Clifford. New York: HarperCollins, 1995. 603–610.

vision that is sometimes hopeful and sometimes violent but always based in reality. And if we listen without prejudice, we might begin to hear the words behind the violence. We might even be able to begin focusing on the real factors of ghetto life rather than constantly blaming the messenger for the delivery of bad news.

—John Herschend

Free Needles Would Be a Help in S. F.

If there is any city to which San Francisco can look for lessons concerning the controversy over providing free needles to drug addicts, it would be far across the Atlantic beneath the brooding bluffs of Scotland's Edinburgh Castle. *1*

The tragedy of AIDS in Edinburgh offers a chilling warning of what San Francisco can expect if this city doesn't move decisively to make needles more freely available. *2*

The Edinburgh experience grew largely out of a shortage of marijuana, a scarcity that quickly made heroin a fashionable drug. The police realized that heroin use was out of control, so they launched a crackdown on drug paraphernalia, confiscating the needles that addicts used to inject the narcotic. *3*

In Scotland's other major metropolis, Glasgow, heroin also spread rapidly among local drug users, but police there took no comparable measures against the possession of syringes. *4*

The lack of clean needles in Edinburgh meant that addicts were forced to share needles. Dr. Roy Robertson, Edinburgh's leading authority on AIDS among drug addicts, estimates that within 18 months of the arrival of AIDS in Scotland, more than half of the city's addicts were infected with the human immunodeficiency virus. *5*

Just 30 miles away in Glasgow, where needles were available, studies have found that only 4 percent to 7 percent of addicts are infected. *6*

Today, Scotland is facing the disastrous consequences of the Edinburgh needle shortage. About 60 percent of the 1200 known HIV-infected people in Scotland are intravenous drug users, most of them in Edinburgh. Problems with heterosexual transmission of the virus from addicts to their girlfriends—and then to the women's babies—have followed. *7*

"Making needles available to addicts is not the only answer to the problem of AIDS among drug users," concludes Robertson, "but certainly, it has to be part of the solution." Just about every health expert who has considered the problem agrees. *8*

To be sure, a society that offered nothing more to its addicts than free needles would be both cruel and cynical. The long-term answer to the connection between AIDS and the drug culture lies in expanded drug treatment centers that can help the addict stop using altogether. *9*

This solution, however, is expensive. President Ronald Reagan's *10* AIDS commission put a $3 billion price tag on its proposal for expanded drug treatment, and neither the Reagan nor Bush administrations have moved to give anything resembling this level of support.

Even if the money were available, neither the facilities nor the *11* personnel to staff them are now in place. Training the number of drug counselors needed would take another year or two, federal officials say.

Moreover, some addicts have shown no willingness to make use *12* of recovery facilities even when they are available. The very nature of drug addiction means that not all those who are sick will want to be cured.

Until these addicts want treatment and until the necessary staff *13* and facilities exist to help them, it only makes sense that needles be made more easily available.

The issue has an unparalleled urgency on the West Coast, particularly in San Francisco. On the East Coast, among the AIDS-ravaged *14* addicts of New York and New Jersey, attempts to prevent AIDS among needle users have come far too late. Between 50 percent and 75 percent of addicts in some of these Eastern cities are HIV-infected.

In San Francisco, HIV infection rates among addicts are substantially lower, generally estimated at between 13 percent and 20 percent. *15* We still have the time and opportunity to stop AIDS from spreading like a prairie wildfire among the addict population. The viral incursion, however, is growing. And the stories of Edinburgh and New York tell us what will happen here if officials don't move fast. The virus will continue to move, even if government officials don't.

Most opposition to free needles has tended to come from black *16* community leaders. They worry that easier access to needles condones drug use and encourages youths to shoot up.

San Francisco Health Commissioner Naomi Gray, the only black *17* on the commission, went so far as to equate free-needle programs with the "genocide" against poor people. The revulsion black leaders feel toward narcotics is understandable; after all, they've seen their communities ravaged by addiction and its related crimes.

But there's no evidence whatsoever that easier access to needles *18* in any way encourages drug use. And rhetorical concerns about hypothetical genocide should not overshadow the stark truth that a real genocide of minorities looms ahead if AIDS is not checked among addicts now.

The distribution of uncontaminated needles to those who already *19* are using drugs is a first, albeit limited, step toward preventing this mass death.

In the past, the history of the AIDS epidemic has largely been *20* written in stories of lost opportunities, unheeded warnings and unnecessary deaths that inevitably follow actions not taken.

The resolution to San Francisco's free-needle controversy in the *21*
weeks ahead will determine whether, in the future, we recall the lives
we saved or the deaths we witnessed.

—Randy Shilts

FOUR APPROACHES TO WRITING ARGUMENTS

The next four writing assignments all focus on argument. Writing Assignment 8 serves as preparation for Writing Assignment 9. Writing Assignment 10 presents a more complex and thus more challenging approach to an issue. Assignment 11 focuses on working collaboratively with classmates on complex issues chosen by the class.

 ### *WRITING ASSIGNMENT 8*

Arguing Both Sides of an Issue

The topic

Below is a list of proposals advocating a position on a social issue. Choose *one* and write two arguments, one defending and one refuting the proposal.

For each argument, convey clearly the position you are taking by writing a short thesis (the conclusion of your argument) at the top of the page. For each position, provide relevant reasons (premises) which are, to the best of your knowledge, accurate. You will have two separate papers with a paragraph for each reason. While each paragraph should be written coherently with fluent sentences, you don't, at this stage, need to provide logical transitions between paragraphs for a coherent whole. And you need not provide an introduction, conclusion, or research. All this will come later in Writing Assignment 9.

Make your selection with care, for you will be spending considerable time on this one issue.

1. Biotechnology firms should be granted patents on genetically engineered products.
2. The federal government should be granted additional investigative powers to combat armed civilian militias.
3. Parental permission should be required for a minor to have an abortion.
4. High school students should have to maintain a C average in order to participate in competitive sports.
5. Doctors should be permitted to perform euthanasia on patients who ask to die.
6. Birth parents should not necessarily be awarded custody of their children after they have given them up for adoption.

7. School administrators should be allowed to censor student newspapers.

8. Colleges should practice affirmative action in their admission policies.

9. Congress should pass legislation making English the official language of the United States Government.

10. If another issue interests you more—for instance, a campus topic or a controversy in your neighborhood—you may write on it. Be sure the issue is one worth arguing from both sides and can be expressed as a proposal similar to those above. You may, of course, change any of the given topics to suit your own purpose.

Audience
A wide range of your peers, those who would agree with you, those who disagree, and those who have not, as yet, formed any opinion.

Purpose
To present both sides of a controversial issue so you and your readers are forced to consider alternatives to one position.

 ### WRITING ASSIGNMENT 9
Taking a Stand

The topic
In this essay you will take a stand on the issue you debated in Writing Assignment 8, constructing as persuasive an argument as possible.

Your thesis may express a strong position either for or against the proposition you addressed in the previous assignment, or may be qualified as appropriate to reflect your view of the issue. (See the discussion of the thesis earlier in this chapter.)

To support your position fully, you will draw on the premises you presented in Writing Assignment 8, discarding reasoning that seems weak or irrelevant, adding reasons where you find gaps in your earlier paper. Strengthen your argument with as much available data as you think necessary to make your case. As you expand your argument, you will probably need to consult outside sources—newspapers, magazines, books, and individual authorities—for supporting information. Be sure to cite all references. For guidelines, consult Appendix I, Research and Documentation.

To address opposing views, you will select the most important premises from your list of arguments on the other side of your position and briefly address them, acknowledging, conceding, and refuting in the manner best suited to your stand on the issue. Do not elaborate the opposing views in the same way you have your own premises.

For help in organizing your paper, refer once again to the sample essays in Exercise 4D.

To complete the assignment, include the following attachments written out on a separate page:

Your issue, question at issue, and thesis

Your principal argument set out in standard form (see Chapter 3)

Peer editing

You may find it useful to edit a first complete draft with classmates. Bring photocopies of your paper to class and exchange papers with one or more students, asking questions, noting strengths and weaknesses on each others' drafts.

Audience

The same as for Writing Assignment 8.

Purpose

To present a convincing, balanced, fair argument for your position on a controversial argument in order to persuade your readers to adopt your point of view.

> **A checklist of essential components for Assignment 9:**
>
> A clear thesis to guide you as a writer and prepare your reader
>
> Support for this thesis—plenty of well-reasoned premises supported with examples, explanation, and analysis
>
> Counterarguments with appropriate concessions and refutations
>
> Sentences logically joined for contrast and concession, cause and effect
>
> Transitions between paragraphs to keep ideas flowing

 WRITING ASSIGNMENT 10

Exploring an Argument in Depth

Not all issues lend themselves to a pro or con, "yes" or "no" argument. In Writing Assignment 8, you argued two opposing positions on the same question at issue, and then in Writing Assignment 9 took a position on that issue. For this paper, you will address an issue in more of its complexity, considering arguments from as many sides as possible and coming to a conclusion that seems reasonable in light of your in-depth exploration. Such topics often present paradoxes in which two contradictory claims may both merit approval.

In such a conclusion, you may incline to one position or another, or may settle for explaining and clarifying the issues without going so far as to make a definitive decision.

The topic

A current controversial issue of interest to you, one that suggests more than a simple pro and con approach. Because you will be presenting a number of viewpoints, you must make sure your readers know which point of view you are expressing at any given point in the paper. Clear and logical transitions between points will help you accomplish this (note discussion of joining words in Chapter 3 and contrast and concession earlier in this chapter), as will smooth attributions of quotations and references to the ideas of others (see Appendix I).

Be prepared to face a degree of chaos as you sort out the different perspectives. Don't be afraid of the inevitable confusion that a more complex issue often produces. It is through such a thinking and writing process that critical thinking takes place.

Once again, you may want to edit a draft with classmates.

Audience

The same as for Assignments 8 and 9.

Purpose

To clarify your audience's understanding of a complex controversial issue.

> **A checklist for Writing Assignment 10:**
>
> An introduction that presents the question at issue with appropriate background and acknowledges its complexity
>
> A detailed discussion of arguments for as many positions as possible
>
> Refutations and concessions as appropriate for a thoughtful examination of alternatives
>
> Your personal recommendation on the issue, based on an evaluation in which you weigh the strengths and weaknesses of the positions you have presented, a synthesis of them, a call for further investigation, or a summary of possible alternatives

 WRITING ASSIGNMENT 11

Collaborating on a Complex Issue

Here we offer an alternative approach to writing the kind of argument presented in Assignment 10. Rather than preparing your paper on your own, you will be working with a group of classmates.

Once out in the world, writing for business, politics, for many jobs, you will find that much of the writing you do is collaborative.

The topic

Each member of the class will submit two or three controversial issues. From this list, the class will select four or five topics around which research groups will form on the basis of preference. You should end up with groups of five or six students.

Here are the guidelines for working with classmates to construct a written argument.

1. The topic research groups will meet in class to narrow the issue to a specific question at issue.
2. Students will conduct research to find at least one relevant article each which addresses the question at issue. They will make copies for members of the group. Because these articles are to represent the various positions on the question at issue, members of the group must confer to ensure that the articles together reflect the diverse points of view.
3. Students will reduce the central argument of their own articles to standard form (see Chapter 3).
4. Each group will meet as often as necessary, in class and out as time permits, to share and discuss these materials. Members of each group will also have an opportunity to discuss the organization and development of their papers.
5. The class will choose whether students complete these papers on their own, or whether they work together as a group to compose one final product as a fully collaborative effort.
6. Each group may want to select the best paper to read to the class, or in the case of collaborative papers, there may be time to hear them all.

Audience

The same as for Writing Assignments 8, 9, and 10.

Purpose

To present different perspectives on an issue and to engage or persuade an audience through collaborative effort.

SUMMARY

Convincing arguments usually contain an introduction to the topic, a thesis stated or clearly implied, well-supported premises, acknowledgment of opposing views, and a conclusion.

Successful written argument depends on a dialectical approach in which writers address both their own position and opposing views.

Expressing relationships between ideas, particularly contrast and concession, requires joining sentences for logic and fluency.

Collaboration on the production of a written argument can be helpful and reflects the process often used in the working world.

KEY TERMS

Issue any topic of concern and controversy.

Question at issue a particular aspect of the issue under consideration.

Thesis a statement of a writer's position; in argument, a response to the question at issue, the conclusion of the central argument in an essay.

Rhetoric the art of using language to good effect, to prove, to convince, to persuade.

Dialectic a method of argument that systematically weighs contradictory ideas with a view to resolution of their contradictions.

Counterargument an opposing view in an argument.

Refutation an explanation of why a position is false or weak.

Concession a statement that grants the opposing view.

Rogerian strategy an explicit effort to see ideas from an opponent's point of view; the cultivation of empathy with the opposition; a concept derived from the research of psychologist Carl Rogers.

Chapter
5

Deductive and Inductive Reasoning

There is a tradition of opposition between adherents of induction and deduction. In my view, it would be just as sensible for the two ends of a worm to quarrel.

—Alfred North Whitehead

As we move from written argument to inductive and deductive reasoning, we need to keep in mind the close relationship between writing and thinking. In this chapter and the two that follow, we examine inference more precisely, sharpening our critical thinking skills and, by extension, our writing skills.

In logic, inferences are said to be arrived at inductively or deductively. Different logicians tend to make different distinctions between deductive and inductive reasoning, with some going so far as to declare, as Whitehead did, that such a distinction is spurious. But classifications, if carefully made, help us to understand abstract concepts, and scientists and humanists alike often refer to patterns of reasoning as deductive or inductive.

KEY DISTINCTIONS

The key distinctions between deduction and induction are generally seen as falling into two categories.

Necessity Versus Probability

In a *deductive argument*, the conclusion will follow by **necessity** from the premises if the method of reasoning is valid, as in this familiar bit of classical wisdom:

1. All men (updated—people) are mortal.
2. Socrates is a man (person).
   ∴ Socrates is mortal.

In an *inductive argument*, the conclusion can only follow with some degree of **probability** (from the unlikely to the highly probable). British philosopher Bertrand Russell made the point implicitly but emphatically in *The Problems of Philosophy:* "The man who has fed the chicken every day throughout its life at last wrings its neck instead." The chicken reasons thus—

1. He has fed me today.
2. He has fed me this next day.
3. He has fed me this day too.
4. He has fed me yet another day, etc.
   ∴ He will feed me tomorrow.

The poor chicken has made a prediction, and a reasonable one, based on its past experience.

A related distinction here becomes clear. The premises of a deductive argument contain all the information needed for the conclusion, whereas the conclusion of an inductive argument goes beyond the premises. For this reason, some prefer the certainty of deduction to the probability of induction. Italian writer Italo Calvino describes such a person in his novel, *Mr. Palomar:*

> To construct a model—as Mr. Palomar was aware—you have to start with something; that is, you have to have principles, from which, by deduction, you develop your own line of reasoning. The principles—also known as axioms or postulates—are not something you select; you have them already, because if you did not have them, you could not even begin thinking. So Mr. Palomar also had some, but since he was neither a mathematician nor a logician, he did not bother to define them. Deduction, in any case, was one of his favorite activities, because he could devote himself to it in silence and alone, without special equipment, at any place and moment, seated in his armchair or strolling. Induction, on the contrary, was something he did not really trust, perhaps because he thought his experiences vague and incomplete. The construction of a model, therefore, was for him a miracle of equilibrium between principles (left in shadow) and experience (elusive), but the result should be more substantial than either.

Ambrose Peré, an Italian Renaissance physician, revealed his distrust of induction when he defined inductive diagnosis as "the rapid means to the wrong conclusion." One assumes that he would have argued for the value of a few well-learned principles behind one's observations.

From General to Specific, Specific to General

In a *deductive* argument the inference usually moves from a generalization to a particular, specific instance or example that fits that generalization. Two examples:

1. All students who complete this course successfully will fulfill the critical thinking requirement.
2. Jane has completed this course successfully.
   ∴ Jane has fulfilled the critical thinking requirement.

1. Children born on a Saturday will "work hard for a living."
2. Nick was born on a Saturday.
　∴ Nick will work hard for his living.

You may not believe this folk wisdom, especially if you were born on a Saturday, but the line of reasoning is still deductive.

In an *inductive* argument the inference usually moves from a series of specific instances to a generalization.

1. Droughts have been more frequent in some areas.
2. Skin cancers related to ultraviolet rays have been increasing.
3. The tree line is moving north about 40 meters a year.
4. Polar ice has been melting more rapidly than in the past.
5. Oceans have been rising at measurable annual rates around the globe.
　∴ The early stages of the dreaded "Greenhouse Effect" are upon us.

Sometimes in inductive reasoning, we begin with a hypothesis, an unproved theory or proposition, and gather the data to support it. For instance, when Jonas Salk thought his vaccine would cure polio, he first had to test it inductively by administering it to a broad sample before concluding that the vaccine prevented polio.

THE RELATIONSHIP BETWEEN INDUCTION AND DEDUCTION

In Exercise 5B we ask you to distinguish between inductive and deductive reasoning, but in reality the two are inextricable. Consider the source for the generalizations upon which deductions are based. In some cases they seem to be the laws of nature (or of God if one is religiously inclined), but more often than not we arrive at these generalizations by means of repeated observations. Throughout history, people have observed their own mortality, so we can now take that generalization—all people are mortal—as a given from which we can deduce conclusions about individual people. Induction has, in this case, led to a trusted generalization which in turn allows us a "necessary," or deductive, inference.

Humorists have sometimes turned these concepts on their heads. Here's Woody Allen reflecting on deduction: "All men are Socrates." And Lewis Carroll, in "The Hunting of the Snark," on induction: "What I tell you three times is true."

In a more serious approach, Robert Pirsig, in his philosophical novel, *Zen and the Art of Motorcycle Maintenance,* and Thomas Huxley, the nineteenth century British scientist and writer, attempt to explain deduction, induction, and the relationships between them in language we can all understand. Their point is that these terms were never intended to be the exclusive domain of academics but, rather, descriptive of the ways in which we all think every day.

Note how the following two excerpts from their work—"The Method of Scientific Investigation" by Huxley and a chapter from Pirsig's novel— explain both the differences between induction and deduction and their dependence on one another.

The Method of Scientific Investigation

The method of scientific investigation is nothing but the expression of the necessary mode of working of the human mind. It is simply the mode at which all phenomena are reasoned about, rendered precise and exact. There is no more difference, but there is just the same kind of difference, between the mental operations of a man of sci-   *1* ence and those of an ordinary person, as there is between the opera- tions and methods of a baker or of a butcher weighing out his goods in common scales, and the operations of a chemist in performing a difficult and complex analysis by means of his balance and finely graduated weights. It is not that the action of the scales in the one case, and the balance in the other, differ in the principles of their construction or manner of working; but the beam of one is set on an infinitely finer axis than the other, and of course turns by the addition of a much smaller weight.

You will understand this better, perhaps, if I give you some famil- iar example. You have all heard it repeated, I dare say, that men of sci- ence work by means of induction and deduction, and that by the help of these operations, they, in a sort of sense, wring from Nature certain other things, which are called natural laws, and causes, and that out of these, by some cunning skill of their own, they build up hypotheses   *2* and theories. And it is imagined by many, that the operations of the common mind can be by no means compared with these processes, and that they have to be acquired by a sort of special apprenticeship to the craft. To hear all these large words, you would think that the mind of a man of science must be constituted differently from that of his fellow men; but if you will not be frightened by terms, you will dis- cover that you are quite wrong, and that all these terrible apparatus are being used by yourselves every day and every hour of your lives.

There is a well-known incident in one of Molière's plays, where the author makes the hero express unbounded delight on being told that he had been talking prose during the whole of his life. In the same way, I trust, that you will take comfort, and be delighted with yourselves, on the discovery that you have been acting on the princi- ples of inductive and deductive philosophy during the same period.   *3* Probably there is not one here who has not in the course of the day had occasion to set in motion a complex train of reasoning, of the very same kind, though differing of course in degree, as that which a scien- tific man goes through in tracing the causes of natural phenomena.

A very trivial circumstance will serve to exemplify this. Suppose you go into a fruiterer's shop, wanting an apple—you take up one, and, on biting it, you find it is sour; you look at it, and see that it is hard and green. You take up another one, and that too is hard, green, and sour. The shopman offers you a third; but, before biting it, you examine it and find that it is hard and green, and you immediately say that you will not have it, as it must be sour, like those that you have already tried. *4*

Nothing can be more simple than that, you think; but if you will take the trouble to analyze and trace out into its logical elements what has been done by the mind, you will be greatly surprised. In the first place you have performed the operation of induction. You found that, in two experiences, hardness and greenness in apples went together with sourness. It was so in the first case, and it was confirmed by the second. True, it is a very small basis, but still it is enough to make an induction from; you generalize the facts, and you expect to find sourness in apples where you get hardness and greenness. You found upon that a general law that all hard and green apples are sour and that, so far as it goes, is a perfect induction. Well, having got your natural law in this way, when you are offered another apple which you find is hard and green, you say, "All hard and green apples are sour; this apple is hard and green, therefore this apple is sour." That train of reasoning is what logicians call a syllogism, and has all its various parts and terms—its major premise, its minor premise and its conclusion. And, by the help of further reasoning, which, if drawn out, would have to be exhibited in two or three other syllogisms, you arrive at your final determination, "I will not have that apple." So that, you see, you have, in the first place, established a law by induction, and upon that you have founded a deduction, and reasoned out the special particular case. Well now, suppose, having got your conclusion of the law, that at some time afterwards, you are discussing the qualities of apples with a friend: you will say to him, "It is a very curious thing—but I find that all hard and green apples are sour!" Your friend says to you, "But how do you know that?" You at once reply, "Oh, because I have tried them over and over again, and have always found them to be so." Well, if we were talking science instead of common sense, we should call that an experimental verification. And, if still opposed, you go further, and say, "I have heard from the people in Somersetshire and Devonshire, where a large number of apples are grown, that they have observed the same thing. It is also found to be the case in Normandy, and in North America. In short, I find it to be the universal experience of mankind wherever attention has been directed to the subject." Whereupon, your friend, unless he is a very unreasonable man, agrees with you, and is convinced that you are quite right in the conclusion you have drawn. He believes, although perhaps he does not know he believes it, that the more extensive verifications are—that the more frequently experiments have been made, and results of the same kind arrived at—that the more varied the conditions under which the same results are attained, the more certain is the ultimate conclusion, and he disputes the question no *5* further. He sees that the experiment has been tried under all sorts of conditions, as to time, place, and people, with the same result; and he says with you, therefore, that the law you have laid down must be a good one, and he must believe it.

In science we do the same thing—the philosopher exercises pre- *6* cisely the same faculties, though in a much more delicate manner. In scientific injury it becomes a matter of duty to expose a supposed law to every possible kind of verification, and to take care, moreover, that this is done intentionally, and not left to a mere accident, as in the case of the apples. And in science, as in common life, our confidence in a law is in exact proportion to the absence of variation in the result of our experimental verifications. For instance, if you let go your grasp on an article you may have in your hand, it will immediately fall to the ground. That is a very common verification of one of the best established laws of nature—that of gravitation. The method by which men of science establish the existence of that law is exactly the same as that by which we have established the trivial proposition about the sourness of hard and green apples. But we believe it in such an extensive, thorough, and unhesitating manner because the universal experience of mankind verifies it, and we can verify it ourselves at any time; and that is the strongest possible foundation on which any natural law can rest.

Mechanics' Logic

Two kinds of logic are used (in motorcycle maintenance), inductive and deductive. Inductive inferences start with observations of the machine and arrive at general conclusions. For example, if the cycle *1* goes over a bump and the engine misfires, and then goes over another bump and the engine misfires, and then goes over another bump and the engine misfires, and then goes over a long smooth stretch of road and there is no misfiring, and then goes over a fourth bump and the engine misfires again, one can logically conclude that the misfiring is caused by the bumps. That is induction: reasoning from particular experiences to general truths.

Deductive inferences do the reverse. They start with general knowledge and predict a specific observation. For example, if, from reading the hierarchy of facts about the machine, the mechanic knows the horn of the cycle is powered exclusively by electricity from the battery, then he can logically infer that if the battery is dead the *2* horn will not work. That is deduction.

Solution of problems too complicated for common sense to solve is achieved by long strings of mixed inductive and deductive infer- ences that weave back and forth between the observed machine and *3* the mental hierarchy of the machine found in the manuals. The cor- rect program for this interweaving is formalized as scientific method.

Actually I've never seen a cycle-maintenance problem complex enough really to require full-scale formal scientific method. Repair problems are not that hard. When I think of formal scientific method an image sometimes comes to mind of an enormous juggernaut, a huge bulldozer—slow, tedious, lumbering, laborious, but invincible. *4* It takes twice as long, five times as long, maybe a dozen times as long as informal mechanic's techniques, but you know in the end you're going to *get* it. There's no fault isolation problem in motorcycle maintenance that can stand up to it. When you've hit a really tough one, tried everything, racked your brain and nothing works, and you know that this time Nature has really decided to be difficult, you say, "Okay, Nature, that's the end of the *nice* guy," and you crank up the formal scientific method.

For this you keep a lab notebook. Everything gets written down, formally, so that you know at all times where you are, where you've been, where you're going and where you want to get. In scientific work and electronics technology this is necessary because otherwise *5* the problems get so complex you get lost in them and confused and forget what you know and what you don't know and have to give up. In cycle maintenance things are not that involved, but when confusion starts it's a good idea to hold it down by making everything formal and exact. Sometimes just the act of writing down the problems straightens out your head as to what they really are.

The logical statements entered into the notebook are broken down into six categories: (1) statement of the problem, (2) hypotheses as to the cause of the problem, (3) experiments designed to test each hypothesis, (4) predicted results of the experiments, (5) observed results of the experiments and (6) conclusions from the results *6* of the experiments. This is not different from the formal arrangement of many college and high-school lab notebooks but the purpose here is no longer just busy-work. The purpose now is precise guidance of thoughts that will fail if they are not accurate.

The real purpose of scientific method is to make sure Nature hasn't misled you into thinking you know something you don't actually know. There's not a mechanic or scientist or technician alive who hasn't suffered from that one so much that he's not instinctively on guard. That's the main reason why so much scientific and mechanical information sounds so dull and so cautious. If you get careless or go romanticizing *7* scientific information, giving it a flourish here and there, Nature will soon make a complete fool out of you. It does it often enough anyway even when you don't give it opportunities. One must be extremely careful and rigidly logical when dealing with Nature: one logical slip and an entire scientific edifice comes tumbling down. One false deduction about the machine and you can get hung up indefinitely.

In Part One of formal scientific method, which is the statement of the problem, the main skill is in stating absolutely no more than you are positive you know. It is much better to enter a statement

"Solve Problem: Why doesn't cycle work?" which sounds dumb but is correct, than it is to enter a statement "Solve Problem: What is wrong with the electrical system?" when you don't absolutely *know* the trouble is *in* the electrical system. What you should state is "Solve Problem: What is wrong with cycle?" and *then* state as the first entry of Part Two: "Hypothesis Number One: The trouble is in the electrical system." You think of as many hypotheses as you can, then you design experiments to test them to see which are true and which are false.   *8*

This careful approach to the beginning questions keeps you from taking a major wrong turn which might cause you weeks of extra work or can even hang you up completely. Scientific questions often have a surface appearance of dumbness for this reason. They are asked in order to prevent dumb mistakes later on.   *9*

Part Three, that part of formal scientific method called experimentation, is sometimes thought of by romantics as all of science itself because that's the only part with much visual surface. They see lots of test tubes and bizarre equipment and people running around making discoveries. They do not see the experiment as part of a larger intellectual process and so they often confuse experiments with demonstrations, which look the same. A man conducting a gee-whiz science show with fifty thousand dollars' worth of Frankenstein equipment is not doing anything scientific if he knows beforehand what the results of his efforts are going to be. A motorcycle mechanic, on the other hand, who honks the horn to see if the battery works is informally conducting a true scientific experiment. He is testing a hypothesis by putting the question to Nature. The TV scientist who mutters sadly, "The experiment is a failure; we have failed to achieve what we had hoped for," is suffering mainly from a bad scriptwriter. An experiment is never a failure solely because it fails to achieve predicted results. An experiment is a failure only when it also fails adequately to test the hypothesis in question, when the data it produces don't prove anything one way or another.   *10*

Skill at this point consists of using experiments that test only the hypothesis in question, nothing less, nothing more. If the horn honks, and the mechanic concludes that the whole electrical system is working, he is in deep trouble. He has reached an illogical conclusion. The honking horn only tells him that the battery and horn are working. To design an experiment properly he has to think very rigidly in terms of what directly causes what. This you know from the hierarchy. The horn doesn't make the cycle go. Neither does the battery, except in a very indirect way. The point at which the electrical system *directly* causes the engine to fire is at the spark plugs, and if you don't test here, at the output of the electrical system, you will never really know whether the failure is electrical or not.   *11*

To test properly the mechanic removes the plug and lays it against the engine so that the base around the plug is electrically grounded, kicks the starter lever and watches the spark-plug gap for a blue spark.

If there isn't any he can conclude one of two things: (a) there is an electrical failure or (b) his experiment is sloppy. If he is experienced *12* he will try it a few more times, checking connections, trying every way he can think of to get that plug to fire. Then, if he can't get it to fire, he finally concludes that *a* is correct, there's an electrical failure, and the experiment is over. He has proved that his hypothesis is correct.

In the final category, conclusions, skill comes in stating no more than the experiment has proved. It hasn't proved that when he fixes the electrical system the motorcycle will start. There may be other things wrong. But he does know that the motorcycle isn't going to run *13* until the electrical system is working and he sets up the next formal question: "Solve problem: what is wrong with the electrical system?"

He then sets up hypotheses for these and tests them. By asking the right questions and choosing the right tests and drawing the right conclusions the mechanic works his way down the echelons of the *14* motorcycle hierarchy until he has found the exact specific cause or causes of the engine failure, and then he changes them so that they no longer cause the failure.

An untrained observer will see only physical labor and often get the idea that physical labor is mainly what the mechanic does. Actually the physical labor is the smallest and easiest part of what the mechanic does. By far the greatest part of his work is careful observation and precise thinking. That is why mechanics sometimes seem so taci- *15* turn and withdrawn when performing tests. They don't like it when you talk to them because they are concentrating on mental images, hierarchies, and not really looking at you or the physical motorcycle at all. They are using the experiment as part of the program to expand their hierarchy of knowledge of the faulty motorcycle and compare it to the correct hierarchy in their mind. They are looking at underlying form.

EXERCISE 5A

Analyzing Pirsig and Huxley

1. In your own words, state Huxley's thesis.
2. According to Pirsig, what is the most important part of the mechanic's work?
3. How does Pirsig define induction and deduction?
4. Which method of reasoning—induction or deduction—does the scientific method rely on?

EXERCISE 5B

Distinguishing Inductive from Deductive Reasoning

Read the following passages carefully and determine which are based on deductive reasoning and which on inductive. Briefly explain your answers.

*1. Marie must be out of town. She hasn't answered her phone in a week, nor has she returned the messages that I have left on her answering machine. When I drove past her house last night, I noted that the lights inside and out were off.

2. Cat lovers do not care for dogs, and since Colette had numerous cats all of her life, I assume she did not care for dogs.

3. According to polls taken prior to the national convention, the candidate I support held a substantial lead in the presidential race. I am now confident that he will win in November.

*4. Every Frenchman is devoted to his glass of *vin rouge*. Philippe is a Frenchman so he too must be devoted to that glass of red wine.

5. For Iranians, life remains a struggle. Personal freedoms are severely curtailed. Through systematic segregation at work and in public places, women remain the second-class citizens that they became during Ayatolla Khomeini's years. And with an average income of $100 a month, the Iranian middle class is straining in the face of 40 percent inflation rates. (from "Iran Gingerly Tries a Bit of Pragmatism" by Youssef M. Ibrahim.)

6. As an expert testified on the MacNeil/Lehrer News Hour following the *Challenger* space shuttle disaster, the solid rocket booster had proved safe in over 200 successful launchings of both space shuttles and Titan missiles. It was reasonable to conclude that the same rocket booster would function properly on the *Challenger* mission.

7. Students educated in the past three decades are not as well informed as were students attending universities prior to the mid–1960s. And since our rising generation of leaders has been educated in the past three decades, they must not be as well informed as those leaders who preceded them.

8. When people are confident and cheerful, they are generally inclined to spend more freely. With this in mind, we have designed these ads to project a feeling of cheerful confidence that should encourage viewers to spend more freely on your product. [Ad agency pitch to a potential client.]

EXERCISE 5C

Identifying Your Own Reasoning Processes

Think about your own reasoning processes for a minute. Calvino (see above) maintains that we can't begin thinking without deductive "principles." But would you get very far in your day without resorting to an inductive thinking process as well?

Jot down two personal examples of your reasoning processes: one illustrating deductive reasoning, the other, inductive.

APPLICATION TO WRITING

Deduction, Induction, and Organizational Patterns

Textbooks about writing frequently describe organizational patterns for essays as being strictly deductive or inductive. It is true that a written argument may start with a broad generalization offered as a given upon which applications to more specific circumstances may be built. Such a shape does resemble one definition of deduction—a generalization applied to a particular instance or example. A paper that assumes the majority of mothers are working outside the home today could then go on to argue for a particular course of action to address problems surrounding the trend of both parents working outside the home. A deductive paper tends to greater formality, a construction based on defined principles, that sets out to prove a stated conclusion.

Often a collection of specific data—empirical observations including personal experience, examples from research, and statistics—can add up to a generalization in the conclusion and thus appear to reflect the inductive process. A survey of urban households, for example, could, with careful analysis, lead to a conclusion about trends in family eating habits. Inductive writing, reflecting its open-ended character, is often looser than its more rigid counterpart.

Legal scholar Patricia J. Williams expresses it this way in describing her personal approach to writing about legal issues:

> Legal writing presumes a methodology that is highly stylized, precedential, and based on deductive reasoning. Most scholarship in law is rather like the "old math": static, stable, formal—rationalism walled against chaos. My writing is an intentional departure from that. I use a model of inductive empiricism, borrowed from—and parodying—systems analysis, in order to enliven thought about complex social problems.

She goes on to explain that she is "trying to create a genre of legal writing to fill the gaps of traditional legal scholarship" by writing "in a way that . . . forces the reader to participate in the construction of meaning."

Ultimately, as Pirsig and Huxley emphasize, it takes an interplay of the two thinking methods to reflect accurately how we arrive at our conclusions. The writer of the paper on family eating habits would be likely to start speculating on why trends in family meals have changed and possibly on what impact such changes would have on society. Such an approach would not be described as inductive, but, in fact, represents a combination of inductive and deductive reasoning

So it would seem that, while an essay may proceed from the particular to the general, mirroring the pattern of inductive reasoning, or from the general to the particular, mirroring deduction, any piece of writing as complex as an essay will involve both inductive and deductive reasoning even if the organization of the essay or the writer's habits of mind resemble one pattern more closely than another.

SUMMARY

Inductive and deductive reasoning are distinct from one another in two ways.

1. In a deductive argument, the conclusion will follow by necessity from the premises if the method of reasoning is valid. But in an inductive argument, the conclusion can only follow with some degree of probability.
2. In a deductive argument, the inference moves from a generalization to a particular instance or example that fits that generalization. In an inductive argument, the inference usually moves from a series of specific instances to a generalization.

Induction and deduction are interdependent; it takes an interplay of the two thinking methods to arrive at our conclusions.

Chapter 6

Deductive Argument

"Contrariwise," continued Tweedledee, "if it was so, it might be; and if it were so, it would be; and if it isn't, it ain't. That's logic."

—Lewis Carroll

All good reasoning depends on seeing relationships between classes. A **class** in logic is all of the individual things—persons, objects, events, ideas—that share a determinate property, a common feature. What is that determinate property? Anything under the sun. A class may consist of any quality or combination of qualities that the classifier assigns to it. A class may be vast, such as a class containing everything in the universe, or it may be quite small, containing only one member, such as Uncle Fred's last girlfriend.

CLASS LOGIC

Making classes and assigning members to those classes is an essential part of everyday reasoning—it's how we order our experience. Indeed, each word in the language serves as a class by which we categorize and communicate experience. We can then take these words in any combination to create the categories or classes that serve our purpose.

A recent article in the *Journal of the American Medical Association,* for example, features a piece titled "Risk of Sexually Transmitted Diseases Among Adolescent Crack Users in Oakland and San Francisco." This title, which identifies one class (and the subject of the article), was created by combining seven classes: the class of things involving risk, the class of things that are sexually transmitted, the class of disease, the class of adolescents, the class of crack users, the class of persons living in Oakland, and the class of persons living in San Francisco.

Relationships Between Classes

There are three possible relationships between classes: **inclusion, exclusion,** and **overlap.**

Inclusion: One class is included in another if every member of one class is a member of the other class. Using letters, we can symbolize this relationship as all As are Bs. Using circle diagrams, also called Euler diagrams after Leonhard Euler, an eighteenth-century mathematician, we can illustrate a relationship of inclusion this way:

For example, the class of professional basketball players is included in the class of professional athletes since all professional basketball players are also professional athletes. The following diagram illustrates this relationship.

Exclusion: One class excludes another if they share no members, if no As are Bs. Such a relationship exists between handguns and rifles.

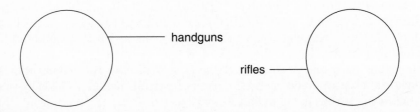

Overlap: One class overlaps with another if they have at least one member in common—if at least one A is also a B—for example, students at this university and students who like rap music.

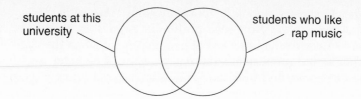

The way our public institutions classify relationships between groups of people can have a significant impact on their lives. The federal department of Housing and Urban Development (HUD) is authorized to allocate housing funds to individuals with disabilities. People with AIDS argue that they are entitled to such funds, but HUD has denied them any such subsidy. Clearly, HUD sees the relationship between disabilities and AIDS as one of exclusion, while those with AIDS see their relationship to those with disabilities as one of inclusion.

EXERCISE 6A

Identifying Relationships Between Classes

Using circle diagrams, illustrate the relationships between the following pairs of classes.

  *1. cantaloupes and watermelons
  2. judges and lawyers
  3. Saabs and convertibles
  4. mollusks and amphibians
  5. cosmetics and hairspray
  6. the homeless and the mentally ill
  7. euthanasia and suicide

Now create your own classes.

  1. Identify two classes, one of which is inclusive of the other.
  2. Identify two classes that are exclusive of one another.
  3. Identify two classes that overlap one another.

Class Logic and the Deductive Syllogism

Both inductive and deductive reasoning often depend on supporting a conclusion on the basis of relationships between classes. Let's look first at deduction. Deductive arguments usually involve more than two classes; in fact, the simplest form of deductive argument involves three classes. Remember this famous argument from Chapter 5?

  All people are mortal.
  Socrates is a person.
  ∴ Socrates is mortal.

The three classes are "people," "mortality," and "Socrates." We can use circle diagrams to illustrate the relationship between these three classes. The first premise asserts that the class of people is included in the class of mortality. The second premise asserts that the class of Socrates is included in the class of people; and thus the conclusion can claim that Socrates is included in the class of mortality.

This type of argument is called a **categorical syllogism**—a deductive argument composed of three classes; such an argument has two premises and one conclusion derived from the two premises.

The subject and the predicate

To help identify the three classes of a categorical syllogism, you may want to identify the subject and predicate of each premise. Categorical propositions, and indeed all English sentences, can be broken down into two parts—the **subject** and **predicate.** These terms are shared by both grammar and logic and mean the same thing in both disciplines. The subject is that part of the sentence about which something is being asserted, and the predicate includes everything being asserted about the subject. In the first premise above, "all people" is the subject and "are mortal" is the predicate; in the second premise, "Socrates" is the subject and "is a person" is the predicate. The subject identifies one class, the predicate the other.

Note: If the premise stated "people are mortal" rather than "all people are mortal," the meaning would be the same since, if a class is not quantified in some way—some, many, few, one—it is assumed that the assertion refers to the entire class.

Truth, validity, and soundness

If the conclusion follows of necessity, inescapably, from the premises, as it does in the syllogism about Socrates, then it is a **valid** argument.

We frequently use the term "valid" in everyday language. For example, we say, "That's a valid point." But in logic **validity** has this very precise meaning: the conclusion follows of necessity from the premises, the form of the argument is correct, the line of reasoning conforms to the rules of logic. When we learn to evaluate the validity of a deductive argument, we can see what it means for a conclusion to follow inescapably from the premises.

Validity, however, is not the only requirement for a successful deductive argument; the premises must also be "**true**" or "**acceptable**." Logicians use the term "true," appropriate when a proposition can be evaluated by absolute or mathematical standards. But proof must often fall short of what can be claimed as "true," an absolute term too imposing, even intimidating, for many assertions which we would nonetheless be inclined to accept. In most of our arguments, we must settle for what is reasonable to believe, what has been adequately supported and explained. Oliver Wendell Holmes, Supreme Court Justice 1902–1932, skirted the issue when he said, "What is true is what I can't help believing." We, like a number of others in the critical thinking field, prefer the term "acceptable" to "true." As Tom Bridges of Montclair State University puts it, "The goal of inquiry is not objective truth, but reasonable belief, *pistis*—the state of being persuaded."

An important point here is that to evaluate an argument successfully, we must begin by evaluating the premises, one by one, rather than moving in on the conclusion first. The conclusion will only be as acceptable as the sum of its premises.

To summarize, two requirements must be met for us to accept the conclusion of a deductive argument.

1. the structure of the argument must be *valid*—that is, the conclusion must follow of necessity from the premises
2. the premises must be *acceptable* (true)

A deductive argument whose premises are acceptable and whose structure is valid is a **sound** argument—a successful deductive argument. Put another way, if the argument is valid and the premises are acceptable, then the conclusion cannot be false. Keep in mind that the terms validity and soundness can refer only to the argument as a whole. In contrast, individual statements can only be described as acceptable or unacceptable (true or false). We can't describe an argument as being true or a premise as valid.

Some examples of sound and unsound arguments:

1. A sound argument—the premises are acceptable and the structure valid.

   Drift-net fishing kills dolphins.
   Mermaid Tuna uses drift nets.
   ∴ Mermaid Tuna kills dolphins.

2. An unsound argument—one of the premises (in this example the first one) is false or not acceptable, even though the structure is valid.

> All Latins are volatile.
> Jesse is a Latin.
> ∴ Jesse is volatile.

3. An unsound argument—the premises are acceptable but the structure is invalid.

> All athletes are people.
> All football players are people.
> ∴ All football players are athletes.

Note that in example 3, all the statements are acceptable, both the premises and the conclusion, but since the structure of the argument is invalid—the premises do not lead inescapably to the conclusion—the argument is unsound. Sketch this argument with circle diagrams to illustrate the principle.

Unreliable syllogisms turn up as accident and humorous intent in a variety of places. Writer and critic Donald Newlove once claimed that while he fell asleep reading Harold Brodkey's *Runaway Soul,* he did the same thing his first time through literary classics *Moby Dick* and *Ulysses,* and thus *Runaway Soul* must also be a great work of literature. Writer Ian Frazier found the following graffiti on a library table at Columbia University:

> David Bowie is supreme.
> God is supreme.
> ∴ David Bowie is God.

Guilt by association

Let's look at another example of an invalid argument with acceptable premises.

> Drug dealers wear electronic pagers.
> Doctors wear electronic pagers.
> ∴ Doctors are drug dealers.

All of us would reject this ridiculous argument, but this pattern of reasoning, erroneous as it is, is fairly common. One famous example took place in 1950 when communism was referred to as the "red menace," and Senator Joseph McCarthy and the House Un-American Activities Committee were beginning their witch-hunt against anyone who had ever had an association, no matter how slight or distant, with communism. It was in this climate of national paranoia that Republican Richard Nixon, running against Democrat Helen Gahagen Douglas for a California senate seat, presented the following argument, allowing the voters to draw their own conclusion.

Communists favor measures x, y, and z.
My opponent, Helen Gahagen Douglas, favors these same measures.
∴ [Helen Gahagen Douglas is a Communist.]

This kind of reasoning, based on guilt by association, is faulty (but often effective—Douglas lost the election) because it assumes that if two classes share one quality, they share all qualities. Such reasoning is a source of much racism and sexism; it assumes that if two people are of the same sex or race, they share not only that characteristic but an entire set of characteristics as well. But a simple diagram can illustrate where the logic fails.

More on syllogisms

Before you examine some syllogisms on your own, we need to look once again at exclusion, overlap, and inclusion. Examine the following example and use circle diagrams to illustrate the relationship between each of the classes to determine the validity of the reasoning.

All Alice's friends are Libertarians.
Deborah is not a Libertarian.
∴ Deborah is not a friend of Alice.

Were you able to illustrate by exclusion that this is a valid argument? Can you do the same for this one?

None of Alice's friends are Libertarians.
Deborah is not a friend of Alice.
∴ Deborah is not a Libertarian.

Can you illustrate why this reasoning is not reliable, why the argument is invalid?

So far we have been dealing with what we call a **universal proposition,** an assertion that refers to all members of a designated class. What happens when we qualify a premise with "some," and then have what logicians call a **particular proposition**? Let's look at an example.

All gamblers are optimists.
Some of my friends are gamblers.
∴ Some of my friends are optimists.

A diagram will illustrate that since the conclusion is qualified, it can follow from one qualified, or "particular," premise. Although it's possible for some friends to fall outside the class of gamblers and thus, perhaps, outside the class of optimists, the second premise guarantees that some (at least two) of my friends are included in the class of gamblers.

This argument is valid. But if the first premise also says "*Some* gamblers are optimists," you can't necessarily claim that even one friend has to be an optimist. Use a diagram to show the possibility that even the qualified conclusion could be false.

EXERCISE 6B

Determining the Validity of Categorical Syllogisms

Use Euler diagrams to determine the validity of the following categorical syllogisms.

Example

1. Stealing is a criminal act.
2. Shoplifting is stealing.
   ∴ Shoplifting is a criminal act.

VALID Inclusion

* **1.** Liberals want to ban offshore drilling.
     Conservationists want to ban offshore drilling.
     ∴ Conservationists are liberals.

* **2.** A cautious pilot wouldn't drink before a flight.
     Maxine is a cautious pilot.
     ∴ Maxine wouldn't drink before a flight.

   3. All Jose's parrots understand Spanish.
     Pepe is his favorite parrot.
     ∴ Pepe understands Spanish.

   4. Gauguin's paintings of Tahiti have brilliant and unrealistic colors.
     "Starry Night" has brilliant and unrealistic colors.
     ∴ "Starry Night" is a Gauguin painting of Tahiti.

5. Young men with shaven heads and swastikas tattooed on their arms are racists.
John is a young man who doesn't shave his head or have a swastika tattooed on his arm.
∴ John is not a racist.

6. Nations that do not respect the rights of American citizens shouldn't receive favored nation status.
China did not respect the rights of American citizen Harry Woo when they imprisoned him without trial.
∴ China didn't deserve favored nation status.

7. Every pediatrician knows that each child develops at his own rate.
Dr. Haskell knows that each child develops at his own rate.
∴ Dr. Haskell is a pediatrician.

8. Some artists are completely self-absorbed.
Frida Kahlo was an artist.
∴ Frida Kahlo was completely self-absorbed.

9. Members of the Christian Coalition believe in family values.
Carlos and Maria believe in family values.
∴ Carlos and Maria are members of the Christian coalition.

10. Killing the innocent is morally wrong.
Modern warfare always involves killing the innocent.
∴ Modern warfare is always morally wrong.

Create three categorical syllogisms of your own—one valid but unsound, one invalid, and one sound.

EXERCISE 6C

Evaluating Deductive Arguments in Everyday Language

Determine whether the following arguments are sound or unsound. For each argument follow these steps: First, reduce each one to a categorical syllogism (supplying any unstated premises or conclusions—see hidden assumptions in Chapter 3); then use circle diagrams to determine validity; and finally, discuss the truth or acceptability of each premise.

***1.** Plagiarism is wrong, and paraphrasing the words of others without proper acknowledgment is the same as plagiarism, so paraphrasing the words of others without proper acknowledgment is wrong.

2. The time has come for the government to ban cigarette smoking on all international flights now that the National Academy of Sciences, in its comprehensive study of air quality in aircraft cabins, has declared that smoke in jetliners is harmful to health and safety. (Hint: The first premise of this argument is not stated.)

3. Mafia member Joe Bonano was guilty of criminal activities because he claimed the Fifth Amendment in the course of his trial. The Fifth Amendment, you will recall, is the privilege of a witness not to testify on the grounds that the evidence called for might be incriminating. One may choose not to testify against oneself, but there is a risk attached to this privilege. For we cannot avoid the fact that people who take the Fifth Amendment have something to hide—their guilt. In the case of Joe Bonano, that something to hide was his criminal activities.

HYPOTHETICAL ARGUMENTS

Another common type of deductive argument is the hypothetical or conditional argument which, unlike the categorical syllogism, is concerned not with classes but with conditions. For example:

If Maria drops that glass, it will break.

A condition is established which, if met, will lead to a a specified consequence. The condition is called the **antecedent;** the consequence or result is called, appropriately enough, the **consequent.** The second premise, or minor premise, establishes whether or not that condition has been met.

Maria dropped the glass.

In this case, the antecedent has been affirmed. The conclusion then follows of necessity: The glass broke. The argument pattern looks like this:

If A, then B.
A.
∴ B.

The Valid Hypothetical Argument

This argument pattern *affirms the antecedent**, and any argument that conforms to this pattern is valid; though of course whether or not the argument is sound, whether or not we accept the conclusion, depends on the acceptability of the premises as well as the validity of the argument.

Another valid argument pattern is one in which the minor premise *denies the consequent.*†

If Maria drops that glass, it will break.
It did not break.
∴ Maria did not drop it.

---

*Logicians refer to this argument pattern as modus ponens.

†Logicians refer to this argument pattern as modus tollens.

It follows that if the glass didn't break, Maria didn't drop it. Here's the form of this argument.

If A, then B.
Not B.
∴ Not A.

The rule governing the validity of a hypothetical argument is really quite simple: *The minor premise must either affirm the antecedent or deny the consequent.*

The Invalid Hypothetical Argument

Conversely, to deny the antecedent or affirm the consequent leads to invalidity.

For example:

If Maria drops the glass, it will break.	[If A, then B.
Maria did not drop the glass.	Not A.
∴ The glass did not break.	Not B.]

It does not follow that if Maria does not drop it, it won't break since there are many other ways for the glass to break: Jack may drop it or someone may pour very hot liquid into it, just to name two possibilities.

To affirm the consequent will also produce an invalid argument.

If Maria drops the glass, it will break.	[If A, then B.
It broke.	B.
∴ Maria dropped it.	A.]

If the glass did break it doesn't necessarily follow that Maria was the cause since, once again, there are many ways for a glass to meet such a fate.

To summarize: These two hypothetical argument patterns are valid.

If A, then B.	If A, then B.
A.	Not B.
∴ B.	∴ Not A.

These two hypothetical argument patterns are invalid.

If A, then B.	If A, then B.
Not A.	B.
Not B.	∴ A.

Determining the validity of hypothetical reasoning reminds us that many conditions or causes can lead to the same result; we can't assume only one specific condition for a particular consequence unless we are told that this is the case.

Necessary and Sufficient Conditions

When there is a condition essential for a particular consequence or result, that condition is called a **necessary condition**—a condition without which something cannot happen. Fire, for example, cannot occur without oxygen; oxygen then is a necessary condition of fire. But oxygen alone cannot start a fire—there must be matter to burn as well as something to ignite it—so oxygen is not a **sufficient condition.** While it is necessary, it is not enough.

During the Senate Judiciary Committee hearings on the nomination of Clarence Thomas to the Supreme Court, a dispute ensued when Senator Alan Simpson maintained that Thomas's acknowledged good character should render him qualified for the Supreme Court. A law professor agreed that good character was an important ingredient for successful service on the Court, but explained that it was not the only desirable characteristic. Good character was indeed *necessary* but it was not *sufficient* to justify approval of Thomas, who many thought lacked judicial experience.

Logicians sometimes express a necessary cause as "if and only if." If, and only if, oxygen is present can fire start. Or, as writer Tobias Wolff (in *This Boy's Life*) remembers his mother warning him: "She said I could have the rifle if, and only if, I promised never to take it out or even touch it"—a necessary condition he failed to honor, unfortunately.

"He is physically able to wag his tail—given sufficient cause."

Hypothetical Chains

Hypothetical arguments may also consist of entire chains of conditions, as in the following example.

> If gun control advocates mount a very strong, well-funded campaign, then Congress will pass a law banning handguns.
> If Congress passes a law banning handguns, then fewer people will be able to purchase them.
> If fewer people are able to purchase them, then there will be fewer guns.
> If there are fewer guns, then there will be less violence in our society.
> ∴ If gun control advocates mount a very strong, well-funded campaign in the fall, then there will be less violence in our society.

The pattern is apparent:

> If A, then B.
> If B, then C.
> If C, then D.
> If D, then E.
> ∴ If A, then E.

If, in such a chain, the first condition is affirmed, the other conditional claims, like falling dominoes, lead us inescapably to the conclusion—providing, of course, that we accept the truth of the claims. In fact, the domino theory, which warned of a Communist threat to the United States and guided foreign policy in, among other places, Central America for much of the twentieth century, is based on this kind of reasoning.

> If Nicaragua falls (to communism), then El Salvador will fall.
> If El Salvador falls, then all of Central America will follow.
> If Central America falls, then Mexico will fall.
> If Mexico falls, communism will be at our border.
> ∴ If Nicaragua falls, communism will be at our border.

Is this a sound argument? If not, why not?

Hypothetical Claims and Everyday Reasoning

As you prepare to do the following exercise on hypothetical arguments, keep in mind that such reasoning is not limited to logic texts. Hypothetical relationships also play a central role when computer programmers design software, and hypothetical reasoning is, in fact, a common feature of the thinking we do every day. For example:

> If I miss that review session, I won't be prepared for the midterm.
> If I don't stop at the grocery store on my way home, I won't have anything to eat for dinner.

As these examples indicate, we continually make conditional claims and decisions based on these claims and the outcome we desire. In the examples above, if the "I" of the sentences fails to affirm the antecedent, he must be prepared to accept the less-than-desirable consequences.

EXERCISE 6D

Determining the Validity of Hypothetical Arguments

Use argument patterns to determine the validity of the following hypothetical arguments. [Keep in mind that you are not evaluating the acceptability of each premise, so even the valid arguments could be unsound according to the principles of reasoning discussed earlier in this chapter.]

*1. If the burglar came in through the window, it would be unlocked. We found the window unlocked. We all agreed that the burglar must have come in through the window.

2. If most nations view ethnic cleansing in Bosnia as a crime against humanity, then military action against the aggressors should be stepped up. Indeed, most nations do view ethnic cleansing as a crime against humanity, so military action against the aggressors should be increased.

3. Doctors claim that if you eat barbecued meats on a regular basis, you increase your risk of developing cancer. Fortunately, Calvin is a vegetarian and thus doesn't eat barbecued meats, so he is not at increased risk for cancer.

4. If the burglar came in through the window, it would be unlocked. We found the window locked, leading us to believe that the burglar couldn't have come in through the window.

5. If you respected my opinion, you would seek my advice. You don't seek my advice, so I can only conclude that you don't respect my opinion.

6. If the government doesn't balance the budget, the deficit will increase. The facts speak for themselves: the deficit is increasing. Clearly, the government is not balancing the budget.

7. If the governor makes a strong speech on the necessity of conserving water, he will be able to convince people to do so. Fortunately, he has scheduled a press conference for that purpose, so people will conserve water.

8. All the sportswriters agreed that if the 49ers didn't play well against the Cowboys, the 49ers were destined to lose the all-important game. As we all remember, they lost in the closing minutes, leaving me with the unhappy knowledge that they didn't play well that day.

9. If the paint is oil-based, the paintbrush cannot be cleaned with water, but the brush is being cleaned with water, so the paint must not be oil-based.

10. If oil supplies from the Persian Gulf are reduced, the price of oil will rise in the United States. If the price of oil in the United States

rises, manufacturing costs will rise, and if this happens, an economic recession could develop. So if an economic recession does develop, we can certainly attribute it to reduced oil supplies from the Persian Gulf.

EXERCISE 6E

Analyzing a Timeless Argument

Reduce the following poem to a hypothetical argument containing two premises and a conclusion, and determine its validity. Hint: The first two stanzas contain the first and second premises, respectively, and the last contains the conclusion.

TO HIS COY MISTRESS

by Andrew Marvell (1621–1678)

Had we but world enough, and time,
This coyness, Lady, were no crime.
We would sit down, and think which way
To walk, and pass our long love's day.
Thou by the Indian Ganges' side
Shouldst rubies find; I by the tide
Of Humber would complain. I would
Love you ten years before the Flood,
And you should, if you please, refuse
Till the Conversion of the Jews.
My vegetable love should grow
Vaster than empires and more slow;
An hundred years should go to praise
Thine eyes, and on thy forehead gaze;
Two hundred to adore each breast;
But thirty thousand to the rest:
An age at least to every part,
And the last age should show your heart.
For, Lady, you deserve this *state*,   (dignity)
Nor would I love at lower rate.

But at my back I always hear
Time's winged chariot hurrying near;
And yonder all before us lie
Deserts of vast eternity.
Thy beauty shall no more be found,
Nor, in thy marble vault, shall sound
My echoing song; then worms shall try
That long-preserved virginity,
And your *quaint* honor turn to dust,   (proud)

And into ashes all my lust:
The grave's a fine and private place,
But none, I think, do there embrace.

Now therefore, while the youthful hue
Sits on thy skin like morning dew,
And while thy willing soul *transpires*   (breathes out)
At every pore with instant fires,
Now let us sport us while we may
And now, like amorous birds of prey,
Rather at once our time devour
Than languish in his slow-*chapped* power.   (jawed)
Let us roll all our strength and all
Our sweetness up into one ball,
And tear our pleasures with rough strife
Through the iron gates of life;
Thus, though we cannot make our sun
Stand still, yet we will make him run.

 ### WRITING ASSIGNMENT 12

Responding to a Poetic Argument

Write a reply (as a poem or a letter) to Marvell's proposal, noting any flaws
you find in his argument.

Audience
The poet

Purpose
To articulate your reaction to the poet's argument.

EXERCISE 6F

Evaluating an Argument for Peace

Using your own words, reduce this poem to a hypothetical argument and
determine its validity. Hint: The first premise is stated in the last stanza,
but the minor premise and the conclusion are implicit.

DULCE ET DECORUM EST

by Wilfred Owen (1893–1918)
Bent double, like old beggars under sacks,
Knock-kneed, coughing like hags, we cursed through sludge,
Till on the haunting flares we turned our backs

And towards our distant rest began to trudge.
Men marched asleep. Many had lost their boots
But limped on, blood-shod. All went lame; all blind;
Drunk with fatigue; deaf even to the hoots
Of tired, outstripped Five Nines that dropped behind.

Gas! Gas! Quick, boys!—An ecstasy of fumbling,
Fitting the clumsy helmets just in time;
But someone still was yelling out and stumbling
And flound'ring like a man in fire or lime . . .
Dim, through the misty panes and thick green light,
As under a green sea, I saw him drowning.

In all my dreams, before my helpless sight,
He plunges at me, guttering, choking, drowning.

If in some smothering dreams you too could pace
Behind the wagon that we flung him in,
And watch the white eyes writhing in his face,
His hanging face, like a devil's sick of sin;
If you could hear, at every jolt, the blood
Come gargling from the froth-corrupted lungs,
Obscene as cancer, bitter as the cud
Of vile, incurable sores on innocent tongues,—
My friend, you would not tell with such high zest
The old Lie: *Dulce et decorum est
Pro patria mori.* *

Biographical note: This poem is especially poignant because its author,
Wilfred Owen, died on the battlefield in the last week of the First World
War at the age of 25.

APPLICATION TO WRITING

Parallel Structure and Class Logic

Our earlier discussion of classes applies not only to logic, syllogisms, and
politics but also to sentence structure, specifically to parallel structure.

Parallel structure is simply a repetition of like grammatical units—a
list of items if you will—often joined by conjunctions. The items in the list,
however, must not only be grammatically similar but also relate logically to
one another. Here's where class logic comes into play. To understand what
we mean, look at the following sentence.

The language used in the text will have to be looked at for sexism, racism, and bias.

---

* "It is sweet and fitting to die for one's country." From the Latin poet Horace.

The list in this sentence is "sexism, racism, and bias." The list is *grammatically* parallel because all three words in the list are nouns, but not *logically* parallel since sexism, racism, and bias are presented as three separate classes when in fact sexism and racism are particular forms of bias; they are included in the class of bias, not separate from it. Here is how the relationships in the sentence above look when sketched with Euler diagrams:

One way to correct this faulty logic would be to replace "bias" with "other forms of bias" thus illustrating the logical and actual relationship—exclusion—that exists between the three classes.

EXERCISE 6G

Editing the Illogical Series

Revise the following sentences for logical classification.

*1. In their attempt to excel, these people will often work extra hours and work through many lunch hours.

2. I have seen city ordinances which do not allow smoking in restaurants popping up all over the place: in offices, in buildings.

3. I asked Linda if she had any materialistic aspirations such as living in a mansion, having a nice car, or being extremely wealthy.

4. The customers at the bank where I work are wealthy depositors, checking account holders, cooperative individuals, and those who are thoughtlessly rude to me.

5. For the most part, he is handsome, active, and well-dressed, usually in expensive clothes or a suit and tie.

A Review of Parallel Structure

Look at the following two sentences:

I came, I saw, I conquered.

They plan to visit Rio, Madrid, and Bangkok.

Though quite different in content they are similar in form: they both illustrate parallel structure. As stated above, parallel structure is simply repetition, usually of the same grammatical structures used in the same way, sometimes of the same word or phrase, often joined by the conjunctions *and, but, or, yet.*

Parallelism is a useful rhetorical device, providing a powerful means of emphasizing relationships by organizing ideas into predictable patterns. We hear a repetition and expect the pattern to continue. Read the two sentences above. Listen to the "ring" of the first sentence and the aid to attention and memory such a rhetorical device provides. Then note the logical organization and its contribution to meaning in the second sentence; the grammatical grouping underscores the implicit relationships between these cities: historical cities of diverse beauty, international centers representing distinct cultures, and interesting travel destinations.

When our expectations are thwarted, we may falter briefly in our reading or even lose the thread of the writer's thought. In most cases, our ear tells us when a series is wandering off the track, but sometimes it can be helpful to check the grammatical structure. Here is a strategy for examining your own sentences.

Think of parallel structures as lists, in the case above a list of cities to visit. We can illustrate this list and the need for it to conform to the principles of parallelism by placing parallel lines at its beginning:

They plan to visit // Rio, Madrid, and Bangkok.

The conjunction "and" joins three proper nouns acting as direct objects of the verb "plan to visit."

We can do the same thing to more complicated sentences taken from Joan Didion's essay on Alcatraz, "Rock of Ages."

It is not an unpleasant place to be, out there on Alcatraz with only // the *flowers* and the *wind* and a bell *buoy* moaning and the *tide* surging through the Golden Gate. . . . [a list of nouns as direct objects of the preposition "with"]

Once a week the Harts take their boat to San Francisco to // *pick up* their mail and *shop* at the big Safeway in the Marina. . . . [a list of two infinitive phrases]

Mr. Scott, whose interest in penology dates from the day his office acquired Alcatraz as a potential property, // *talked about* // *escapes* and *security routines* and *pointed out* the beach where Ma Barker's son Doc was killed trying to escape. [This sentence contains two lists, one within the other—two verbs for the subject "Mr. Scott"; and two nouns acting as direct objects of "talked about."]

Now read the next sentence (aloud if possible) and hear how the loss of expected balance or harmony offends the ear.

When I should be studying, I will, instead, waste time by watching television or daydream.

The two verbs are not in the same form and are therefore not parallel. They can be made parallel by simply changing "daydream" to "daydreaming."

Sometimes faulty parallelism offends not only our ear but also our reason.

> People who have "book smarts" usually work in places like // *libraries* or *assistants* to attorneys.

Though the writer has joined two nouns (grammatically compatible elements), an assistant of any kind cannot be a "place." He has lost control of the sentence because he has forgotten where the list begins. There is more than one way to fix this sentence, to make it logical and balanced. How would you correct it?

English, however, can be somewhat flexible when it comes to parallelism. For example, few readers would object to this sentence:

> The bus system is economical, but it is crowded, uncomfortable, and may not be depended on.

Here the third element does not conform to the grammatical structure of the first two, yet it is neither confusing nor harsh in its rhythm. We could easily revise the ending to read "undependable," but some writers might prefer the original. Careful writers, however, make such decisions judiciously, generally preferring to maintain the grammatical and rhetorical integrity of a parallel series.

Before doing Exercise 6H, note the rhetorical effects of parallel structure on the following passage taken from *The Road to Coorain,* an autobiography of Jill Ker Conway, the first woman president of Smith College. Use our system of notation to mark off the different series or lists.

> Those night train journeys had their own mystery because of the clicking of the rails, the shafts of light pouring through the shutters of the sleeping compartment as we passed stations, and the slamming of doors when the train stopped to take on passengers. In the morning there was the odd sight of green landscape, trees, grass, banks of streams—an entirely different palette of colors, as though during the night we had journeyed to another country. Usually I slept soundly, registering the unaccustomed sounds and images only faintly. This time I lay awake and listened, opened the shutters and scanned unknown platforms, and wondered about the future.

This passage has several parallel lists. Did you find them all?

EXERCISE 6H

Supplying Parallel Elements

Complete these sentences with a parallel element.

1. Writing a good paper is a task that demands // hard work, patience, and . . .
*2. She // rushed home, threw her assorted debris into a closet, and . . .
3. Fewer and fewer Americans are buying houses these days // not because they don't want to own their own home but . . .
4. The first lady is a woman who // has an open mind but . . .

5. The first lady is a woman who has // an open mind and . . .

In the following sentences, identify the misfits—the element of the sentence which is not parallel—and revise the sentence so that all the elements of the list are parallel.

6. Many influences shape a child's development: family, church, peer groups, economic, social, and school.

7. Do you live in an area where knife wounds, killings, and people are raped are as common as the sun rising in the morning?

8. He helped to wash the car and with cleaning out the garage.

9. Free inquiry in the search for truth sometimes necessitates the abandonment of law and order but which always demands freedom of expression.

10. Pineapple juice is my favorite because it is a good source of energy, it isn't artificially sweetened, and because of its low cost.

11. The president launched a campaign against drunk driving and promoting the use of seat belts.

As a final exercise in parallel structure, write three of your own sentences—one with three or more verbs sharing the same subject, one with three or more adjectives, and one with three or more nouns. Use as your subject a topic you are currently writing on for this or another class.

Parallelism—The Open and Closed Series

And now for a rhetorical fine point—the open and closed series. For example:

> The state must balance its budget by eliminating free school lunches, afterschool childcare, and driver education classes.

The list is complete. The writer is recommending that three government benefits be terminated. But what if the writer only wants to suggest the kinds of cuts the legislature should make? He might write,

> The state must balance its budget by eliminating free school lunches, afterschool childcare, driver education classes, etc.

This version indicates an open series, one that may not be complete but is, instead, representative. A writer of a memo can use "etc." to indicate the representative nature of his list, but "etc." is not appropriate in a more formal piece of writing such as an editorial, an essay, or a business report. So how can we write an open series without resorting to the vague and lazy "etc."? Simply remove the "and" from the list. Joan Didion uses this strategy in describing Alcatraz:

> Alcatraz Island is covered with flowers now: orange and yellow nasturtiums, geraniums, sweet grass, blue iris, black-eyed Susans.

The absence of the "and" before the final element implies that the list is not exhaustive, that there may be other flowers on the island in addition to those she names.

Emphasizing Ideas with Parallelism

As we mentioned above, parallelism can be a powerful rhetorical device. Beyond the sentence, parallelism can provide emphasis and organize major ideas in paragraphs, particularly in argument. Note how writer Alan Brinkley uses parallelism in his piece on Senator Packwood's expulsion from the Senate for sexual harassment charges.

> Bob Packwood's tortured departure from the Senate has many similarities to Richard Nixon's tortured departure from the White House twenty-one years ago. Like Nixon, Packwood remained in office long after his reputation was destroyed, and resigned only when his last remaining supporters abandoned him. Like Nixon, he meticulously recorded incriminating information and then tried to suppress and alter it. Like Nixon, he denied his offenses to the end, tried to discredit his accusers, and relied heavily on procedural and legal arguments to avoid facing the substance of the charges against him. Like Nixon, he insisted that he was resigning for the good of the country. And, like Nixon, in leaving by the door he has saved himself from almost certain defenestration.

Note how the repetition of the phrase "Like Nixon" provides not only emphasis but also coherence.

SUMMARY

There are three possible relationships between classes: inclusion, exclusion, and overlap.

Both inductive and deductive reasoning often depend on supporting a conclusion on the basis of relationships between classes.

For a categorical argument to be sound, the structure of the argument must be valid and the premises acceptable.

For a hypothetical argument to be valid the second, or minor premise, must either affirm the antecedent or deny the consequent.

Parallelism is a useful rhetorical device, providing a powerful means of emphasizing relationships by organizing ideas into predictable patterns.

KEY TERMS

Class in logic is all of the individual things—persons, objects, events, ideas—that share a determinate property.

Inclusion a relationship between classes in which every member of one class is a member of another class.

Exclusion a relationship between classes in which classes share no members.

Overlap a relationship between classes in which classes share at least one member.

Categorical syllogism a deductive argument composed of three classes; the argument has two premises and one conclusion derived from the two premises.

Subject that part of the sentence about which something is being asserted.

Predicate includes everything being asserted about the subject.

Validity the conclusion follows of necessity from the premises; the form of the argument is correct.

Soundness describes a deductive argument whose premises are acceptable and whose structure is valid.

Universal proposition refers to all members of a designated class.

Particular proposition refers to some members of a designated class.

Antecedent the part of a hypothetical argument that establishes a condition.

Consequent the part of a hypothetical argument that results from the antecedent.

Necessary condition a condition without which the consequence cannot occur; for example, fire cannot occur without oxygen.

Sufficient condition one condition, among others, that leads to a particular consequence; for example, a match is one way to start a fire but not the only way.

Parallel structure a repetition of like grammatical units, often joined by the conjunctions and, but, or, yet.

Chapter
7

Inductive Argument

He uses statistics as a drunken man used lamp-posts—for support rather than illumination.

—Andrew Lang

*T*he fundamental distinction between deductive and inductive reasoning lies in the relative certainty with which we can accept a conclusion (see Chapter 5). The certainty guaranteed when a deductive argument is validly reasoned from acceptable premises cannot be assumed in an inductive argument, no matter how carefully one supports the inference. The terms most appropriate for inductive arguments then are strong and weak, reliable or unreliable rather than valid and invalid.

Some logicians prefer the categories deductive and nondeductive to deductive and inductive, given the varied forms arguments can take when they don't conform to the rigorous rules of inference required for deduction.

GENERALIZATION

Determining cause and effect, formulating hypotheses, drawing analogies, arriving at statistical generalizations are all examples of nondeductive reasoning, or as we have chosen to call it, inductive reasoning. But in this chapter we concentrate on the **statistical generalization.** Such generalizations are best characterized as predictions, as claims about the distribution of a **projected property** in a given group or population, the **target population.** From the distribution of such a property in *part* of the target population, the **sample,** we infer a proposition, a conclusion that is either strong or weak depending on how carefully we conduct our survey. We make a prediction, an inference, about the unknown on the basis of the known; on the basis of our observations of the sample, we make a generalization about all of the population, including that part we have not observed closely.

Suppose we want to determine whether New York taxpayers will support a tax designated specifically for building shelters for the homeless.

Here the **projected property** would be the willingness to support this particular tax (what we want to find out). The **target population** would be New York taxpayers. The **sample** would be that portion of New York taxpayers polled. From their answers, we would draw a conclusion, make a generalization about New York taxpayers in general: unanimous support, strong support, marginal support, little support, no support—whatever their answers warrant. But no matter how precise the numbers from the sample, we cannot predict with absolute certainty what the entire population of New York taxpayers will actually do. When we make an inference from some to all, the conclusion will always remain logically doubtful to some degree.

R. Ch

Let's look at another example.

For several years now, scientists and health officials have been alerting the public to the increased risk of skin cancer as the thinning of the ozone layer allows more of the harmful ultraviolet rays to penetrate the atmosphere. Imagine that the student health center at your school wanted to find out if students were aware of this danger and were protecting themselves from it. In this case, the **projected property** would be taking preventive measures to protect oneself from the sun. The **target population** would be all the students attending your school, and the **sample** would be the number of students polled. Once again, any conclusions reached by the health center on the basis of its survey would be tentative rather than certain, with the certainty increasing in proportion to the size of the sample—the greater the number of students polled, the more reliable the conclusion, assuming the sample is representative as well.

The Direction of Inductive Reasoning

The direction of inductive reasoning can vary. We may start by noting specific instances and from them make general inferences, or we may begin with a general idea and seek specific examples or data to support it. The following example moves from specific cases to a generalization.

Observing a sudden increase in the number of measles cases in several communities, public health officials in 1990 inferred that too many infants were going unvaccinated.

Even here you may notice that our ability to think both deductively and inductively has a way of intertwining the two modes of thought, but the structure of this argument is still inductive, the conclusion being probable rather than guaranteed.

But often we start with a tentative generalization, a possible conclusion called a **hypothesis,** an assertion we are interested in proving.

Rousel Uclaf, the French manufacturers of a revolutionary new pill to prevent pregnancy and avoid abortion, hoped to prove that it was both effective and safe. In order to do so they had to conduct elaborate studies with varied groups of women over time. Until they had gathered such statistical support in a sample population, their claim that it was effective and safe was only a hypothesis, not a reliable conclusion. But once they had tested their product, RU 486, on 40,000 women in several European countries and found only two "incidents" of pregnancies and no apparent harm, they were ready to claim that RU 486 is reasonably safe and statistically effective.

Even here, the conclusion remains inductive—it is a highly probable conclusion but not a necessary one as it would be in deduction. Unfortunately, there are examples of such inductive reasoning leading to false (and disastrous) conclusions. Approved for use in Europe, the drug

Thalidomide, given to pregnant women for nausea in the 1960s, caused many children to be born with grave deformities. And the Dalkon Shield, an intrauterine birth control device of the 1970s, although tested before being made available, caused sterility in many of its users.

Testing Inductive Generalizations

With inductive arguments, we accept a conclusion with varying degrees of probability and must be willing to live with at least a fraction of uncertainty. But the question will always remain, how much uncertainty is acceptable?

Criteria for evaluating statistical generalizations

How we infer our conclusions, the way in which we conduct our surveys, is crucial to determining the strength of an inductive argument. Whether we are constructing our own arguments or evaluating those of others, we need to be discriminating. Many of our decisions on political, economic, socio-logical, even personal issues depend on inductive reasoning. Scarcely a day goes by without an inductive study or poll reaching the news sections of daily papers or the evening news on TV—surveys show the president's popularity is rising or falling, Americans favor socialized medicine, one in five nongovernment workers is employed at firms with drug testing pro-grams. A few principles for evaluating such generalizations can help us all examine the conclusions with the critical perspective necessary for our self-defense.

In order to accept a conclusion as warranted or reliable, we need to control or interpret the conditions of the supporting survey.

Two features of the sample are essential:

1. The *size* must be adequate. The proportion of those in the sample must be sufficient to reflect the total size of the target population. Statisticians have developed complex formulas for determining ade-quate size proportionate to a given population, but for our general purposes common sense and a little well-reasoned practice will serve. The Gallup Organization polls 2,500 to 3,000 to determine how 80 million will vote in a presidential election and allows for only a 3 percent margin of error. This suggests that the size of a sur-vey can often be smaller than we might initially assume.
2. The sample must be *representative*. It must represent the target population in at least two different ways.
   a. The sample must be selected *randomly* from the target popula-tion.
   b. It must also be *spread* across the population so that all significant differences within the population are represented. Such a con-trived approach might seem contradictory to a random sample, but some conscious manipulation is often necessary to assure a sample that is genuinely typical of the target population.

Examine the following diagram to see these principles illustrated.

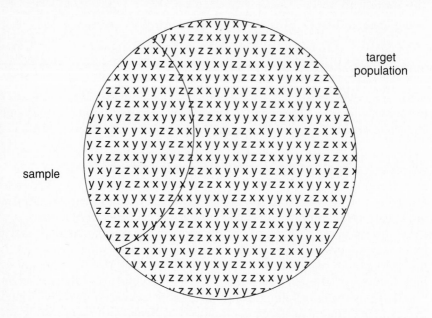

As you can see, we are back to classes (Chapter 6). The sample is a sub-class included in the larger class of the target population. As we make inferences, we move from a conclusion about the smaller class, the sample, to a conclusion about the larger class, the target population.

If they remove all the fools from Congress, it wouldn't be a representative Congress.

Political commentator Molly Ivins

Let's evaluate the reasoning in the following argument:

A visitor of modest means from a midwestern city comes to San Francisco for five days and is instructed by her friends to assess the prices of San Francisco's restaurants; some of them are considering a trip there in the near future. Our tourist, let's call her Martha, picks up a guidebook and takes the first five restaurants listed in the book: Masas, Campton Place, Postrio, the Ritz Carlton, and Aqua, all of which are located downtown. Verging on bankruptcy, poor Martha returns home with the report that restaurants in San Francisco are staggeringly expensive. For a resident of San Francisco, the error in her conclusion and the flaw in the reasoning that led to her false conclusion are easy to spot—she has inadvertently chosen five of the most expensive restaurants in the city. Before selecting her restaurants, she should have examined her guidebook carefully to be sure that her survey of restaurants was, to some degree, representative. The book clearly began with a list of the major splurges, and that was as far as Martha went.

With only five days, she was necessarily limited when it came to the *size* of her sample, and thus she would have to place a strong qualifier on any conclusion she drew. But with a little care, she could have aimed for a more *random* sample by investigating different sections of her guidebook, referring to more than one guide, and visiting various geographical areas of San Francisco. Such a sampling would also have helped her arrive at examples spread more effectively over different types of cuisine. A visitor intent on savoring the best fare regardless of cost would have done well following Martha's approach, but one interested in the prices was doomed to a distorted picture.

Can you identify the projected property, the target population, the sample, and the conclusion for this inductive argument?

Hasty Generalizations

When, like Martha, we leap to an unwarranted conclusion, we commit the common logical fallacy of hasty generalization. If, for example, after one semester at a university as a student having had two professors who failed to return work, often missed class, or arrived late, you concluded that the university had a rotten faculty, you would be guilty of hasty generalization. The sample is clearly too small to warrant such a conclusion. For further discussion of this familiar weakness in reasoning, look ahead to Chapter 8.

COUNTEREXAMPLES

With any generalization supported by specific examples, one counterexample can discredit, or "embarrass," the conclusion. Warranted conclusions must be consistent with the data used in their support, and where necessary, qualified appropriately—"most," "some," "usually," "occasionally," "in most cases."

Garfield doubts his conclusion when he discovers three counterexamples.

Thinking Critically About Surveys and Statistics

Because surveys and statistics suggest an authority they may not warrant, we must think critically about them rather than accept them without question. Statistics should contribute to reasoning, not serve as a substitute for it.

The following *Los Angeles Times* editorial on the much publicized decline in the Scholastic Aptitude Test scores points out that relying on numbers without thinking about alternative explanations can quickly lead to false conclusions.

SAT Slippage Is an Illusion

Every fall since 1972, the College Board has issued a report showing how the nation's high school seniors scored on the Scholastic Aptitude Test.

This fall, headlines throughout the United States echoed the College Board's own summary: "SAT Verbal, Math Scores Decline." The data show that the average SAT verbal score has declined from 453 to 422 over the past 20 years, and the average SAT math score has declined from 484 to 474 during the same period.

Are today's students less able than students of the past?

Actually, the decline in SAT scores is more apparent than real and is mainly because of the increased number of test takers. In 1972, 25 percent of 17-year-olds took the test. In 1991, it was 31 percent. As more students take the test, the average score is likely to go down.

It is better to compare the number of individuals who got a good score on the SAT to the total number of individuals in the same age group. This comparison yields different and more positive conclusions.

On the verbal part of the SAT, about 9 percent of all 17-year-olds scored 500 or better in 1972. By 1980 only about 6 percent scored 500 or better. However, during the 1980s the percent of high-scoring 17-year-olds has increased and is now up to about 8 percent.

On the math part of the SAT, about 11 percent of all 17-year-olds scored 500 or better in 1972. The percent of good math scores reached a low of 9 percent in 1978. Since then, the percent of good math scores has risen to 13 percent in 1991—the highest level in 20 years.

In summary, the SAT data suggest that today's college-bound students are doing somewhat better in math and somewhat worse in verbal skills than they did 20 years ago.

Roger Rasmussen
Los Angeles Times

Roger Rasmussen is director of the Independent Analysis Unit, a watchdog group for the Los Angeles Board of Education.

Rasmussen is pointing out that a simple percentage of the total number taking the SAT gives a distorted picture of how the scores of high school seniors have fluctuated over 20 years. Larger numbers taking the test and thus a larger spread at the lower end of expected scores will logically produce lower average scores. Those likely to achieve high scores have traditionally been preparing for college and thus were more likely to take the SAT. A comparison of those with higher scores (over 500 out of the 800 possible) reveals a different picture. While scores did decline initially as larger numbers of students moved into the pool, in less than ten years, scores on the verbal and math tests were rising for that group and by 1991 the verbal scores were almost back to 1972 levels. The math scores were actually higher by two percentage points—a brighter picture than the headlines painted. Numbers without critical thinking can distort reality.

General Foods learned the danger of placing blind faith in statistical marketing research when they tested Great Shakes, a new drink mix. Surveys of customers in several cities indicated they were enthusiastically buying all the flavors, and General Foods immediately began marketing the product nationally. They were surprised by the disappointing sales. What they had failed to consider was the possibility that customers were simply sampling all the flavors, hoping to find one they liked, and once they had rejected all flavors they lost interest in Great Shakes.

The following exchange of letters in *The Nation* also illustrates just how tricky numbers can be and reminds us that we should not judge without reflection.

Sexism Rampant

Hunter, NY

Your poetry competition and its result were remarkable. Competitiveness is one of those traits of our present system I'd think you'd eschew. But what really irks me is your result: Four female poets win a competition cosponsored by a publication with a female poetry editor [Grace Schulman]. Yes, there were males on the judging panel just as the queens of old had eunuchs to attend them. Does *The Nation* mean to tell us there were no entries by male poets that remotely approached the quality (however that's judged) of the winners? I can imagine the screams from the gallery if the results were as one-sided in the other direction—four male winners of a prize offered by a publication with a male poetry editor.

If progressive principles include freedom from gender bias, you're as regressive as anyone, only you've exchanged Neanderthal attitudes for Amazonian. You're as helplessly carried about by the raging beast of gender prejudice as anyone you've ever criticized.

Dominick Amarante

Schulman Replies

New York City

The Discovery—*The Nation* contest is nearly unique in that it is judged anonymously. Neither the judges nor I know the gender or the names of the poets who enter the competition. However, this information might enlighten Dominick Amarante: According to the laws of probability, if an equal number of male and female poets submit entries, one out of sixteen times all the winners will be female, or male.

Grace Schulman

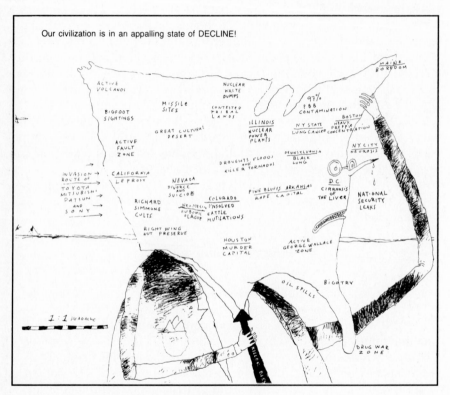

Our civilization is in an appalling state of DECLINE!

How reliable is this alarming conclusion?

When evaluating surveys and their conclusions, we must also consider the source of the survey; in other words, who conducted the survey and who paid for it?

A recent study of silicone breast implants concluded that there was no link between ruptured implants and connective tissue disease. Lawyer and consumer advocate Mary Alexander criticizes this study not only for the limited size of its sample and its failure to allow for the 8.5 years of latency between implantation and silicone disease, but also for two of its authors who "admitted on the threat of perjury that they were paid consultants of breast implant manufacturers." Furthermore, Dow Corning, the world's largest silicone breast implant manufacturer, had donated $5 million to one of the hospitals involved in the study. Such a study is riddled with conflict of interest. It is not in the best interest of those who benefit directly from Dow Corning to find fault with the company's product.

Note also subtle slants in the emphasis given to statistics. In the same issue of a major daily newspaper, the summary caption on page one stated that, "A new poll finds that 1 in 5 Californians still resent Japan for the attack on Pearl Harbor," while the inside story was headed, "50 years after attack on Pearl Harbor, only 1 in 5 is still resentful, poll shows." What are the different implications of these two captions?

EXERCISE 7A

Evaluating Inductive Arguments

In the following inductive arguments, identify the conclusion, the projected property, the target population, and the sample. Then, drawing on the principles of reliable inductive generalizations, evaluate the argument.

*1. The quality control inspector at Sweet and Sour Yogurt removes and tests one container out of approximately every thousand (about one every 15 minutes) and finds it safe for consumption. She then guarantees as safe all the containers filled that day.

2. In her book *Women and Love,* Shere Hite claims that a large percentage of American women are unhappy in their marriages and feel that men don't listen to them. She felt confident in her conclusions after mailing out 100,000 questionnaires to women's political, professional, and religious organizations and having 4 percent of the questionnaires returned.

3. Setting out to document her theory on the prevalence of racism on television, a sociologist examines 40 episodes from the new fall primetime situation comedies and finds that 36 of them contain racist stereotypes. She concludes that 90 percent of television drama is racist.

4. On November 1, businessman Eric Nichols decided to select one domestic airline from his two favorites in order to consolidate his frequent flier mileage. He planned to base his decision on each airline's reliability. From November through April he made 20 evenly spaced trips on United, experiencing two cancellations, nine delayed departures, and eight late arrivals. From May through October, he flew American Airlines 22 times, but improved his record with only one cancellation, seven delays, and five late arrivals. Without further consideration, he chose American as the more reliable of the two.

5. The French Ministry of Social Affairs reported that three well-known research physicians at the Laennec Hospital in Paris had observed "dramatic biological improvements" in a group of patients with AIDS. The physicians reported a "dramatic" slowing of Acquired Immune Deficiency Syndrome in one of the six patients and a complete halt in the disease's progress in another after only five

days of treatment with a compound called cyclosporine. (Hint: The conclusion is implicit.)

6. A recent study by the University of Medicine and Dentistry of New Jersey concluded that "women who were abused [physically, emotionally, or sexually] as children have more health problems and require more hospital care than women who were not abused." Seven hundred women from a private gynecological practice were interviewed. Mostly white, middle class with college degrees, they ranged in age from 16 to 76.

EXERCISE 7B

Finding Weaknesses in Inductive Arguments

In the following article, a critic points out weaknesses in an inductive argument. Analyze the original inductive study, then the critic's response, and summarize your findings according to these steps:

1. Identify the projected property, the target population, the sample, and the conclusion.
2. Explain the weaknesses as discussed by the critic and conclude with discussion of your own opinion. Do you support the critic or the researchers who first presented the conclusions?

Dispute Over Claims of Ibuprofen Dangers

United Press International

Washington

Federal officials and makers of ibuprofen medicines yesterday disputed the conclusions of medical researchers who claim that a 12-patient study indicates that over-the-counter doses of the pain killer may cause kidney failure in high-risk people.

In a study published in the Annals of Internal Medicine, doctors from Johns Hopkins University medical school in Baltimore looked at the effects of ibuprofen and two other types of nonsteroidal, anti-inflammatory drugs in 12 women with chronic kidney problems but no obvious symptoms. Three of the patients developed complications.

But Food and Drug Administration spokeswoman Bonnie Aikman said yesterday that consumers have no cause for alarm about taking over-the-counter ibuprofen, as long as they read the label telling them to contact a doctor if they experience any unusual symptoms. That advice will be highlighted on ibuprofen labels starting in June, Aikman added.

The patients in the study were given the prescription-level dose of ibuprofen—2,400 milligrams a day—two times the maximum daily dose recommended for over-the-counter versions of the drug. Eight days into an 11-day course of treatment, three of the patients were judged to have severe enough kidney impairment that researchers stopped giving them the drug. When researchers later tried giving them lower doses of ibuprofen, 1,200 milligrams per day—or the top over-the-counter dose, two of the three patients again developed evidence of acute kidney failure.

Ibuprofen was recommended to patients by doctors nearly 50 million times in 1987, according to the National Disease and Therapeutic Index. An estimated 100 million people have used the nonprescription drug since it was introduced in 1984.

T. R. Reid, a spokesman for the Upjohn Co. of Kalamazoo, Mich., maker of Motrin, a prescription ibuprofen medication, and Motrin IB, the over-the-counter version, called the conclusions of the Johns Hopkins study "warped."

Reid noted the study only looked at 12 patients, and all patients were predisposed to kidney failure. But his major objection was that its authors extended the findings about prescription ibuprofen to over-the-counter ibuprofen.

Other common over-the-counter products containing ibuprofen are Nuprin, made by Bristol-Myers Squibb Co. of New York, and Advil, made by Whitehall Laboratories Inc. of New York.

"We do not believe the findings of this study apply to the safety of nonprescription ibuprofen in the general population," Whitehall said in a statement.

Reid said labels on prescription Motrin already inform doctors there is a slim risk—1 percent or less—of kidney complications from prolonged use of the drug.

In addition, the Upjohn Company said labels on nonprescription ibuprofen tell people with serious medical conditions, such as poor kidney function, to consult with their doctors before starting any new over-the-counter medication.

EXERCISE 7C

Collecting Generalizations

Humorist James Thurber, celebrated for his long association with *The New Yorker* magazine, had fun exploiting our tendency to overgeneralize in his essay, "What a Lovely Generalization." Many of his examples are absurd, but some suggest the dangers that can spring from such patterns of thought. For those interested in collecting generalizations, he suggests listening "in particular to women, whose average generalization is from three to five times as broad as a man's." Was he sexist or making a not so funny joke? He listed many others from his collection, labelling some "true," some "untrue," others "debatable," "libellous," "ridiculous," and so on. Some examples from his collection: "Women don't sleep very well," "There are no pianos in Japan," "Doctors don't know what they're doing,"

"Gamblers hate women," "Cops off duty always shoot somebody," "Intellectual women dress funny." And so his collection ran, brimming with hasty generalizations.

Your task is to collect two "Lovely Generalizations" from the world around you, comment on the accuracy, absurdity, and dangers of each and discuss the implications of your generalizations for those who seem to be the target.

EXERCISE 7D

Putting Induction and Deduction Together

Read the following passage taken from Arthur Conan Doyle's story, *A Study in Scarlet*. Some critical thinkers have presented this passage as an example of deduction, others as induction. What do you think? Try to construct a deductive syllogism (see Chapter 6) and then list the inductions that led to your premises. How sound is your syllogism?

A Study in Scarlet

"I wonder what that fellow is looking for?" I asked, pointing to a stalwart, plainly dressed individual who was walking slowly down the other side of the street, looking anxiously at the numbers. He had a large blue envelope in his hand, and was evidently the bearer of a message.

"You mean the retired sergeant of Marines," said Sherlock Holmes.

"Brag and bounce!" thought I to myself. "He knows that I cannot verify his guess."

The thought had hardly passed through my mind when the man whom we were watching caught sight of the number on our door, and ran rapidly across the roadway. We heard a loud knock, a deep voice below, and heavy steps ascending the stair.

"For Mr. Sherlock Holmes," he said, stepping into the room and handing my friend the letter.

Here was an opportunity of taking the conceit out of him. He little thought of this when he made that random shot. "May I ask, my lad," I said, in the blandest voice, "what your trade may be?"

"Commissionaire, sir," he said, gruffly. "Uniform away for repairs."

"And you were?" I asked, with a slightly malicious glance at my companion.

"A sergeant, sir, Royal Marine Light Infantry, sir. No answer? Right, sir."

He clicked his heels together, raised his hand in salute, and was gone.

I confess that I was considerably startled by this fresh proof of the practical nature of my companion's theories. My respect for his powers of analysis increased wondrously. There still remained some lurking suspicion in my mind, however, that the whole thing was a prearranged episode, intended to dazzle me, though what earthly object he could have in taking me in was past my comprehension. When I looked at him, he had finished reading the note, and his eyes had assumed the vacant, lack-lustre expression which showed mental abstraction.

"How in the world did you deduce that?" I asked.

"Deduce what?" said he, petulantly.

"Why, that he was a retired sergeant of Marines."

"I have no time for trifles," he answered, brusquely; then with a smile, "Excuse my rudeness. You broke the thread of my thoughts; but perhaps it is as well. So you actually were not able to see that that man was a sergeant of Marines?"

"No, indeed."

"It was easier to know it than to explain why I know it. If you were asked to prove that two and two made four, you might find some difficulty, and yet you are quite sure of the fact. Even across the street I could see a great blue anchor tattooed on the back of the fellow's hand. That smacked of the sea. He had a military carriage, however, and regulation side whiskers. There we have the marine. He was a man with some amount of self-importance and a certain air of command. You must have observed the way in which he held his head and swung his cane. A steady, respectable, middle-aged man, too, on the face of him—all facts which led me to believe that he had been a sergeant."

"Wonderful!" I ejaculated.

"Commonplace," said Holmes, though I thought from his expression that he was pleased at my evident surprise and admiration.

WRITING ASSIGNMENT 13

Questioning Generalizations

Add the two generalizations you chose for Exercise 7C "Collecting Generalizations" to the following list of generalizations and choose one to write a paper in support of, or in opposition to. This list could be even longer and more diverse if your instructor collects the entire classes' generalizations and makes them available to you.

1. Women are better dancers than men.
2. Men are better athletes than women.
3. Everyone is capable of being creative.
4. Nice guys finish last.

5. Appearances can be deceiving.

6. The purpose of a college degree is to prepare an individual for a career.

7. A college graduate will get a higher paying job than a high school graduate.

8. A woman will never be elected president of the United States.

9. All people are created equal.

10. War is a necessary evil.

Audience

A reader who is not strongly invested in the proposition one way or another but who is interested in hearing your point of view.

Purpose

To cast a critical eye on a generalization which people tend to accept without question.

 ### *WRITING ASSIGNMENT 14*

Conducting a Survey: A Collaborative Project

Conduct a survey at your school to determine something of significance about the student body, and then write a report in which you state either a question or a hypothesis, describe the survey, and speculate on the results. (Apologies to statisticians for the oversimplification of a very complex task.)

The class as a whole can brainstorm possible questions to ask the student body, the target population. What do students think about the current administration on campus or in Washington? Our nation's involvement in foreign wars? Or a host of other political issues. How many students take a full academic load and work part-time as well? There are many possibilities.

Choose five or six topics from these many possibilities and divide into groups around them. These groups will then create a survey—a questionnaire appropriate to the topic they are researching—and a strategy for distributing it to a representative sample.

The next step is to collect, tabulate, and discuss the data. Either each student can then write her own report or the group can write a single report, assigning a section to each member of the group.

The report will contain the following:

1. A description of the survey

What questions did you ask?
When and where did you ask them?

2. A description of the sample

Whom did you ask?
How many did you ask?

3. Evaluation of the survey

Was the sample large enough?
Was it representative?
Were your questions unbiased?
What could you do to make it better?

4. Analysis of the results

How does it compare to what you expected the results to be before
you began gathering the data?
What do you imagine are the causes which led to these results?
What are the implications of the results?

Audience
Your campus community—students, faculty, and staff.

Purpose
To inform your campus community about its student members.

SUMMARY

The statistical generalization, based as it is on an inductive leap from some
to all, will never be as certain as a conclusion drawn from sound deductive
reasoning.

The direction of inductive reasoning can vary. We may note specific instances and from them make general inferences, or we may begin with a
general idea and seek specific examples or data to support it.

For a statistical generalization to be reliable, the sample must be adequate
in size and representative of the target population.

With any generalization supported by specific examples, one counterexample can discredit the conclusion.

KEY TERMS

Statistical generalization a prediction about the distribution of a partic-
ular feature in a given group.
Projected property what is to be determined about the target population.
Target population the group about which the conclusion will be drawn.
Sample the surveyed members of the target population.
Hypothesis a tentative generalization, a possible conclusion, an assertion
we are interested in proving.

Chapter
8

Logical Fallacies

So convenient a thing it is to be a reasonable creature, since it enables one to find or make a reason for everything one has a mind to do.

—Benjamin Franklin

WHAT IS A FALLACIOUS ARGUMENT?

A fallacious argument is one that is persuasive but does not logically support its conclusion. All fallacious arguments are therefore unsound; in other words, the conclusion does not follow from the premises. But not all unsound arguments are fallacious. What's the difference? A fallacious argument will usually be persuasive while not all unsound arguments are.

We can demonstrate the relationship between fallacious arguments and unsound arguments with Euler diagrams (see Chapter 6).

As this diagram indicates, all fallacious arguments are unsound, but not all unsound arguments are fallacious.

To further illustrate this distinction between an unsound and a fallacious argument, look at the following example.

Short people do not make good presidents.
The democratic candidate is short.
Therefore, the democratic candidate will not be a good president.

This argument is obviously unsound, but it is not persuasive and would convince no one. Technically, the line of reasoning is logical since the two premises lead inescapably to the conclusion. There is nothing fallacious in the *form* of this argument. The difficulty lies in the first premise. Because this is an absurd claim, and thus an unacceptable premise, we consider the argument unsound, but this is not the same as finding the reasoning fallacious.

Now let's look at a fallacious argument.

> Senator X was expelled from college for cheating on an exam.
> His wife divorced him because of his numerous affairs.
> Therefore, he is a man without honor, a politician who cannot be trusted, and we should not support his National Health Bill.

This argument is also unsound but some may find it persuasive, believing that such a man could not propose worthwhile legislation. But since there is nothing in the premises which indicates flaws in the bill—only flaws in the man—the conclusion is not logically supported. The bill may be worthwhile despite the nature of the man who proposes it.

Fallacious reasoning may be intentional, as is sometimes the case with unscrupulous merchandisers and politicians, or it may be an innocent mistake resulting from fuzzy thinking or unexamined bias. In any case, if we are familiar with fallacies we can avoid them in our own thinking and writing. We can also spot them in the arguments of others, a skill that makes us wiser consumers and citizens.

There are many fallacies, a number of which tend to overlap. Our intention here is not to overwhelm you with an exhaustive list of fallacies and a complex classification scheme. Instead, we offer a list of the more common fallacies, presented in alphabetical order for easy reference.

Appeal to Authority

The opinion of an authority can support an argument only when it reflects his special area of expertise; the authority must be an expert on the subject being argued as is the case in the following examples.

> The Surgeon General warns that smoking is injurious to health.
> Vladimir Horowitz, the internationally acclaimed pianist, preferred the Steinway piano.
> Studies conducted by *The New York Times, the Los Angeles Times,* and the ABC Network suggest that increasing numbers of viewers object to TV violence.

But if the appeal is to an authority who is not appropriate, the appeal is fallacious, as is the case in the following example.

> Abortion to save the life of a mother is an irrelevant issue because a former surgeon general, a well-known pediatric surgeon, claimed that in all his years of surgical practice he had never seen a case in which such a dilemma had arisen.

The problem here is that a pediatric surgeon is not an appropriate authority on an issue involving obstetrics.

Fallacious appeals to authority are bountiful in advertising which employs well-known actors and athletes to sell us everything from banking services to automobiles to coffee. Since many of these celebrities have no specialized knowledge—no authority—on the particular service or product they are promoting, they are not credible sources. Some may remember an actor known for his role as a TV doctor who endorsed a painkiller on television commercials.

Appeals to authority also appear in the form of snob appeal or appeal to the authority of the select few. The following advertisement for a resort hotel illustrates this fallacy which appeals to people's desire for prestige and exclusivity.

> Palmilla's not for everyone. The best never is.

Keep in mind that fallacious appeals to authority should not cause us to doubt all authorities, but rather encourage us to distinguish between reliable and unreliable sources. In constructing your own arguments be prepared to cite, explain, and, if necessary, defend your sources when relying on authority.

Appeal to Fear

THE FAR SIDE   By GARY LARSON

"Why, yes . . . we do have two children who won't
eat their vegetables."

Parents often rely on appeals to fear to persuade their children.

An appeal to fear attempts to convince by implicitly threatening the audience. Its efforts to persuade are based on emotion rather than reason. An ad for a business college uses this approach.

Will there be a *job* waiting when *you* leave college?

This ad attempts to frighten students by implying that unless they attend this business college, they will be unable to get a job after attending a four-year traditional college.

Senator Jesse Helms of North Carolina raised millions in campaign funds by sending voters a letter that contained the following warning:

> Your tax dollars are being used to pay for grade school classes that teach our children that **CANNIBALISM, WIFE-SWAPPING** and the **MURDER** of infants and the elderly are acceptable behavior.

Appeal to Pity

An appeal to pity attempts to win our sympathy in order to convince us of the conclusion. Like an appeal to fear, it appeals to our emotions rather than our intellect. Some students use this approach when arguing for a particular grade.

> Professor Hall, I must get an A in your course. If you don't give me an A, I won't be able to go to law school.

As we know, a student's work in a course—papers, exams, participation—determines the final grade. The consequences of a grade, no matter how dire they may be, should have no effect in determining that grade.

Emotion may play a part in argument, but its role must be secondary, a backdrop to logical reasoning. In fact, effective arguments often begin with frightening statistics—"If nothing is done about the Greenhouse Effect, the earth's temperature will increase 10 degrees by the year 2000 with disastrous consequences for our environment." Or they may begin with an emotional illustration. For example, an argument for mandatory fencing around all private swimming pools may open with a description of a mother caring for a child who is brain damaged as a result of almost drowning in a private pool. Either of these introductions will capture the emotions and interest of the audience, but they should be followed by facts, appropriate appeals to authority, and logical reasoning.

Begging the Question

When a person begs the question, he offers no actual support for his conclusion while appearing to do so. Instead, he may argue in a circle, just restating, as a premise, his conclusion in different words.

> Students like rock music because it is the most enjoyable music around.

The writer is simply stating that students find rock music enjoyable because it is enjoyable. He begs the question. "They like it" means the same as "They find it enjoyable."

Or, take a couple of classics:

Parallel lines will never meet because they are parallel.

. . . your noble son is mad.
Mad call I it, for to define true madness,
What is't but to be nothing else but mad?
—Polonius to Queen Gertrude in *Hamlet,* II.ii

[We can discern something of Polonius' character from the manner of his argument.]

DENNIS the MENACE

"IT WAS SURE LUCKY YOU NAMED ME DENNIS...
'CAUSE THAT'S WHAT EVERBODY CALLS ME."

Dennis, like many children, follows a circular pattern of reasoning.

Some such fallacious arguments beg the question not by restating the conclusion, but by supporting the conclusion with assumptions (stated or hidden) that are as much in need of proof as the conclusion.

A familiar example is frequently offered by those opposed to rent control who argue that rent controls should be removed because such decontrol could result in a significant rise in housing construction and thus relieve the shortage of affordable rental units. A letter to the editor points out the weakness.

> Editor: In your editorial concerning the housing crisis, you rely on one of the oldest rhetorical tricks of accepting as a given that which you could not possibly prove, that is, "There can be little question that removal of rent controls would result in a boom in apartment house construction. . . ." If rent control is such an important factor, construction should have been booming in the '70s before rent control laws existed in our state. It wasn't. . . .

Before we can accept the conclusion, the "truth" of the premise—that construction of new housing will increase if rent control laws are abolished—must be established.

We can also encounter question begging (avoiding the issue) in the form of an actual question, *a loaded question.* An example: Have you started paying your fair share of taxes yet? First, the questioner would have to establish what he means by "fair share," and then establish that the person to whom he addressed the question had not been paying it.

In some arguments, just a single word—reactionary, negligent, warmonger, deadbeat—can beg the question. Be on the alert for such prejudicial language.

Equivocation

Equivocation is the shifting of the meaning of a given term within a single argument. This fallacy stems from the often ambiguous nature of language. A term may be ambiguous because it has more than one meaning; for instance, the word "affair" may mean a party, a controversial incident, or an extramarital relationship. Look at this example:

> We are told by the government that to discriminate against a person in employment or housing is wrong and punishable by law. But we must discriminate when we hire an individual (Does he have the necessary experience?) or rent an apartment (Does he have sufficient income?). Discrimination is a necessary part of making such decisions.

The word "discriminate" is the culprit. In the first sentence, "discriminate" refers to prejudice, to denying an individual employment or housing because of his or her race, sex, or religion. In the second sentence, "discriminate" refers to making careful distinctions between applicants on the basis of relevant issues.

Often equivocation is used to manipulate the language for rhetorical effect and positive associations, especially in advertising. A color film company refers to its product as "The Color of America," a slogan that is superimposed over images of Black and Asian American families. Hence, color refers to color film and to race, a clear case of equivocation.

In writing our own arguments, we can avoid equivocation by defining all ambiguous terms and being consistent in our use of them. (See Chapter 9 for definition strategies.)

**"Tonto, when I said put silver on the table,
I meant knives, forks, spoons."**

Tonto annoys the Lone Ranger when he equivocates, mistaking the horse Silver for tableware.

False Analogy

One creative way to mount an argument can be through analogy. An argument by analogy compares two or more things, alike in certain respects, and suggests that since they share certain characteristics, they probably share other characteristics as well. A doctor argues effectively for drug therapy over psychotherapy as the best treatment for schizophrenia or severe depression by comparing the brain to the heart. "The brain is an organ, like the heart, and like that organ, can malfunction as a result of biochemical imbalances."

But in a false analogy, one compares two things in which the key features are different. A mountain climber offers this analogy to minimize the danger of his sport.

I don't want to die falling off a rock. . . . But you can kill yourself falling in the bathtub, too.

—*John Bachar*

He is comparing two acts that are quite dissimilar, climbing a mountain and taking a bath, one a sport, the other a daily routine. And while it is possible to kill oneself slipping in the bathtub, if we were to compare the number of deaths in proportion to the number of bathers and the number of mountain climbers, we would surely find a higher incidence of deaths in mountain climbing than in bathing. In order to construct a more convincing analogy, the mountain climber should compare the risk in mountain climbing to another high-risk sport such as race car driving.

A "Dear Abby" reader writes in response to Abby's recommendation that young people use contraceptives for premarital sex, "We know that premarital sex is wrong, just as we know shoplifting is wrong." Dear Abby's reply points out the fallaciousness of this comparison.

> One of the most powerful urges inborn in the human animal is the sex drive. Nature intended it to ensure perpetuation of our species. It is not comparable with the temptation to swipe a candy bar or a T-shirt.

In debating whether or not it is appropriate for Miss America beauty contestants to have plastic surgery, those in favor of allowing such surgery compare it with other practices women use to improve their appearance such as makeup and hair color. *Boston Globe* columnist Ellen Goodman points out that this analogy is false since cosmetics are superficial while cosmetic surgery, such as breast implants, is physically invasive. She then offers a more accurate analogy—cosmetic surgery for beauty contestants is like steroids for athletes—each gives an unfair advantage to contestants involved in a competition.

The following letter to "Miss Manners" argues on the basis of analogy, an analogy that in her reply Miss Manners shows to be false.

> Dear Miss Manners:
> If I were to entertain someone at dinner whom I knew to be a vegetarian, I would make certain there would be plenty of things on the menu that a vegetarian could eat. Besides my lamb chop, there would be plenty of vegetables, breads, salads, etc. I would not feel compelled to become a vegetarian myself for the occasion.
>
> Were I to dine at the home of vegetarians, I would expect of them a similar accommodation, so that in addition to their usual fare, they might serve me a small steak, perhaps, though of course they wouldn't need to partake of it themselves.
>
> Miss Manners replies:
>
> Gentle Reader:
> You lose the argument. Here is the problem: Serving vegetables to guests does not violate your principles, nor does it make you a vegetarian. However, expecting your vegetarian friends to serve you something that they exclude from their households would require their violating their principles.

Reasoning by analogy is appealing because it is vivid and accessible. But we must not accept analogies without careful examination. We must ask if the two things being compared are similar in ways that are significant to the point being made.

"For all his brilliance, we're going to have to replace Trewell. He never quite seems able to reduce his ideas to football analogies."

False Cause

The fallacy of false cause is also called post hoc reasoning, from the Latin *post hoc, ergo propter hoc* which means "after this, therefore because of this." As this translation indicates, the fallacy of false cause assumes a cause-effect relationship between two events because one precedes another. It claims a causal relationship solely on the basis of a chronological relationship. Mark Twain uses this relationship for humorous effect.

I joined the Confederacy for two weeks. Then I deserted. The Confederacy fell.

We know, as Twain did, that his desertion did nothing to end the Civil War, but this fallacy is not always so obvious. Look at the following example:

Governor Robinson took office in 1995.
In 1996, the state suffered a severe recession.
Therefore, Governor Robinson should not be re-elected.
(Hidden assumption: The governor caused the recession.)

Elected officials are often credited with the success or blamed for the failure of the economy. But in fact, anything as complex as the economy is affected by numerous factors such as inflation, environmental changes, the laws of supply and demand, just to name a few. Elected officials may indeed affect the economy but are unlikely to be the sole cause of its success or failure.

In a letter to the *New York Times Book Review,* a doctor takes exception with a book in which the author claims that his nephew's autism resulted from brain damage due to a vaccination.

> To the Editor:
> There will always be people who are convinced that because the signs of mental retardation or a seizure disorder or autism first became evident after an immunization, then certainly the immunization caused their problems; millions of dollars have been awarded in damages because some such people served on juries.
>
> For those people of reason who remember that **post hoc, ergo propter hoc** is a logical fallacy and not a standard of proof, let me state categorically that careful review of the literature confirms that a DPT shot might result in a fever or a sore leg or an irritable child. But it will not cause retardation, it will not precipitate epilepsy, and it never has and never will lead to autism.
>
> Diane Lind Fenster, M.D.
> Green Bay, Wis.

Some have argued that the atomic bombs we dropped in Hiroshima and Nagasaki caused Japan to surrender at the end of World War II. Others argue that this is a case of post hoc reasoning, that other factors such as Russia's threat to enter the war against Japan caused Japan to surrender, so that the killing of 110,000 Japanese, many of them women and children, was unnecessary.

Determining the cause of all but the simplest events is extremely difficult. Post hoc reasoning is appealing because it offers simple explanations for complex events.

False Dilemma

A false dilemma presents two and only two alternatives for consideration when other possibilities exist. For this reason, a false dilemma is often referred to as either/or reasoning.

> Either you are in favor of recalling the mayor, or you are a supporter of his political platform.

We are presented with only two positions when in fact we may hold neither. We may want the mayor to continue in office because we believe him to be a strong administrator, but we may object to his proposal to encourage big business by lowering the business tax.

In his essay, "Love One, Hate the Other," movie critic Mick LaSalle rails against what he calls "false polarities." He offers the following examples: Lennon or McCartney, Monroe or Bardot, Hemingway or Fitzgerald, Freud or Jung. He calls them false "because, in each case, two elements are arbitrarily set apart as opposites when they are not opposite at all, and the idea is that we must choose between the two when there's no legitimate need to do that."

Narrowing to two choices is a strategy designed to forestall clear thinking and force a quick decision. This kind of reasoning can be seductive because it reduces the often difficult decisions and judgments we must make by narrowing complex problems and issues to two simple options.

Columnist Anna Quindlen comments on how this either/or reasoning shaped the public's opinion and the trial of Erik and Lyle Menendez, two brothers accused of murdering their parents for financial gain.

> . . . the question has become: venal rich kids or tormented victims? Which are the Menendez brothers? Few seem to consider a third possibility: maybe both. . . . Lyle and Erik [are] either tormented, abused child-men or cold-blooded climbers in Porsches. Not both. Never both.
>
> The ultimate either-or decision belongs to the jurors in the Menendez case. But perhaps they will consider things that we overlook when we are turning public tragedy into social mythology: sometimes bad things happen to bad people, that it is possible to be both victim and victimizer. Life is so messy that the temptation to straighten it up is very strong. And the result's always illusory.

"Damn it, Eddie! If you don't believe in nuclear war and you don't believe in conventional war, what the hell kind of war do you believe in?"

What alternative has the speaker completely overlooked?

Hasty Generalization

A hasty generalization is a conclusion based on a sample that is too small or in some other way unrepresentative of the larger population.

Students in Professor Hall's eight o'clock freshman composition class are often late. There's no doubt that people are right when they claim today's college students are irresponsible and unreliable.

In this case the sample is both unrepresentative and too small; unrepresentative because we would expect an eight o'clock class to have more late students than classes offered later in the day, and too small because one section can't represent an entire freshman class.

It is impossible to avoid making generalizations, nor should we try to. But we must examine the basis for our generalizations to determine their reliability (see Chapter 7).

One way to avoid this fallacy is to qualify your generalizations with words such as "many" or "some." Most of us would accept the claim that "some women are bad drivers," but would reject and even be offended by the claim that "women are bad drivers."

Personal Attack

Often called by its Latin name, *ad hominem* ("against the man"), this fallacy substitutes for a reasoned evaluation of an argument an attack against the person presenting the argument. By discrediting the source, often in an abusive or irrelevant way, a person can disguise the absence of a substantive position.

> Because she is extremely wealthy and owns two luxurious homes, our mayor, Carolyn Quinn, cannot properly represent the people of this city.

But does a person's economic status necessarily rule out understanding of those in different circumstances?

A few years ago, conservative John H. Bunzel wrote a controversial book, *Challenge to American Schools.* In it he attacked the National Education Association for criticizing some reform ideas he admired—merit pay and standardized tests. He focused on their "leftist" politics rather than examining the reasons for their opposition.

When Rachel Carson's *Silent Spring,* a seminal work on the health hazards of insecticides and pesticides, was published in 1962, a leading scientist (male), questioned her concern for future generations since she was a spinster who had no children. He attacked her personally, not her argument that certain commonly used chemicals caused cancer.

Those given to Latin names like to label a particular kind of personal attack as *tu quoque*—"you also." In this instance, a person and thus his arguments are discredited because his own behavior does not strictly conform to the position he holds. We've all heard about the parent who drinks too much but admonishes his child about the dangers of drinking.

Antigun control groups were delighted when Carl Rowan, a prominent Washington columnist and a staunch advocate of gun control, used an unregistered pistol to wound a young man who broke into his backyard. But Rowan's failure to follow his own beliefs does not necessarily make his argument for gun control a weak one.

Poisoning the Well

A person poisons the well when he makes an assertion that precludes or discourages an open discussion of the issue. This assertion will intimidate the listener, who fears that any resistance on his part will lead to a personal disagreement rather than a critical discussion.

> Every patriotic American supports legislation condemning the desecration of the flag.

The listener must now prove his patriotism rather than express his doubts about the legislation, and the speaker avoids having to defend his conclusion with relevant premises.

Slippery Slope

We know this one by other names too: the domino theory, the ripple effect. One thing leads to another. People often claim that an action should be avoided because it will inevitably lead to a series of extremely undesirable consequences. Sometimes such a chain reaction is probable, but often it can be exaggerated for effect.

Look, if you give them a nuclear freeze, the next thing you know they'll want to outlaw war altogether.

If only all slippery slopes led to such a desirable outcome.

Writer Wendy Kaminer, reviewing *Under Fire: The NRA and the Battle for Gun Control,* presents one group's position on gun control:

> What seems like reasonable restrictions on guns with no legitimate civilian purpose (assault rifles, for example) will lead inevitably to total prohibition of gun ownership that ends in virtual slavery at the hands of a totalitarian regime.

The argument here is that if we allow the government to take one step—the banning of assault weapons—the next step will be the banning of all guns—and the final step, loss of all freedom for all citizens.

In this argument, the downward slope is more precipitous than the evidence warrants, leading to an erroneous conclusion and, tragically, to private militias and the bombing of Oklahoma City.

Special Pleading

When an argument contains the fallacy of special pleading, it judges and labels the same act differently depending on the person or group who performs the act. It is the application of a double standard.

> The supplying of weapons to Central America by the Russians was an act of aggression. Our military aid to the region, however, helped the Freedom Fighters in their quest for peace.

In the 1980s, both the United States and Russia supplied military aid to Central America. But the language used to describe this act makes it appear as if what the United States did was admirable while what the Soviets did was reprehensible.

In a similar manipulation of language, a well-known defense lawyer, while discussing legal strategies on television, stated that he "prepares" his witnesses while the prosecution "coaches" theirs.

Straw Man

In a straw man argument, a person creates and then attacks a distorted version of the opposition's argument.

> The democratic candidate wants the federal government to house everyone, feed everyone, care for everyone's children, and provide medical care for everyone. And he's going to take 50 percent of every dime you make to do it.

This argument overlooks the candidate's proposal to reduce defense spending in order to meet his goals. Hence, this is an unfair presentation of the opposing view, but one that could be very effective in discouraging votes for the democratic candidate. And this is the purpose of a straw man argument: to frighten supporters away from the opponent's camp and into one's own.

Boston Globe columnist Ellen Goodman comments on this strategy in an essay titled "The Straw Feminist."

The straw man has been a useful creature throughout history. Whenever people argued, he could be pulled together quickly out of the nearest available haystack, and set up as an opponent. The beauty of the straw man was that he was easily defeated. The straw man was also useful as a scarecrow. The arguments attributed to him were not only flimsy, they were frightening.

So I wasn't surprised when the straw feminist was sighted burning her bra at a "Miss America" pageant. The fact that there never was a bra-burning was irrelevant. Feminists became bra-burners. Not to mention man-haters.

The straw feminist wanted to drive all women out of their happy homes and into the workforce. The straw feminist had an abortion as casually as she had a tooth pulled. The straw feminist was hostile to family life and wanted children warehoused in government-run day and night care. At times, the straw feminist was painted slightly pinko by the anti-Communists or rather lavender by the anti-lesbians. But it was generally agreed upon that she was a castrating—well, you fill in the blank.

This creature was most helpful for discrediting real feminists but also handy for scaring supporters away.

A caution: German philosopher Arthur Schopenhauer [1788–1860] pointed out that "It would be a very good thing if every trick could receive some short and obviously appropriate name, so that when a man used this or that particular trick, he could at once be reproved for it." Fallacies provide us with those short and appropriate names for tricks or errors in reasoning, but we must not assume that all such errors can be labeled. Whenever we find fault with a particular line of reasoning, we should not hesitate to articulate that fault, whether or not we have a label for it. On the other hand, we must be careful not to see fallacies everywhere, perhaps even where they don't exist. We must read critically, informed by our knowledge of fallacies; at the same time we should avoid tedious witch-hunts on the charitable assumption that most arguments are offered in good faith.

EXERCISE 8A

Identifying Fallacies

Identify by name the fallacies in each of the following arguments and justify your responses. You may want to turn to the end of the chapter for a chart of the fallacies.

Competition and collaboration: An interesting approach to this exercise combines competition and cooperation. The class is divided into two teams who compete in identifying the fallacies, with team members cooperating on responses.

1. "I think if you look at the problems that are before us, on the whole they are problems that they have created. And so a willingness to be less creative is what is called for here." (Former Secretary of State George Shultz emphasizing that it would be up to the Soviet Union to initiate improved relations.)

*2. "Students should not be allowed any grace whatsoever on late assignments. Before you know it, they will no longer complete their work at all. If they don't do their assignments, they will be ignorant. If the students who are being educated are ignorant, then all of America will become more ignorant." (Thanks to a former student.)

3. America: Love it or leave it.

4. You can't expect insight and credibility from the recent book *The Feminist Challenge* because its author David Bouchier is, obviously, a man.

5. Politicians can't be trusted because they lack integrity.

6. Closing the gay baths to prevent the spread of AIDS is like closing bars to prevent the spread of alcoholism.

7. How long must we allow our courts to go on coddling criminals?

8. "I'm firm. You are stubborn. He's pig-headed." (philosopher Bertrand Russell)

*9. Anyone who truly cares about preserving the American way of life will vote Republican this fall.

10. "Why is it okay for people to choose the best house, the best schools, the best surgeon, the best car, but not try to have the best baby possible?" (A father's defense of the Nobel Prize winners' sperm bank.)

11. Socrates, during his trial in 399 B.C.: "My friend, I am a man, and like other men, a creature of flesh and blood, and not of wood or stone, as Homer says; and I have a family, yes, and sons, O Athenians, three in number, one almost a man, and two others who are still young; and yet I will not bring any of them hither in order to petition you for an acquittal." (Plato, the "Apology")

12. "All Latins are volatile people." (Senator Jesse Helms, on Mexican protests against Senate Foreign Affairs subcommittee hearings on corruption south of the border.)

13. Mark R. Hughes, owner of Herbalife International, was questioned by a Senate subcommittee about the safety of the controversial diet products marketed by his company. Referring to a panel of three nutrition and weight-control authorities, Hughes asked: "If they're such experts, then why are they fat?"

14. During these same hearings, Senator William Roth, R-Delaware, the Senate subcommittee chairman, reminded Hughes of criticism by some physicians that Herbalife fails to recommend that consumers seek guidance from doctors about their diets. "Do you believe it's safe to use your products without consulting a doctor?" Roth asked. "Sure," replied Hughes, 29. "Everybody needs good, sound, basic nutrition. We all know that."

15. When the Supreme Court ruled that school officials need not obtain search warrants or find "probable cause" while conducting reasonable searches of students, they violated freedoms guaranteed under the Bill of Rights. If you allow a teacher to look for a knife or drugs you'll soon have strip searches and next, torture.

*16. Since I walked under that ladder yesterday, I've lost my wallet and received a speeding ticket.

17. Sometimes, the *best* is not for everyone. (an ad for a "Parisian boutique")

18. "I intensely believe that service is the highest form of being." (Susan Ford Vance, daughter of former President Jerry Ford, in an ad for a luxury hotel.)

19. We are going to have to ease up on environmental protection legislation or see the costs overwhelm us.

20. Any rational person will accept that a fetus is a human being.

21. "Editor—Is anyone really surprised that students' grades haven't improved when all they do is listen to rock 'n' roll? Rock lyrics don't ever develop into anything cohesive and the music never expands itself like real music does. All it does is just sit there and make a lot of very loud noise that goes boom, boom, boom, boom, boom that blots off the mind completely. How can a mind ever expand when that's all it ever takes in? It all started about 35 years ago with bubble-gum rock and then went into heavy metal and grades have been going down steadily ever since." (Bob Grimes in a Letter to the Editor, *San Francisco Chronicle*)

22. Heat Wave Blamed For Record Temperatures Across U.S. (a *Grass Valley Union* headline)

23. The erosion of traditional male leadership has led to an increase in divorce because men no longer possess leadership roles.

24. "**Dear Ann Landers**: I have been a nudist for 36 years and am firmly convinced that if everyone would accept the concept of nudism, there would be no more wars, no crime and no greed, and we would live together in perfect harmony as God intended us to. Anyone who reads the Bible knows that all the trouble started when Eve ate that apple and put on the fig leaf." (*San Francisco Examiner*)

25. Now, all young men, a warning take,
And shun the poisoned bowl; (alcohol)
'Twill lead you down to hell's dark gate,
And ruin your own soul.
(Anonymous, from Carl Sandburg, ed., *The American Songbag*)

26. While our diplomats in France were gathering intelligence, their diplomats in Washington were practicing espionage.

*27. I recently read about a homeless man with a burst appendix who was turned away from a hospital emergency room to die in the street. It's obvious that hospitals don't care about people, only money.

28. "You didn't have to come from Mars to direct *E.T.,* did you?" (Quincy Jones, producer of the film, *The Color Purple,* to Steven Spielberg, who was chosen to direct the film over the objections of the black community.)

29. I wouldn't consider reading William Safire's weekly language columns. How can you possibly respect him when you know that he wrote speeches for Nixon?

30. Do the vastly inflated salaries paid to professional athletes lead them into drug abuse?

31. The Nuclear Freeze movement was misguided and dangerous from the beginning, dependent as it was on "unilateral" disarmament. (A common argument of the movement's opponents. Those supporting the Nuclear Freeze movement actually proposed "bilateral" disarmament.)

32. Haemon: So, father, pause, and put aside your anger.
        I think, for what my young opinion's worth,
        That, good as it is to have infallible wisdom,
        Since this is rarely found, the next best thing
        Is to be willing to listen to wise advice.
       Creon: Indeed! Am I to take lessons at my time of life
            From a fellow of his age?
                                (Sophocles, *Antigone*)

*33. S & W vegetables are the best because they use only premium quality.

34. "We would not tolerate a proposal that states that because teenage drug use is a given we should make drugs more easily available." (Archbishop John R. Quinn in response to a National Research Council's recommendation that contraceptives and abortion be made readily available to teenagers.)

35. Reading test scores in public schools have declined dramatically. This decline was caused by the radical changes in teaching strategies introduced in the 1960s.

36. The rates of teen pregnancy, youth violence, and drug use have increased rapidly in the years since school prayer was banned. The evidence is clear: we must bring prayer back to the classroom.

37. "Just as instructors could prune sentences for poor grammar, so the principal was entitled to find certain articles inappropriate for publication—in this situation because they might reveal the identity of pregnant students and because references to sexual activity were deemed improper for young students to see." (From an editorial on the U.S. Supreme Court's decision to give public school officials broad powers to censor school-sponsored student publications.)

38. "**Editor:** Now that it has been definitely established that nonsmokers have the right to tell smokers not to pollute their air, it follows that people who don't own cars have the right to tell car owners not to drive. Right?" (Jim Hodge, *San Francisco Chronicle*)

39. We must either give up some of our constitutional liberties to ensure the government can protect us against terrorism or we will again fall prey to terrorists.

40. Cartoon

The Final Four.

 WRITING ASSIGNMENT 15

Analyzing an Extended Argument

From the following collection of editorials, choose one (or find one in a periodical) on which to write an essay evaluating the argument. We suggest the following process for approaching this paper. Analyze each paragraph of your chosen editorial in order. Compose a list of the fallacies you find in each paragraph—give names of fallacies or identify weaknesses in reasoning (not all weaknesses can be precisely named) and illustrate with specific examples from the editorial. Avoid the trap of being too picky; you won't necessarily find significant fallacies in every paragraph. During this paragraph by paragraph analysis, keep the argument's conclusion in mind and ask yourself if the author provides adequate support for it.

Next, review your paragraph by paragraph analysis to determine the two or three major problems in the argument. Then group and condense your list of faults or fallacies, and in a coherently written essay organized around these two or three principal categories of weakness, present your evaluation of the argument. For example, if you find more than one instance of personal attack, you will devote one of your paragraphs to this fallacy and cite all the examples you find to support your claim. Follow the same procedure for other weaknesses. Identify each specific example you cite either by paraphrase or direct quotation, imagining as you write that the reader is not familiar with the editorial you are critiquing.

Audience

College age readers who have not read the editorial and who are not familiar with all of the fallacies listed in the text.

Purpose

To illustrate to a less critical reader that published arguments written by established professionals are not necessarily free of fallacious reasoning.

On Date Rape:

Dating is a very recent phenomenon in world history. Throughout history, women have been chaperoned. As late as 1964, when I arrived in college, we had strict rules. We had to be in the dorm under lock and key by 11 o'clock. My generation was the one that broke these rules. We said, "We want freedom—no more double standard!" When I went to stay at a male friend's apartment in New York, my aunts flew into a frenzy: "You can't do that, it's dangerous!" But I said, "No, we're not going to be like that anymore." Still, we understood in the '60s that we were taking a risk.

Today these young women want the freedoms that we won, but they don't want to acknowledge the risk. That's the problem. The minute you go out with a man, the minute you go to a bar to have a drink, there is a risk. You have to accept the fact that part of the sizzle of sex comes from the danger of sex. You can be overpowered.

So it is women's personal responsibility to be aware of the dangers of the world. But these young feminists today are deluded. They come from a protected, white, middle-class world, and they expect everything to be safe. Notice it's not black or Hispanic women who are making a fuss about this—they come from cultures that are fully sexual and they are fully realistic about sex. But these other women are sexually repressed girls, coming out of pampered homes, and when they arrive at these colleges and suddenly hit male lust, they go, "Oh, no!"

These girls say, "Well, I should be able to get drunk at a fraternity party and go upstairs to a guy's room without anything happening." And I say, "Oh, really? And when you drive your car to New York City, do you leave your keys on the hood?" My point is that if your car is stolen after you do something like that, yes, the police should pursue the thief and he should be punished. But at the same time, the police—and I—have the right to say to you, "You stupid idiot, what the hell were you thinking?"

I mean, wake up to reality. This is male sex. Guess what, it's hot. Male sex is hot. There's an attraction between the sexes that we're not totally in control of. The idea that we can regulate it by passing campus grievance committee rules is madness. My kind of feminism stresses personal responsibility. I've never been raped, but I've been very vigilant—I'm constantly reading the signals. If I ever got into a dating situation where I was overpowered and raped, I would say, "Oh well, I misread the signals." But I don't think I would ever press charges.

The girl in the Kennedy rape case is an idiot. You go back to the Kennedy compound late at night and you're surprised at what happens? She's the one who should be charged—with ignorance. Because everyone knows that Kennedy is spelled S-E-X. Give me a break, this is not rape. And it's going to erode the real outrage that we should feel about actual rape. This is just over-privileged people saying they want the world to be a bowl of cherries. Guess what? It's not and it never will be.

Camille Paglia
A humanities professor and cultural critic
San Francisco Examiner

QUALITY TIME   Gail Machlis

Boxing, Doctors—Round Two

Before I went on vacation a few weeks ago, I wrote a column criticizing the American Medical Association for its call to abolish boxing. As you might have expected, I have received letters from doctors telling me I'm misinformed and scientifically naive. One doctor even said I must have had terrible experiences with doctors to have written what I wrote.

That just shows how arrogant doctors are. It never would occur to them that I might have a defensible position. If I disagree with them, it's because I'm ignorant.

Doctors are used to being right. We come into their offices sick and generally not knowing what's wrong with us. We are in awe of their expertise and afraid for our well-being. We have a tendency to act like children in front of them. "If you can only make me well, Doc, I will love you for life." Doctors, who start out as regular human beings, come to expect us to worship them. They thrive on the power that comes from having knowledge about life and death.

Which brings us to their misguided stand against boxing. Doctors are offended by injuries in boxing, although they don't seem as mortified by the people who die skiing or bike riding or swimming every year. You rarely hear a peep out of them about the many injuries football players sustain—that includes kids in the peewee leagues and high school. Why the outrage over boxing?

Because many doctors are social snobs. They see people from ethnic minorities punching each other in a ring and they reach the conclusion that these poor, dumb blacks and Latinos must be protected from themselves because they don't know any better. The AMA is acting like a glorified SPCA, arrogantly trying to prevent cruelty to animals. They would never dare preach this way to football players, because most of them went to college. Nor would they come out against skiing, because many doctors love to ski.

Boxers know the risks of taking a right cross to the jaw better than doctors, and they take up the sport with a full understanding of its risks. A man should have the right to take a risk. Doctors may want to save us from adventure, but there still is honor in freely choosing to put yourself on the line. Risk is why race-car drivers speed around treacherous tracks. Danger is why mountain climbers continue to explore the mystery of Mount Everest. Yet doctors do not come out against auto racing or mountain climbing.

One physician wrote a letter to the Sporting Green saying the AMA's position against boxing is based on medical evidence. As I read the letter's twisted logic, I wondered if the AMA causes brain damage in doctors. "Skiing, bicycle riding and swimming kill more people each year (than boxing)," he writes. "Obviously, far more people engage in those activities than enter a boxing ring."

Does his position make sense to you? We should eliminate boxing, the sport with fewer negative consequences, but allow the real killer sports to survive. Amazing. If this doctor were really concerned with medical evidence, as he claims, he would attack all dangerous sports, not just boxing.

But he doesn't. The truth is, boxing offends the delicate sensibilities of doctors. They don't like the idea that two men *intentionally* try to hurt each other. They feel more comfortable when injuries are a byproduct of a sport—although ask any batter who has been beaned by a fastball if his broken skull was an innocent byproduct.

In other words, doctors are making a moral judgment, not a medical judgment, about which sports are acceptable. Every joker is entitled to ethical opinions, but doctors have no more expertise than you or I when it comes to right and wrong. If preaching excites them, let them become priests.

What if the AMA is successful in getting boxing banned? Will the sport disappear? No way. As long as man is man, he will want to see two guys of equal weight and ability solve their elemental little problem in a ring. If the sport becomes illegal, it will drift off to barges and back alleys, where men will fight in secret without proper supervision. And then you will see deaths and maiming like you never saw before.

Whom will the AMA blame then?

Lowell Cohn, a sportswriter
The San Francisco Chronicle

Abbie Hoffman—Pol Pot in Style

Abbie Hoffman died. Old hippies and Yippies and followers of social reform all lamented his passing. The TV cameras interviewed bearded burn-out cases who all knew Hoffman. It was the end of an era, they all said.

No. The era had ended long ago. The era ended when Pol Pot butchered 2 million Cambodians and the same phony revolutionaries, the college kids whose parents had fat incomes and red convertibles, failed to say one word against the slaughter.

I've been itching to write some sort of nasty column about how my generation, the war babies born after WWII, grew up with a superiority complex and a sense of righteousness that was based on nothing more than ego. And how this same crowd ranted and raved about one injustice or another and then collectively closed its eyes when a New Holocaust took place smack dab in the middle of the generation's ego trip. It's a column I haven't been able to do.

When the war babies single-handedly beat back the escalation of the Vietnam war and caused Lyndon Johnson to leave office in disgrace (ironically leading to a rebirth of the Republican Party), it figured it was on a mission from God. The mission was to save the world. Unfortunately, this group had no methodology. In fact, the war babies were so shallow that their intellectual heroes turned out to be rock stars—the Beatles!

Rock stars as intellectual heroes has since become the model for every generation since the 60s. It's pathetic. Since the Beatles, we have seen a parade of nerdy singers and introverts with a message, a beat and a twanging guitar.

The Beatles were also goofballs. They wore weird clothes, followed cults, made faces into national TV cameras, said dumb things to serious questions. This became the model for behavior—Abbie Hoffman epitomized the techniques. He formed the wacky Youth International Party—members were called Yippies. He wrote "Steal This Book." He said dumb things, acted weird and lifted his shirt to show his chest on the David Susskind Show. It was a laugh riot and Hoffman was the king of gag masters.

Eventually, through a series of run-ins with the law, mostly over petty offenses blown out of proportion by a government that couldn't take a joke, Hoffman was under arrest. He took off and made the authorities look like fools by effortlessly hiding out for years while in the public eye posing as another person. What a wacky crazy guy. Hahahaha.

All the while Pol Pot was torturing millions of helpless Cambodians in the New Holocaust. It was fascinating how all that was ignored despite the reports of savagery coming out of Southeast Asia. While the same community a few years earlier railed against American racism practiced in Vietnam because of too many GIs calling the South Vietnam allies "gooks," not a word was said when millions of Cambodians were being systematically slaughtered. Here was the real racism of the rich war babies coming to the front. After all, who needs more Asians? Pol Pot wasn't like Hitler, these people aren't Jewish. So forget about them and let's protest the treatment of blacks in South Africa. Heck, one was beaten up the other day. And let's not forget Nicaragua. Keep U.S. troops out. We don't want another Vietnam, do we?

So the war babies continue to party to this day with Loni Hancock still fighting for People's Park in Berkeley. She now equates the park to Gettysburg. Sure it is, Loni—Gettysburg, Kan. What People's Park really represents is the net accomplishments of a generation of pot smoking, drug using, free-sexers who cared about nothing more than themselves. It's a weed patch for burn-out cases to flop. How glorious. The war babies promoted drug use, now cocaine terrorizes and corrupts the country. The war babies promoted indiscriminate sex and now AIDS haunts the land. The war babies promoted racial equality for all, as long as it wasn't in Asia.

I'm sorry about the death of Hoffman. I thought he was a funny guy—a performance artist of sorts. Unfortunately too many people used him and his mentors, The Beatles, as role models.

By the way, Pol Pot is still alive and expected to again take over Cambodia. Hey, but who cares?

John C. Dvorak
A radio talk show host

Guns Save Lives

The data from the 1990 Harvard Medical Practice Study suggest that 150,000 Americans die every year from doctors' negligence—compared with 38,000 gun deaths annually. Why are doctors not declared a public health menace? Because they save many more lives than they take. And so it is with guns.

Every year, good Americans use guns about 2.5 million times to protect themselves and their families, which means 65 lives are protected by guns for every life lost to a gun. For every 101 California tragedy, many others are averted.

An unsurprising 1 percent of America's 240 million guns are used for protection annually. The U.S. Bureau of Justice Statistics has repeatedly shown that guns are the most effective means of self-protection. If guns are as dangerous for self-defense as the alarmists claim, why does their leading researcher, Dr. Arthur Kellermann, want his wife to have a gun for defense?

Physicians who advocate gun prohibition have promoted confiscatory taxation and fees on guns, ammunition, and gun owners, in hopes that those taxes will be funneled into their research and their emergency rooms. To strengthen their case, they ignore the lives protected by guns and exaggerate the medical costs, claiming $20 billion per year in costs from gun violence.

In fact, the cost of medical care for gun violence is about $1.5 billion per year, less than 0.2 percent of our $800 billion annual health care costs. So advocates of gun prohibition routinely include estimates of "lost lifetime earnings," assuming gang bangers, drug dealers and rapists to be as productive as teachers and factory workers.

Even the virulently anti-self defense New England Journal of Medicine and Journal of Trauma have published studies showing that three-fourths of gun homicide "victims" are drug dealers or their customers. On the street, they cost society an average of $400,000 per criminal per year. In prison, they cost an average of $30,000 per criminal per year and, some cold-hearted analysts have noted, in the ground, they hurt no one and cost us nothing.

Cost-benefit analysis is necessarily hardhearted and, though it may be repugnant to consider, the gun deaths of those predators may be a savings to society on the order of $5.5 billion annually, more than three times the medical "costs" of guns.

Edgar A. Sutter
National Chairman of Doctors for Integrity in Research
and Public Policy.

KEY TERMS

Fallacy	Description	Example
Appeal to authority (2 forms)	**1.** Appeals to an authority who is not an expert on the issue under discussion.	Abortion to save the mother is irrelevant because a pediatric surgeon has never seen a case in which such a dilemma has risen.
Snob appeal	**2.** Appeals to people's desire for prestige and exclusivity.	Pamilla's not for everyone. The best never is.
Appeal to fear	Implicitly threatens the audience.	Will there be a *job* waiting when *you* leave college?
Appeal to pity	Attempts to win sympathy.	Professor Hall, I must get an A in your course. If you don't give me an A, I won't be able to go to law school.
Begging the question (3 forms)	**1.** Offers no actual support; may restate as a premise the conclusion in different words.	Students like rock music because it is the most enjoyable music around.
Loaded question	**2.** Asks a question that contains an assumption that must be proven.	Have you started to pay your fair share of taxes yet?
Question begging epithet	**3.** Uses a single word to assert a claim that must be proven.	Reactionary, negligent, warmonger, deadbeat.
Equivocation	Shifts the meaning of a term within a single argument.	We are told that to discriminate in employment or housing is punishable by law. But we must discrimi-nate when we hire an individual or rent an apartment.
False analogy	Compares two or more things that are not in essence similar and suggests that since they share certain characteristics, they share others as well.	I don't want to die falling off a rock. But you can kill yourself falling in the bathtub too.

False cause [Latin name: *post hoc, ergo* *propter hoc*]	Claims a causal re- lationship between events solely on the basis of a chrono- logical relationship.	I joined the Confederacy for two weeks. Then I deserted. The Confederacy fell.
False dilemma	Presents two and only two alternatives for consideration when other possibilities exist.	Either you are in favor of recalling the mayor, or you are a supporter of her political platform.
Hasty **generalization**	Generalizes from a sample that is too small or in some other way unrepresentative of the target population.	Students in Professor Hall's eight o'clock freshman composition class are often late. Today's college students are irresponsible and unreliable.
Personal attack [Latin name: *ad hominem*] (2 forms)	**1.** Attacks the person presenting the argu- ment rather than the argument itself.	Because she is extremely wealthy, our mayor cannot properly represent this city.
Tu quoque ("you also")	**2.** Discredits an argu- ment because the behavior of the person proposing it does not conform to the posi- tion he's supporting.	A teenager to his father: Don't tell me not to drink. You drink all the time.
Poisoning the **well**	Makes an assertion which will intimidate the audience and therefore discourage an open discussion.	Every patriotic American supports legislation condemning the desecration of the flag.
Slippery slope	Claims that an action should be avoided because it will lead to a series of ex- tremely undesirable consequences.	What seems like reasonable restrictions on guns with no legitimate civilian purpose will lead inevitably to total prohibition of gun ownership that ends in virtual slavery at the hands of a totalitarian regime.

Special pleading	Judges and labels the same act differently depending on the person or group who performs the act.	The supplying of weapons to Central America by the Russians was an act of aggression. Our military aid to the region, however, helped the Freedom Fighters in their quest for peace.
Straw man	Creates and then attacks a distorted version of the opposition's argument.	The democratic candidate wants the federal government to house everyone, feed everyone, care for everyone's children, and provide medical care for everyone. And he's going to take 50 percent of every dime you make to do it.

Chapter
9

Language: Meaning and Style

"When I use a word," Humpty Dumpty said in rather a scornful tone, "it means just what I choose it to mean—neither more nor less."

—Lewis Carroll, *Alice Through the Looking Glass*

*I*n Chapter 8, we note how fallacious arguments can be built on the misuse of language; you will remember circular definitions in begging the question and the danger of equivocation, subtle shifts in the meaning of a given term within the same argument.

Now we'd like to concentrate on the precise use of language, on paying close attention to how we choose our words and how we construct our sentences. As Francis Bacon put it four hundred years ago, "Men imagine that their minds have the command of language, but it often happens that language bears rule over their minds." Language itself, he suggests, can shape—even control—our thoughts. Poet W. H. Auden agrees: "Language is the mother, not the handmaiden, of thought; words will tell you things you never thought or felt before." Thus it is enormously important that we know the meaning of the words we use and that when we write, our readers, to the degree possible, share our understanding of words. To achieve this clarity in our writing, we must, when necessary, define our terms and prefer, usually, the concrete to the abstract.

Cicero, the Roman orator, claimed that every discourse should begin with a definition in order to make clear what the subject under consideration is. French philosopher Voltaire wrote, "If you would argue with me, first define your terms." And in more recent times, Ellen Willis, writing in *Rolling Stone,* admonishes us "Find out who controls the definitions, and you have a pretty good clue who controls everything else."

Why is definition so crucial?

LOGICAL DEFINITION

To answer that question, let's examine the following sentences:

1. Was Richard Nixon an effective president?
2. Does money mean success?
3. Was the violence in the movie "Pulp Fiction" obscene?
4. Is television addictive?
5. Is alcoholism an illness?
6. Should we encourage entrepreneurs?

Remembering our discussion in Chapter 4, you will note that each sentence is a question at issue. Examine these questions more closely, and you will notice that each contains at least one key term that is open to interpretation. For example, what does it mean to be an "effective" president? If you were to write a paper based on this question at issue, you would first have to define "effective," to list the criteria for such a presidency before applying them to Richard Nixon.

You need to define, to stipulate, to pin down precise meaning for terms such as these. To supply useful definitions, where do you begin? A good dictionary is the best *initial* source. Following the tradition of classical rhetoric laid down by Plato and Aristotle, first place the term in its general *class* and then narrow the definition by determining the **distinguishing characteristics,** the ways in which it differs from other terms in the same class.

Such a rigorous process is hardly necessary for a concrete term such as "fork," which belongs to the class of eating utensils and is distinguished from other members of its class, other eating utensils, by its shape, a handle at one end with two or more pointed prongs at the other. But abstract terms such as "success" and "obscene" must be carefully defined.

A definition of key terms in questions two and three above would look like this:

Term	Class	Distinguishing Characteristics
Success	(is) a favorable result	(which) implies economic and social achievement in one's chosen professional field.
Obscene	(is) a negative quality	(which) offends prevailing notions of modesty or decency

Note that the distinguishing characteristics are still subject to interpretation, to individual assessment. Another writer could define success in terms of personal relationships or contributions to the community rather than professional achievement. And, of course, stipulating the precise meaning of "obscene" is a task that has long bedeviled our courts and has continued to do so with cases such as the violence in the lyrics of Ice-T and the sexually explicit photographs of Robert Mapplethorpe.

GUINDON

John White is my idea of an intellectual. He buys Playboy magazine, cuts out the interviews and hangs them all over his bedroom.

EXERCISE 9A

Defining Key Terms

For the remaining three questions at issue above (4–6), identify terms that require clarification and stipulate a definition. Place each term first in its general class and then narrow your definition with distinguishing characteristics as we have done above. You may find it interesting to compare your definitions with those of classmates.

DEFINITION AND THE SOCIAL SCIENCES

In a study on child abuse and health, which we cited in Chapter 7, the researchers first had to define child abuse before they could determine its effect on women's health. They separated child abuse into three categories—emotional, physical, and sexual. Then they defined each category.

emotional abuse: repeated rejection or serious physical threats from parents, tension in the home more than 25 percent of the time, and frequent violent fighting among parents.

physical abuse: strong blows from an adult or forced eating of caustic substances; firm slaps were excluded.

sexual abuse: any nonvoluntary sexual activity with a person at least five years older.

Researchers interviewed 700 women from a private gynecological practice and tabulated their responses according to these categories. Without clear-cut definitions to guide them, social scientists would be left with subjective impressions rather than quantifiable results.

DEFINITION AND PERCEPTION

Our definitions can reveal how we see people—as individuals and collectively. In his book *Days of Obligation,* writer Richard Rodriquez points out that American feminists have appropriated the word *macho* "to name their American antithesis," a man who is "boorish" and "counterdomestic." But in Mexican Spanish, he tells us that *"Machismo* is more akin to the Latin *gravitas.* The male is serious. The male provides. The Mexican male never abandons those who depend upon him." As this example illustrates, when different cultures share languages, shifts in meaning often occur, reflecting cultural bias.

Feminist Gloria Steinem points out our culture's sexual bias in its traditional definitions of the following terms, definitions that have played crucial roles in determining how women and men view themselves and others.

work: something men do, go to; as distinguished from housework and childcare, which is what women do

art: what white men produce

crafts: what women and ethnic minorities do

We can hope that these definitions are changing. And indeed, we have historical precedent for scientific definitions shifting to conform to new ways of thinking. In the nineteenth century, alcoholism was defined as criminal behavior. When the term was redefined as an illness after World War I, considerable progress in treatment became possible.

Conversely, when the American Psychological Association recently stopped classifying homosexuality as an illness, the homosexual community was understandably gratified by the revision of a definition it found unjust and damaging to its members.

Writer Katie Roiphe, author of *The Morning After: Sex, Fear, and Feminism on Campus,* inspired angry responses when she claimed that the definition of date rape had gone too far. "It's creating stereotypes of men as predatory beasts and women as delicate vessels. It's destructive. When you use rape to mean so many things, the word itself loses its meaning."

Language evolves over time. It's a natural process. But when expanded meaning results in loss of precision, we do well to examine the causes and effects of the revised meaning.

LANGUAGE: AN ABSTRACT SYSTEM OF SYMBOLS

As you have noticed from the preceding discussion, abstract words can present particular difficulties when it comes to stipulating precise meaning. But language itself, whether it refers to an abstract concept or a concrete object, is an abstract system of symbols. The word is not the thing itself, but a *symbol* or *signifier* used to represent the thing we refer to, which is the *signified.* For example, the word "cat" is a symbol or signifier for the animal itself, the signified.

"Cat"

THE SYMBOL or SIGNIFIER	THE SIGNIFIED
(the word)	(the thing being referred to)

But meaning is made only when the signified is processed through the mind of someone using or receiving the words. This process serves as an endlessly destabilizing force. Whenever a speaker, writer, listener, or reader encounters a word, a lifetime of associations renders the word, and thus the image it conjures up, distinct for each individual.

As literary theorist Stanley Fish points out, meaning is dependent not only on the individual but also on the context, situation, and interpretive community.

To illustrate this point, let's look at the word "host." It means one thing if we are at a party, something different if we're discussing parasites with a biologist, and something else entirely if we are at church. Hence, the context or situation determines our understanding of "host."

If, however, you are not a member of a religion that practices the ritual of communion or are not conversant with parasitology, then you may understand the meaning of "host" *only* as the giver of a party. You are not part of the interpretive community, in this case a religious community or a scientific discipline, which understands "host" as a consecrated wafer, a religious symbol, or as an organism on which another lives.

As you can see, language remains perpetually contingent, and thus as a means of communication, slippery. Even when the signified is *concrete,* individual experience and perception will always deny the word complete stability; the range of possible images will still be vast. Take the word "table." Nothing of the essence of table is part of the word "table." Although most words in English (or any modern language) have roots and a history in older languages, the assignation of a particular meaning to a given term remains essentially arbitrary. While all English speakers share a *general* understanding of the word "table," each user or receiver of this word, without having considerably more detail, will create a different picture.

If the symbolic representation of a *concrete,* visible object such as a table is as unstable as our discussion suggests, think how much more problematic *abstract* terms must be. Were we to substitute the abstraction "freedom" for the concrete "table," the range of interpretations would be considerably more diverse and much more challenging to convey to others. Visual pictures, which arise when concrete objects are signaled, don't come to mind as readily when we refer to abstractions, a distinction that required us to define the abstract terms in the questions at issue above and led Shakespeare to explain why poets give "to airy nothing a local habitation and a name."

Semanticist S. I. Hayakawa discusses the idea of an abstraction ladder in which language starts on the ground, so to speak, with an object available to our sense of perception, and moves up to concepts abstracted from, derived from, the concrete source—for example, from a specific cow to livestock to farm assets to assets. He stresses that our powers of abstraction are indispensable. "The ability to climb to higher and higher levels of abstraction is a distinctively human trait without which none of our philosophical or scientific insights would be possible." But he cautions against staying at too high a level of abstraction.

> The kind of "thinking" we must be extremely wary of is that which *never* leaves the higher verbal levels of abstraction, the kind that never points *down* the abstraction ladder to lower levels of abstraction and from there to the extensional world:
>
> > "What do you mean by *democracy*?"
> > "Democracy means the preservation of human *rights.*"
> > "What do you mean by *rights*?"
> > "By rights I mean those privileges God grants to all of us—I mean man's inherent privileges."
> > "Such as?"
> > "Liberty, for example."
> > "What do you mean by *liberty*?"
> > "Religious and political freedom."
> > "And what does that mean?"
> > "Religious and political freedom is what we enjoy under a democracy."

The writer never moves down to the essential lower levels on the abstraction ladder, and a discourse consisting only of abstractions, devoid of concrete details and examples, is necessarily vague, often difficult for the reader to understand, and, in this definition of democracy, circular.

The Importance of Specificity

To avoid the confusion that unclarified abstractions can generate, Hayakawa suggests pointing down "to extensional levels wherever necessary; in writing and speaking, this means giving *specific examples* of what we are talking about," grounding our arguments in experience.

Compare the empty, circular definition of democracy Hayakawa quotes above with the concrete illustrations that illuminate E. B. White's celebrated World War II definition of the same term.

July 3, 1943

We received a letter from the Writers' War Board the other day asking for a statement on "The Meaning of Democracy." It presumably is our duty to comply with such a request, and it is certainly our pleasure. Surely the Board knows what democracy is. It is the line that forms on the right. It is the don't in don't shove. It is the hole in the stuffed shirt through which the sawdust slowly trickles; it is the dent in the high hat. Democracy is the recurrent suspicion that more than half of the people are right more than half of the time. It is the feeling of privacy in the voting booths, the feeling of communion in the libraries, the feeling of vitality everywhere. Democracy is a letter to the Editor. Democracy is the score at the beginning of the ninth. It is an idea that hasn't been disproved yet, a song the words of which have not gone bad. It's the mustard on the hot dog and the cream in the rationed coffee. Democracy is a request from a War Board, in the middle of a morning in the middle of a war, wanting to know what democracy is.

Such specificity is what writer Annie Dillard values when she says, "This is what life is all about: salamanders, fiddle tunes, you and me and things . . . the fiz into particulars" (*Teaching a Stone to Talk*). And what novelist Vladimir Nabokov prizes when he asks us to "Caress the details, the divine details" (*Lectures on Literature*).

The Manipulation of Language

Sometimes abstractions are used, consciously or unconsciously, to confuse, distort, conceal, or evade, in short, to manipulate others—a practice Hemingway comments on in *A Farewell to Arms,* his World War I novel.

I was always embarrassed by the words sacred, glorious, and sacrifice and the expression in vain. We had heard them, sometimes standing in the rain almost out of earshot, so that only the shouted words came through, and had read them, on proclamations that were slapped up by billposters over other proclamations, now for a long time, and I had seen nothing sacred, and the things that were glorious had no glory and the sacrifices were like the stockyards at Chicago if nothing was done with the meat except to bury it. There were many words that you could not stand to hear and finally only the names of places had dignity. Certain numbers were the same way and certain dates and these with the names of the places were all you could say and have them mean anything. Abstract words such as glory, honor, courage, or hallow were obscene beside the concrete names of villages, the numbers of roads, the names of rivers, the numbers of regiments and the dates.

Hemingway eloquently indicates the power of concrete nouns to generate precise meaning readily visualized.

Closer to home, during debates on the complex environmental issue of preserving wetlands in the early nineties, then-President Bush declared that "All existing wetlands, no matter how small, should be preserved." But when pressured by real estate, oil, and mining interests to open protected wetlands to development and exploration, Bush expediently redefined the word, a definition that left at least 10 million acres of wetlands unprotected.

These examples lend fresh meaning to our opening claims of power for those who control the definitions.

In the 1940s, British writer George Orwell addressed the political significance of language in his celebrated essay, "Politics and the English Language," claiming that "political speech and writing are largely the defence of the indefensibles. . . . Defenceless villages are bombarded from the air, the inhabitants driven out into the countryside, the cattle machine-gunned, the huts set on fire with incendiary bullets: this is called *pacification*." In his novel *1984,* he satirizes the official use of deceptive language, coining, among other terms, the words "doublethink" and "newspeak."

In more recent times, we have had our own share of befuddling language, dubbed psychobabble, spacespeak, doublespeak, gobbledygook. Sometimes a euphemism is justified as a means of sparing feelings—someone passed away rather than died, or a large woman is referred to as mature in size. And the specialized lingo of a particular discipline may be necessary even though it appears as needless jargon to a lay person. Later in this chapter a writer refers to the terms metonymy and synecdoche—both useful to rhetoricians, but obscure to others.

But we must be wary of language that camouflages precise meaning. Note how language dulls reality in the following examples:

The "peacemaker" for the MX missile
"offshore" for foreign
"unlawful or arbitrary deprivation of life" for killing
"revenue enhancement" for taxes
"negative growth" for economic recession
"collateral damage" for civilian losses

One institution that is especially guilty of manipulating language for its own purposes is advertising. The poultry industry, for example, has long been under fire for their ambiguous use of "fresh" in labeling and promoting their products—the suggestion being that their chickens had not been frozen when, in fact, they were often stored below 32°F. For exaggerated, sometimes amusing, distortions of definition, examine cosmetic and fashion advertising.

"Well, actually, Doreen, I rather resent being called a 'swamp thing.' ... I prefer the term 'wetlands-challenged mutant.'"

 WRITING ASSIGNMENT 16

Composing an Extended Definition of an Abstract Term

Step 1

Choose a word from the list of abstract terms below, think about its implications for a few minutes, and then start writing a definition that captures its meaning and significance for you. (If an abstract term other than one of those on the list comes to mind and interests you, substitute it, but clear it with your instructor first.) Using a freewriting approach, keep going for about 20 minutes. If time and your instructor permit, do this in class; you will find the combination of spontaneity and structure imposed by writing during class to be an aid to composing. You can't get up to make a phone call or clean the refrigerator.

education	gossip
sportsmanship	leadership
originality	imagination
machismo	character
courage	sexual harassment
defeat	marriage
maturity	soul
leisure	generosity
creativity	intelligence
progress	burn-out
trend	heroism
rationality	responsibility

Volunteers can enlighten (and entertain) the class by reading these drafts aloud.

THE LOCKHORNS

"IT'S NOT GOSSIP....IT'S ORAL HISTORY!"

Step 2

With more time for reflection and revision, take the spontaneous draft you have written and, in a page or two, expand and edit your definition. In the process of defining your term, analyze and clarify what it means to you, arriving at, or at least implying, a significant point. You may find yourself actually arguing a point, although in this assignment argument is not a requirement. As the discussion in this chapter has emphasized, you must include specific detail to animate your abstraction.

If time permits, multiple definitions of the same term can be read to the class for comparison and discussion.

Here are some possible strategies for writing an extended definition; do not feel compelled to use them all.

- stipulate your precise meaning (see logical definition above), but don't include a dictionary definition unless you plan to use it or disagree with it.
- provide examples of the term
- explain the function or purpose of the term
- explore etymology (origin and history of a word). The most fruitful source for such explorations is *The Oxford English Dictionary*, a multivolume work available in most college libraries, and a dictionary well worth your acquaintance. Use the history of a term to help make a point.
- examine the connotations of the term
- discuss what it is not (Use this sparingly.)
- draw analogies (Here you will want to be precise; be sure the analogy really fits.)

A few cautions:

- define or illustrate more complex words with more familiar ones
- stick to one sense of the word unless you clarify an intended distinction
- avoid circularity

Look ahead in this chapter to *Writing with Style* for helpful sentence hints:

appositives for inserting short definitions, identifications, and concrete examples into your sentences (page 183)

clear *"focus"*—appropriate sentence subjects and active verbs (page 189)

Audience
The instructor and other members of the class.

Purpose
To make an abstraction concrete.

Extended definitions: Student examples Several of our students have contributed their efforts on this topic. Here is a sampling.

Two different approaches to the same term:

Radical

The word "radical" has been defined in *The Oxford-English Dictionary* as "going to the root or origin, touching or acting upon what is essential and fundamental." Thus, a radical reform is said to be a fundamental, "thorough reform." In a political sense, an advocate of "radical reform" was described as "one who holds the most advanced views of political reform on democratic lines, and thus belongs to the extreme section of the Liberal party." While this may have been a commonly accepted usage of the term in England at the time, the word "radical" has drifted away from its original specific meaning to a rather vague term for anyone who appears to be trying to disrupt the status quo.

In the late 1800s and early 1900s, socialists, Communists, and anarchists alike were popularly categorized by the general American public with the term "radical." With the controversy surrounding the political goals of these different activists, "a radical" was at the very least a controversial figure. More often than not, the word "radical" brought to mind some sort of disruptive character, a nonspecific image of an extremist, most probably from the far left. On the political spectrum the "radical" is still viewed as an individual on the extreme left, opposite the "right" or "conservative" parties. "Conservatives" holding radically different views and goals are not normally termed "radicals"; they are merely part of the "ultraright."

The term "radical" today is used less as a description of political intent and more as a critique of overall manner and appearance. While many of the "radicals" in the 1960s did indeed advocate numerous political reforms, the general public was more impressed by their personal character and style of advocacy. It is not surprising that when asked to define "a radical," most individuals conjure up a vague image of some young person wearing ragged clothes and long hair. It is a pity that in this society, where progressive change is so essential, the term "radical" has been imbued with so much negativity, so many connotations which really have nothing to do with political reform.

Radical

A radical is an algebraic symbol which tells a person to carry out a certain mathematical operation. The end result of this operation will tell a person the root or origin of a number or problem.

Recently, while in Los Angeles, I overheard someone describe a car as radical. I immediately thought to myself, something is wrong here. Radicals do not have engines. They may contain a number, like 32, underneath their top line, but never a stock Chevy 302 engine. It simply would not fit. When I asked this person why he called the car a radical, he replied, "Because the car is different and unusual." Once again, I thought to myself, he has made a mistake. Radicals are quite common. In fact, they are an essential part of most algebraic theories. I had to infer that this man knew nothing about algebra. If he did, he would have realized that radicals are not different or unusual at all, and would not have called the car one.

While I was in New York this past summer, I happened to see a group of people carrying signs of protest in front of the United Nations Building. As I watched them, a man came over to me, pointed at the group and muttered, "Radicals." I thought to myself, man are you ever wrong. Radicals do not carry signs saying, "Feed the Poor." They may carry a number, like 2, in their top right hand corner, but this number only means to find the root of a problem. It does not mean, "Feed the Poor."

These two events show that there is a great deal of misunderstanding throughout the country in regards to what a radical is. At their simplest level, radicals tell us to find the root of a problem. At their most complex level, they tell us the same thing.

A student's definition in which the approach reflects the word itself:

Fun

What's fun? In the black community fun means trippin'.[1] For example, the fellas pitchin' pennies, shootin' dice, playin' three-card molly[2] on the back of the bus, or playin' stick ball in the streets from the time they are five until they are 25. Little girls and big girls playin' Double Dutch,[3] jumpin' ropes and singin' to the rhythm of their feet. Blastin' the ghetto box to the latest beat and watching the brothuhs break. Bustin' open the fire hydrants on a hot day in order to cool off by runnin' through the water. Listenin' to the dudes standing on the street corner rappin' to a sistuh as she strolls down the street. "Hey, Mamma, what it is! You sho' is lookin' mighty fine today! How 'bout slidin' by my pad for a bit?" Gettin' happy in church and callin' out, "Lordy, Lordy! Lordy have mercy! Yes, Lord! Help me Lord!" Helpin' Mamma wash the collard greens and sweet potatoes, stirrin' the corn bread and slicin' the fatback[4] for Sunday supper after church. The whole family sittin' on the stoop in the evening listenin' to grandmamma tell stories 'bout the ol' days while fussin' about the young folk. All of this comes down to trippin', enjoying one's self, and havin' fun in the hood.[5]

---

[1]trippin'—enjoying yourself

[2]three-card Molly—a card game involving three different-colored cards

[3]double dutch—a jump rope game involving two ropes swung in opposite directions. The jumping technique involves intricate rhythm and style and is often accompanied by a song or a chant recited by a child.

[4]fatback—discarded meat in the back of a butcher shop

[5]hood—the African-American community or neighborhood

STIPULATING PERSONAL MEANING

Through the centuries, people have been defining what they consider themselves to be, using the term "man" in a number of inventive ways.

Plato
First, he put man in the class "biped" and differentiated him from others in the class by describing him as "a featherless biped." When his rival, Diogenes, produced a plucked chicken, Plato had to add "having broad nails" as a further distinguishing characteristic.

Shakespeare
"What a piece of work is a man! How noble in reason! how infinite in faculty! in form, in moving, how express and admirable! in action how like an angel! in apprehension how like a god! the beauty of the world! the paragon of animals! And yet, to me what is this quintessence of dust? Man delights not me; no, nor woman neither." (*Hamlet,* II.ii. 316)

Ambrose Bierce
"An animal so lost in rapturous contemplation of what he thinks he is as to overlook what he indubitably ought to be. His chief occupation is extermination of other animals and his own species, which, however, multiplies with such insistent rapidity as to infest the whole habitable earth and Canada." (*Devil's Dictionary*)

Inventing New Words to Fill a Need

Contemporary American writer Alice Walker sought to rectify some of the linguistic imbalance in gender representation when she coined the term *womanist* for her collection of nonfiction, *In Search of Our Mothers' Gardens, Womanist Prose by Alice Walker.* Why, we might ask, did she need to invent such a word? We can assume that she experienced a condition for which there was no term, so she created one. To stipulate the meaning of her neologism (a newly coined word or phrase), she opens the book with a series of definitions.

> *WOMANIST:*
> 1. From womanish. (Opp. of "girlish," i.e., frivolous, irresponsible not serious.) A black feminist or feminist of color. From the black folk expression of mothers to female children, "You acting womanish," i.e., like a woman. Usually referring to outrageous, audacious, courageous or *willful* behavior. Wanting to know more and in greater depth than is considered "good" for one. Interested in grown-up doings. Acting grown up. Being grown up. Interchangeable with another black folk expression: "You trying to be grown." Responsible. In charge. *Serious.*
> 2. Also: A woman who loves other women, sexually and/or nonsexually. Appreciates and prefers women's culture, women's emotional flexibility (values tears as natural counter-balance of laughter), and

women's strength. Sometimes loves individual men, sexually and/or nonsexually. Committed to survival and wholeness of entire people, male *and* female. Not a separatist, except periodically, for health. Traditionally universalist, as in: "Mama, why are we brown, pink, and yellow, and our cousins are white, beige, and black?" Ans.: Well, you know the colored race is just like a flower garden, with every color flower represented." Traditionally capable, as in: "Mama, I'm walking to Canada and I'm taking you and a bunch of other slaves with me." Reply: "It wouldn't be the first time."

3. Loves music. Loves dance. Loves the moon. *Loves* the Spirit. Loves love and food and roundness. Loves struggle. *Loves* the Folk. Loves herself. *Regardless.*

4. Womanist is to feminist as purple to lavender.

Writer and performer Rich Hall created the word *sniglet* for "any word that doesn't appear in the dictionary, but should." Two examples from his collection:

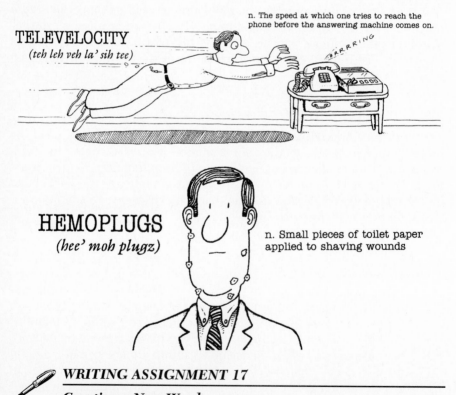

TELEVELOCITY
(*teh leh veh la' sih tee*)

n. The speed at which one tries to reach the phone before the answering machine comes on.

HEMOPLUGS
(*hee' moh plugz*)

n. Small pieces of toilet paper applied to shaving wounds

✎ **WRITING ASSIGNMENT 17**

Creating a New Word

Now it's your turn to create a new word. Give the word an extended definition so that those in your class can see how to use it and why our culture needs such an addition to the language.

Audience

The instructor and other members of the class.

Purpose

To identify a meaning in need of a name.

APPLICATION TO WRITING—WRITING WITH STYLE

Some may dismiss style as ornament, as the decorative frills of writing, or as something limited to matters of correct grammar and usage. A wiser definition of style would encompass more: choices of diction and word order that aim to strengthen our ideas and render them more precisely. An effective style chosen with your audience, your purpose, even your personal integrity in mind, can capture your reader's attention and possibly win the day for your argument. Style plays a central role in clear communication.

Sentence Length

How many times have you heard, "Keep it short, write short sentences?" Too many, probably. To be clear, direct, and concise, you do not always have to fall back on repetitive short sentences. As the discussion of logical joining in Chapter 3 and of appositives and verbal modifiers to follow in this chapter suggests, you can extend the flow of your ideas and insert necessary information by expanding your repertoire of sentence structures.

Appositives—A Strategy for Defining and Identifying Terms within the Sentence

As we have illustrated above, abstract terms need defining so that our readers understand what we mean. One might agree in theory but question in practice how a writer defines terms without derailing the organization of the paper or paragraph. Often, the answer is to use **appositives**— noun phrases placed beside nouns to elaborate on their meaning.

Here is Joan Didion, contemporary American essayist, giving us a vivid picture of the Los Angeles climate:

> In fact the climate is characterized by infrequent but violent extremes: *two periods of torrential subtropical rains* which continue for weeks and wash out the hills and send subdivisions sliding down toward the sea; about *twenty scattered days a year of the Santa Ana,* which, with its incendiary dryness, invariably means fire.

Didion has added details and combined ideas into one sentence by using appositives. In each case, the appositive (underlined) modifies the noun "extremes," explains or defines what the extremes are, all within one sentence.

Appositives usually follow the nouns they modify, but some writers introduce a sentence with an appositive: *An expression of frustrated rage,* "gangsta rap tries to be outrageous in order to provoke strong reactions."

The phrase, "an expression of frustrated rage" modifies "gangsta rap." Such additions allow a writer to include essential information or background details that may not warrant separate sentences. The effect is streamlined thought in fluent prose, as the following examples in Exercise 9B illustrate.

"I lost the spelling bee on the word 'gangsta.'"

EXERCISE 9B

Recognizing Appositives

In the three passages that follow, identify the appositives and the nouns they modify by underlining the appositives and circling the nouns.

*1. A descriptive passage with examples

> The Evertons are introduced to a second national peculiarity, one they will soon recognize on the streets of Ibarra and in towns and cities beyond. It is something they will see everywhere—a disregard for danger, a companionship with death. By the end of a year they will know it well: the antic bravado, the fatal games, the coffin shop beside the cantina, the sugar skulls on the frosted cake.
>
> —Harriet Doerr, *Stones for Ibarra*

2. Identification

> Cotton Mather was an exception, one who so fully accepted and magnified the outlook of his locality that he has entered folklore as the archetypal Puritan, not only a villainous figure in the pages of Hawthorne, William Carlos Williams and Robert Lowell, but an object of parody even to his fellow townsmen in 18th-century Boston.
>
> —Larzer Ziff, *New York Times Book Review*

3. Definition

> As Baranczak points out, Milosz [Nobel Prize–winning poet] rejects symbols in favor of metonymy and synecdoche, those figures of speech which represent a whole by a thing allied to it or by a part of it.
>
> —Helen Vendler in *The New Yorker*

Punctuation of Appositives

Punctuation choices are simple and logical. In most cases, the appositive phrase is set off from the noun it modifies with commas. If you want greater emphasis, you can do as Harriet Doerr did and use a dash: "It is something they will see everywhere—a disregard for danger, a companionship with death."

Or choose a colon (appropriate only when the appositive ends a sentence) for an even sharper break as Joan Didion did:

> In fact the climate is characterized by infrequent but violent extremes: two periods of torrential subtropical rains which continue for weeks and wash out the hills and send subdivisions sliding down toward the sea; about twenty scattered days a year of the Santa Ana, which, with its incendiary dryness, invariably means fire.

This passage also illustrates the way in which Didion varies punctuation to control all the information in this long sentence, providing logical markers for the reader: the colon sets off the appositive series; the semicolon marks the major division in the series, separating these points from the lesser pauses marked by commas.

Punctuation rules in English are surprisingly relaxed; punctuation is there simply to organize patterns of thought and guide the reader through the meaning of our sentences. It is in this role that punctuation provides a vital service.

EXERCISE 9C

Creating Appositives

Most of you already use appositives to some extent in your writing whether you recognize them or not. But a little conscious practice may expand your knowledge of this useful device.

A. Combine the following sets of sentences by reducing one or more sentences to appositives. You may find more than one way to combine them.

Example:
Unilateral disarmament was considered dangerous and impractical. It was a policy that would require only one side to reduce its arms.
becomes
Unilateral disarmament, *a policy* that would require only one side to reduce its arms, was considered dangerous and impractical.
or
Unilateral disarmament, *a policy* that was considered dangerous and impractical, would require only one side to reduce its arms.

*1. New York has long been the destination of America's adventurous young. It is a city of danger and opportunity.

2. Punk was a return to the roots of rock 'n' roll. It was a revolt against the predictability of disco.

*3. People have very different ideas about the meaning of poverty. It is a condition that to some suggests insufficient income, to others laziness, and to still others a state of unwarranted discomfort.

4. Writing ability can have far-reaching effects on a college graduate's future accomplishments. Writing ability is the capacity to generate and organize relevant ideas, compose coherent sentences, choose precise diction, control mechanics.

5. They regarded the dictator with a mixture of fear and awe. These feelings were not conducive to an attitude of respect and trust toward their government.

6. According to the lieutenant's testimony during his court-martial, he was simply following orders as any military man is trained to do. These orders came from his commanding officers.

7. When the Soviets sent troops into Vilnius, Vytautas Landsbergis isolated himself and members of his government in a fortified parliament building. Vilnius is the capital of Lithuania and Landsbergis was the Lithuanian president.

8. Lisa read only spare modern novels. She liked ones with quirky characters, subtle structure, and ambiguous turns in plot, if they had plots at all.

9. During the 1980s, psychiatrists expanded the definition of the term "addiction." It is a word whose meaning has undergone revision to cover a broader range of compulsive behaviors. These compulsions now include sex, television viewing, designer clothes, shopping. These extend to a whole spectrum of dependencies.

10. Concrete has spread over wider and wider areas of the American landscape. It has covered not just the weed patches, deserted lots, infertile acres but whole pastures, hillsides, and portions of the sea and sky.

B. Finally, write a sentence about your major, your job, or another interest, being sure to include a related technical term. Then add an appositive which defines or illustrates the term.

C. Read the following passage:

James R. Johnson, general manager of the city zoo and a noted authority on reptiles and amphibians, died shortly after his morning run on Thursday, June 25. He was 47.

Mr. Johnson's body was found in his home, on Marsh Lane, a landmark craftsman house constructed by Johnson and his wife Marie out of unusual woods gathered all over the United States. Zoo staffers Jeffrey Kelley and Susan McMillan became concerned when Johnson failed to show up at the zoo and went to his house to investigate. James Kincaid, a spokesman for the zoo, notified authorities yesterday morning.

Mr. Johnson, manager of the zoo since 1988 and an expert on reptiles and amphibians since earning a PhD from Johns Hopkins University in 1977, was an avid runner and noted collector of books and manuscripts relating to his field. He was also well known for his personal collection of iguanas and rare lizards—particularly those found in Mexico, a favorite travel destination.

The coroner, Jacob Feinstein, reported that Johnson died suddenly of a cerebral hemorrhage. He was alone in the house at the time of his death.

Johnson is survived by his wife, Marie Coleman Johnson, daughter of Marvin Coleman, the district attorney from 1966 to 1989; his parents, Laura and Daniel Johnson of St. Louis; and three children: Beverly, Anna, and Robert, all residing at home. Funeral arrangements are pending.

Using this as a model, write an obituary for either a public figure or a fictional character you make up as you go along. Feel free to embroider upon the life of the person you choose for this assignment. Write as many *appositives* as you can think of, and underline each of them. You will find it helpful to first identify the appositives in the passage above.

You may choose to do this exercise in small groups in class.

SENTENCE FOCUS—TECHNIQUES FOR SHARPENING THE FLOW OF IDEAS

He draweth out the thread of his verbosity finer than the staple of his argument.

—Shakespeare, Love's Labor's Lost

We are all familiar with the confusion and obfuscation of much official prose today—political, bureaucratic, academic. Some of this muddled language may be deliberate, to conceal meaning, but often it is inadvertent, a result of writers surrendering to the abstractness of language, of fuzzy language overwhelming complex ideas. We refer to such writing as "unfocused," in much the same way that fuzzy, confused thought is often unfocused. It may help you to understand our discussion of sentence **focus** to think in terms of focusing a camera. When you take a picture, you select and concentrate on a given image—you focus your camera to sharpen that image. An unfocused photograph will be blurred. In much the same way, unfocused writing may be easy to write, but it is usually difficult to read.

The New Yorker found this example of unfocused writing:

> Agreement on the overall objective of decision usefulness was a prerequisite to the establishment of a conceptual framework. Now, at least, we know where we are headed. (The Week in Review, newsletter of Deloitte Haskins & Sells)

After this, do we know where they are going?

Compare the following memo from the Internal Revenue Service and a possible revision.

> Advice has been requested concerning tax deductions for research expenses, including traveling expenses, incurred by college and university professors. (original)

> College and university professors have requested advice about tax deductions for their research expenses, including traveling expenses. (possible revision)

Which version is clearer, easier to read? We assume that the majority of readers will prefer the second. What are the differences? The possible revision is shorter by two words. But is this the only distinction? Make your evaluation before reading on.

Calvin and Hobbes   by Bill Watterson

Concrete Subjects

Look at the grammatical subjects in the two sentences above—"advice" in the first, "professors" in the second—and notice what kind of nouns they are. One is an *abstract noun*, the other a *concrete noun*. Because the sentence subject tends to reflect what a passage is about, the subject is where the *focus* of a sentence usually sits. A concrete noun is capable of producing a visual picture and thus can also *focus* a reader's attention more closely. And when that concrete noun is a person or people, readers can visualize an action and so more readily follow the precise progression of ideas in a sentence. Hence, "professors" as the subject of the second sentence is preferable to the "advice" of the original. The reader can see the "professor" but not the abstraction "advice."

Active and Passive Verbs

Now look at the verbs. In the original sentence on tax deduction, the verb is "has been requested" while in the revision the verb is "has requested." The first is **passive voice,** the second, **active voice.** The basic distinction is that *with a passive verb, the subject is acted upon; the subject is not doing anything in the sentence—it is passive.* "Advice" is being requested, not, obviously, doing the requesting. *When the verb is active, its subject is performing the action of the sentence,* and thus the reader can see a subject doing something. The "professors" are doing the requesting.

We must wade through the original IRS memo to understand the point, whereas in the possible revision we see from the beginning that professors are requesting advice, people are doing something. A possible confusion about who is doing the requesting is made clear.

Sentences written in the passive are easy to spot because they always follow a grammatical pattern:

> subject + a form of the verb "to be" (am, is, are, was, were) + the past participle of the verb (usually with an *-ed* ending) + an expressed or implied "by" phrase, which contains the agent of the verb.

(subject)	(to be)	(past participle)	(optional by phrase)
Mistakes	were	made	(by the chief of staff)

The following two sentences say essentially the same thing, but note how the change in the form of the sentence shifts the emphasis from the concrete subject, "J. Robert Oppenheimer," to the abstract, "elemental danger."

Active   J. Robert Oppenheimer, one of the creators of the atom bomb, *felt* the elemental danger loosed on the earth.

Passive   The elemental danger loosed on the earth *was felt* by J. Robert Oppenheimer, one of the creators of the atom bomb.

Which version do you prefer? Why?

When the Passive Is Appropriate

Aiming for direct, assertive prose, careful writers usually prefer active verbs. But on occasion, when one wants to emphasize someone or something not performing the action in a sentence, the passive is useful. Scientists and social scientists, for example, must often focus on the content of their research rather than on themselves as researchers. Under such circumstances, the passive serves a useful purpose.

> This research *was undertaken* with a grant from the National Science Foundation.

rather than

> I *undertook* this research with a grant from the National Science Foundation.

In this case, "I" should not be the focus of the sentence and thus should not be the grammatical sentence subject.

There is a less honorable use of the passive, however, one politicians have a tendency to rely on—that is, to evade responsibility. William Safire in his *New York Times* column, "On Language," comments on this predilection, focusing on former White House chief of staff John Sununu, who, when asked at a press conference about the use of government funds for personal expenses, replied, "Obviously, some mistakes were made."

Safire notes that "The passive voice acknowledges the errors, but it avoids the blame entirely. . . . When deniability is impossible, dissociation is the way, and the [passive voice] allows the actor to separate himself from the act."

Not surprisingly, when you rely on concrete nouns as your sentence subject, you stand a better chance of automatically using an active verb. Concrete subjects, as we point out above, can do something while abstract nouns usually cannot.

More Ways to Sharpen Focus

Beyond the issues of concrete subjects and active verbs, we can note four additional features to be alert for when considering sharp focus.

1. The logical progression of focus

Central to good paragraph focus is the logical progression of ideas within a paragraph. Read the following paragraph closely to see how research physician and writer Lewis Thomas maintains consistent sentence subjects, emphasizing the topic of the paragraph—how we relate to the concept of death. Note how the grammatical subjects provide a coherent line of reasoning even though at the heart of the passage lies an abstract idea.

> **We** continue to share with our remotest ancestors the most tangled and evasive attitudes about death, despite the great distance **we** have come in understanding some of the profound aspects of biology. **We** have as much distaste for talking about personal death as for thinking about it; *it* is an indelicacy, like talking in mixed company about venereal disease or abortion in the old days. **Death** on a grand scale does not bother us in the same special way; **we** can sit around a dinner table and discuss war, involving 60 million volatilized human deaths, as though **we** were talking about bad weather; **we** can watch abrupt bloody death every day, in color, on films and television, without blinking back a tear. But when the numbers of dead are very small, and very close, **we** begin to think in scurrying circles. At the very center of the problem is the naked cold **deadness** of one's own self, the only reality in nature of which **we** can have absolute certainty, and **it** is unquestionable, unthinkable. **We** may be even less willing to face the issue at first hand than our predecessors because of a secret new hope that maybe **it** will go away. **We** like to think, hiding the thought, that with all the marvelous ways in which *we* seem now to lead nature around by the nose, perhaps **we** can avoid the central problem if **we** just become, next year, say, a bit smarter.

2. The expletive "there is"

The expletive "there is" ("there are," "there were") are useful when a writer means that something exists:

> There are several reasons for recycling.
> There is every reason to believe that a third political party will grow stronger in the future.

But when you can use a concrete noun paired with a more vigorous verb, the prose will be tighter. If you are unconvinced on the "there" issue, read the following paragraph from an essay on Writing Assignment 4 (Chapter 2).

> Children and the ability to have them are equally important to the society of the Small People. *There is* only one word for sex in their language and it translates as "to plant a wise one." To me this implies the final product is more important than the act of "planting a wise one." *There is* also a great emphasis put on childhood. *There are* seven terms used to describe stages of life from birth to puberty. *There is* only one word describing life after puberty.

This paragraph conveys the existence of the terms but very little additional reasoning. Poor focus is combined with choppy prose and needless passive verbs. Note how easy it is to avoid vigorous, active prose once you let the "there disease" take over. Let's fix the focus in three of these sentences.

Original

> There is also a great emphasis put on childhood. There are seven terms used to describe stages of life from birth to puberty. There is only one word describing life after childhood. (original)

Revision

> They clearly emphasize childhood, using seven terms to describe stages of life from birth to puberty, with only one word describing life after childhood. (revision)

The revision is tighter and reveals the logical relationship between each point. When the sentences stood isolated with their "theres," that logic was less obvious.

3. Overuse of "to be"

Beware of the verb "to be" (am, is, are, was, were). It is, of course, an important verb, but again, it states existence (being) only, and you often want your prose to be more expressive than that. Here's another reason to use passive verbs sparingly; they always, by definition, contain a form of the verb "to be." The same applies to "there are" sentences.

4. Dangling modifiers

Experienced writers often turn verbs into **verbal modifiers** (participles such as running, buying, avoiding). Such transformations increase sentence fluency and combine ideas to express logical relationships. Look at the examples below.

(two choppy sentences)

She *thought* critically about the issue. She *recognized* that her opponents had a good argument.

(one revision)

Thinking critically about the issue, she recognized that her opponents had a good argument.

(another option)

She thought critically about the issue, *recognizing* that her opponents had a good argument.

Such modifiers can enhance the fluency of your prose, but you need to be cautious about their logic. When you use a verbal as a modifier, the person or object serving as the sentence subject must usually also work logically as the agent of the modifier.

In the two revisions above, "she" is logical as the agent of "thinking" or "recognizing" as well as the grammatical subject of the actual verb in each variant of the sentence.

When the logical agent is missing from the sentence, the verbal modifier is said to dangle, hence the term **dangling modifier.**

Newspaper columnist Herb Caen, a stickler for sound sentence structure, was disgusted with himself when he fell into the dangling modifier trap:

"Having used up all his frequent-flier miles to Paris to woo and win her, Attorney Joe Freitas and Douce Francois . . ."

Had Caen looked back, he would have noticed that it wasn't logical for both of them to have used his frequent flier miles in this context, and Douce was unlikely to have been wooing herself. As he wrote in a future correction, "right there I should have stopped and started over."

EXERCISE 9D

Revising Dangling Modifiers

Many an experienced writer has lost track of the logic in her sentence. Identify the illogical dangling modifiers in these examples from published writers and recommend a remedy.

*1. While writing today's piece, Gerald Nachman's column was lost in the computer. (Did his column write itself?)

2. After passing around pictures of Christopher, the couple's conversation returned to the movie, *El Norte.* (Can a conversation pass pictures around?)

3. Walking up the staircase to Joyce Carol Oates' office in the Creative Arts building, through the halls that smell of artists' paint, past the neat rows of studios and classrooms, the blood-stained story of her most recent book, "Angel of Light," seems a tale told on another planet. (Did her blood-stained story walk up the staircase?)

4. Speaking as an old friend, there has been a disturbing tendency in statements emanating from Beijing to question the good faith of President Reagan on issues like Taiwan. (Do you see how the "there"construction has led former President Nixon astray? Did a disturbing tendency speak as an old friend?)

A wrap-up on writing style

1. Focus your thoughts and your writing on precisely what you want to say. When logically possible, prefer concrete, consistent subjects. As ideas develop through a paragraph, your sentence subjects may also develop and change, reflecting the new information introduced in the previous sentence.

2. Unless you have compelling reasons for preferring the passive voice, choose active verbs which allow for more direct, vigorous expression of your ideas.

3. Unless you intend to express the existence of something, avoid the over-used, empty phrases "there are" and "it is" and in the process look for more vigorous verbs.

4. To increase the flow of ideas, expand your sentence repertoire with appositives and verbal modifiers.

Revising for sharp sentence and paragraph focus will help to maintain the clear, direct expression you and your readers demand, no matter what your academic or professional discipline. But keep in mind that revising is often most effective as a late stage in the writing process. We may expect a first draft to have several poorly focused sentences and paragraphs. Look back at Chapter 1 to refresh your memory on the writing process.

EXERCISE 9E

Sharpening Sentence Focus for Clear Expression and Fluent Style

A. Revise the following sentences for good focus, combining where appropriate for a smooth, logical flow of ideas.

Example: It was while I was waiting in the registration line that the realization came to me of how complicated a university is.

(revision)

While I was waiting in the registration line, I came to realize (or I realized) how complicated a university is.

1. Fear of brutality from customers is a concern many prostitutes have.

2. When it is seen that a criminal act is being committed, a call should be placed to the police.

3. A strike is used when employees want things their employers are unwilling to provide.

4. The leaders have determined that the spiritual initiate has no need of worldly things, so only minimum wages are paid.

5. There is a much bigger emphasis placed on the role of the individual in this generation than in our parents' generation.

6. Teenagers are easily influenced by TV. Specific violent acts have been committed by teenagers after such acts have been shown on prime time.

7. The people of this tribe are literate, given that they have twenty terms for "book." There also may be several kinds of artwork they create, since they have nine words for "artist."

8. Having developed a complex social order, cultural patterns have been shown by the people of this tribe. These patterns are reflected in their arts and their theater.

B. Now try your hand at revising this student paragraph with the same strategies in mind. Note how difficult it is to follow the writer's reasoning in this poorly focused paragraph.

> There are many ways to be a bad teacher. There are mistakes made by bad teachers that come in a variety of forms. Assignments are given unclearly so that when papers are graded it isn't known what students are graded on or what the grade means. Grading by the ineffective teacher is according to arbitrary standards, so students think their grades are unfair. There are problems with explanations given by bad teachers and understanding is hard to arrive at. This disorganization can be seen by students when the poor teacher fails to bring all materials to class. There are many explanations given, but the dissatisfaction of students is clearly not done away with. In such cases, it is not clear who is responsible for a bad grade—the student or the teacher.

 ## WRITING ASSIGNMENT 18

Revising an Essay

For your final assignment in this text, we would like you to choose one of the assignments you completed earlier and revise it in light of material covered in later chapters. For example, in assignment #9, Chapter 4, you were asked to write a formal argument which included the opposition's point of view, the counterargument. Now you can review the counterargument (and your own reasoning) to see if it contains any fallacies (Chapter 8) or inadequately defined terms (Chapter 9). You can review and revise your writing style for parallel structure (Chapter 6), appropriate use of the passive, concrete sentence subjects and appositives (Chapter 9). You may choose to follow a similar revision process for a different writing assignment.

Whichever assignment you choose, these skills and the passage of time will enable you to do an excellent job of revision.

SUMMARY

Words at a high level of abstraction such as "success" and "obscene" must be defined.

Definitions can affect how people view themselves and others, "addiction" being only one example.

Language is an abstract system of symbols.

The assignation of a particular meaning to a given term remains essentially arbitrary.

Meaning is dependent to a large degree on the individual, the context, and the interpretative community.

Political systems and advertising often manipulate abstract language for their own purposes.

The power to abstract is what makes us human. Specific, concrete details are what flesh out our ideas so our readers can grasp, visualize, and retain meaning.

Rather than contradictory, these two imperatives—the abstract and the concrete—are best seen as complementary in both our writing and our thinking.

For a vigorous and concise writing style, writers prefer concrete subjects and active verbs, and use "there is" only to express existence.

Combining and expanding sentences with appositives and verbal modifiers will increase the logical flow of ideas.

KEY TERMS

Distinguishing characteristics in logical definition, the ways in which a term differs from other terms in the same class.

Appositives noun phrases placed beside nouns to elaborate on their meaning; useful for describing, identifying, and defining.

Passive voice a sentence construction in which the subject is acted upon, not doing anything in the sentence. Example: The constitutionality of the 1991 civil rights legislation was ruled on by the Supreme Court.

Active voice a sentence construction in which the subject performs the action of the sentence. Example: The Supreme Court ruled on the constitutionality of the 1991 civil rights legislation.

Verbal modifier participles—verb forms usually ending in *-ing*—used as sentence modifiers. Example: *Before resorting to violence,* we must thoroughly investigate all other means of resolution.

Dangling modifier a verbal modifier that lacks a logical agent in the clause it modifies. Example: *Before resorting to violence,* all other means of resolution must be thoroughly investigated.

"You've taught me how to think."

Appendix
I

Research and Documentation

RESEARCH

Think First

Before you rush to the library, topic in hand, to begin your research, there are two important preliminary steps.

First, narrow your topic to a clear question at issue (see Chapter 4), since such a question will help you to focus your research efforts. With only a topic to guide you, you might become lost in an avalanche of material, taking voluminous notes, most of which would have no application to your final paper.

Look at the difference in scope between an issue and a related question at issue:

Issue: Protection of the environment

Question at issue: Should endangered species be protected at the cost of jobs?

Imagine what it would be like to research the issue, and then imagine what it would be like to research the question at issue. Which would be easier?

Sometimes, however, you will need to do a little investigating in the library before you are able to arrive at a question at issue. Or you may be led to revise your question at issue as your research leads you in unexpected directions. But generally, narrowing the focus of your research will pay substantial dividends in time and energy.

As well as establishing, if possible, a question at issue before beginning your research, you should also construct an argument both for and against the question at issue. This argument will consist of premises in their roughest form—not developed, not supported, not refined.

You will already have some knowledge based on your experience, your reading. This may be general knowledge, but it will be sufficient to enable you to construct a preliminary argument.

The two advantages to this approach are:

1. You are not overwhelmed by the opinions of experts, feeling as if they have left you nothing to say.
2. Your research has a focused, precise purpose as you look for support for your premises, discovering in the process gaps in your reasoning and counterarguments that had not occurred to you.

How to Begin Your Research

Most libraries are equipped with computer databases in which you can research your topic under subject, author, or title headings. Resources vary from library to library, but most offer databases that list recent newspapers, magazines, and journals. If you need sources dated earlier than the past decade or so, you may need to consult your librarian about traditional indexes.

DOCUMENTATION

What Information Should Be Documented?

1. All direct quotations.
2. All indirect quotations in which you summarize the thoughts of others without quoting them directly. For example:

   Semanticist S. I. Hayakawa notes that although poetry and advertising seem unrelated, they actually share many characteristics (162).

3. All facts and statistics that are not common knowledge. If we were to state that many modern marriages end in divorce, documentation would not be necessary because the assertion reflects common knowledge. But if we state that 25 percent of the high school seniors in this country have tried cocaine, we must provide documentation; our readers would want to know the source of this conclusion to evaluate for themselves its reliability.

How Should It Be Documented?

Although each discipline has its preferred style of documentation, the two most common styles are set forth in the Modern Language Association (MLA) and the American Psychological Association (APA) style guides. English and the humanities prefer the MLA, whereas the social sciences prefer the APA.

Both guides rely on parenthetical documentation—author and page number identified in the text of the paper—with a list of cited works and all relevant publishing information at the end of the paper.

Although a teacher may require a certain style of documentation, most are more concerned about consistency than about which style the student uses. Following is a brief introduction to the MLA and the APA styles of documentation as they apply to a quotation taken from a book by one author and to a quotation taken from a magazine article.

The MLA Style of Documentation

For a book by one author (MLA):

Introduce the material being cited with a signal phrase, usually the author's name, and use a parenthetical citation stating the page number of the sentence.

```
S. I. Hayakawa points out that advertising and poetry are
alike in that "they both strive to give meaning to the data
of everyday experience" (162).
```

Readers can then turn to the list of works cited at the end of the paper to discover the title and publishing information, which will be listed under the author's last name.

When the author is not identified in the text—when there is no signal phrase—the author is identified in the parenthetical citation.

```
Consumers want to identify with the happy, attractive peo-
ple featured in advertisements (Hayakawa 164).
```

Note that there is no punctuation between the author's name and the page reference.

For a magazine article (MLA):

Once again, you may identify the work and/or author in a signal phrase, placing the page number in a parenthetical citation.

```
In "Reinventing Baltimore," author Tony Hiss tells us that,
"A city [Baltimore] that was almost two-thirds white in
1960 is now almost three-fifths black" (41).
```

Or, in the absence of a signal phrase, you may identify both the author and the page number in a parenthetical citation.

```
Baltimore, "almost two-thirds white in 1960 is now almost
three-fifths black" (Hiss 41).
```

The list of works cited (MLA):

This list, to be titled "Works Cited," will be the final page of your paper and include all of the works cited in it. These works are listed in alphabetical order according to the last name of the author. It does not include works that you read but did not cite.

For a book by one author (MLA):

```
Hayakawa, S. I. Language in Thought and Action. Orlando:
Harcourt Brace Jovanovich, 1990.
```

Note that the information comes in three units—author, title, and publishing information—each separated by a period, and that they second line is indented five spaces under the first. You can find the publishing information on the reverse side of the title page of the book.

For a magazine article (MLA):

```
Hiss, Tony. "Annals of Place: Reinventing Baltimore." The
New Yorker 29 April 1991: 40-73.
```

The APA Style of Documentation

For a book by one author (APA):

Introduce the quotation using the author's name followed by the date of publication in parentheses. Place the page reference in parentheses at the end of the passage.

> Semanticist S. I. Hayakawa (1990) points out that advertis-
> ing and poetry are alike in that "they both strive to give
> meaning to the data of everyday experience" (p. 162).

If paraphrasing rather than quoting directly, include the author's name in a signal phrase followed by the publication date in parentheses, similar to the example above. Or, if the author is not identified in a signal phrase, place his/her name and the publication data in parentheses at the end of the sentence. Note that a page number is not required for a paraphrase.

> Consumers want to identify with the happy, attractive peo-
> ple featured in advertisements (Hayakawa, 1990).

For a magazine article (APA):

For a quotation taken from a magazine article, follow the same format required for a book by one author.

The list of works cited (APA):

In APA style, the alphabetical list of works cited is entitled "References" and conforms to the following guidelines:

1. List the authors by last names, and use initials instead of first names.
2. Place the date of publication in parentheses after the author's name.
3. Underline titles and subtitles, capitalizing only the first word of the title and proper nouns.

For a book by one author (APA):

> Hayakawa, S. I. (1990). <u>Language in thought and action.</u> Or-
> lando: Harcourt Brace Jovanovich.

For a magazine article (APA):

> Hiss, T. (1991, April 29). Annals of place: reinventing
> Baltimore. <u>The New Yorker,</u> pp. 40–73.

This discussion of documentation is a brief overview of the choices and formats available to you. For a complete guide to documentation, refer to a contemporary English handbook or to the Modern Language Association or American Psychological Association style guides.

Incorporating the Ideas of Others into Your Own Writing

If you want your paper to read smoothly, you must take care to integrate direct quotations and paraphrases of other people's ideas into the grammatical flow of your sentences. Don't just "drop" them with a thud into a paragraph. Rely, rather, on a ready supply of introductory phrases with which to slide them in gracefully, such as "As Freud discovered," "Justice O'Connor notes," and "According to *The New York Times.*"

Sometimes, to make a quotation fit in smoothly with your own writing, you must add a word or words. Such additions are placed in brackets. For example:

> Carson McCullers sets a strangely luminous night scene:

> > There was a party at the banquet table in the center, and green-white August moths had found their way in from the night and fluttered about the clear candle flames.

She seems to make a point of the "green-white August moths [that] had found their way in from the night. . . ."

As well as introducing quotations and paraphrases smoothly into the syntax of your sentence, you must also pay attention to semantics. Don't assume that the relevance of the quotation is self-evident. Make its relationship to your reasoning explicit. Is it an example? an appeal to authority? premise support? a counterargument? Whatever the case, the purpose of the quotation—how it relates to the point you are making—should be made explicit.

Punctuation and Format of Quotations

Periods and commas are placed *inside* quotations marks unless the quotation is followed by a parenthetical citation, in which case the period follows the citation.

> "Writing, like life itself, is a voyage of discovery," said Henry Miller, author of <u>Tropic of Cancer</u>.

> "Thinking is the activity I love best, and writing to me is simply thinking through my fingers."

> —Isaac Asimov

> "The true relationship between a leader and his people is often revealed through small, spontaneous gestures" (Friedman 106).

Colons and semicolons go outside quotation marks.

> Read Hemingway's "Hill Like White Elephants"; we'll discuss it at our next meeting.

Use single quotation marks [' '] for quotations within quotations.

> "In coping with the violence of their city, Beirutis also seemed to disprove Hobbes's prediction that life in the 'state of nature' would be 'solitary.'"

> —Thomas Friedman, From Beirut to Jerusalem

If the quotation is more than three lines long, it should be indented and single spaced. No quotation marks are necessary.

Omitting Words from a Direct Quotation

Sometimes we don't want to include all of a quotation, but just certain sections of it that apply to the point we are making. In this case, we may eliminate a part or parts of the quotation by the use of *ellipsis:* three spaced periods that indicate the intentional omission of words.

1. Something left out at the beginning.

> ". . . writers should be read but not seen. Rarely are they a winsome sight."
>
> —Edna Ferber

2. Something left out in the middle.

> "Everything goes by the board: honor, pride, decency . . . to get the book written. If a writer has to rob his mother, he will not hesitate; the 'Ode on a Grecian Urn' is worth any number of old ladies."
>
> —William Faulkner

3. Something left out at the end.

> "I'd like to have money. And I'd like to be a good writer. These two can come together. . . ." [Note: the first dot is the period that ends the sentence.]
>
> —Dorothy Parker

Appendix
II

He or She?

*I*n recent decades we have become increasingly aware of how inadequate English is when we need to make specific gender references. We find no problem when we know a person's name, but often we need to refer to individuals in a more general way. *They* and *them* work well for people or things, but do you know anyone who answers to *it*?

This deficiency in our language reflects more than a simple inconvenience. The way we use language—the choices we make, the emphasis we place—suggests a broad range of personal and community attitudes, a world view, conscious and subliminal. A world described only in terms of masculine references assumes a world dominated by men. It is not surprising, therefore, that as women began to share the public worlds of business, politics, medicine, art, and sport, the universal masculine referents presented a bruising contradiction and a linguistic dilemma for writers and public speakers.

Not so many years ago, readers were content to let the masculine pronouns stand for all humanity. No longer. While some traditionalists still prefer the familiar surface of prose to be uncluttered by the complications to which revision of pronouns leads, a growing majority is no longer willing to accept a discourse that renders females invisible.

Attempts to invent a new singular pronoun comparable to the helpful plural "they" to solve this problem have so far failed. In the meantime we are left with a number of choices. We must choose carefully on the basis of audience, purpose, circumstance, context, and, ultimately, personal inclination, all the time recognizing the implications of our choice.

Often we can use a plural noun to which the all-purpose plural pronouns—they, their, them—refer:

Writers need to be aware of *their* audience when choosing language.

But when the noun we are referring to is singular, we have various choices, many of which may displease some readers:

Each writer must consider the audience when revising <u>his or her</u> [<u>his/her</u>] paper.

First, <u>he/she</u> [<u>she/he, s/he</u>] must decide how much background information the particular audience will need.

First, <u>he</u> must decide how much background information the particular audience will need. [This represents the traditional use of "he" as a referent for both males and females.]

First, <u>she</u> must decide how much background information the particular audience will need. [This choice redresses centuries of exclusion.]

Or we can sometimes drop the pronoun:

Each writer must consider the audience when revising a paper. [A simplification of" . . . when revising his/her paper."]

Many readers object to the awkwardness that multiple pronouns create in the flow of a sentence. Others are offended by the implicit sexism of relying exclusively on the third person masculine pronoun [he, him, his].

Usage is changing, slowly, to allow <u>they/them/their</u> to refer to grammatically singular nouns and particularly to the pronoun "everyone," a practice that is standard in spoken English.

<u>Everyone</u> should remember to include opposing views in <u>their</u> written arguments.

Almost <u>everyone</u> knows someone, often someone in <u>their</u> own family, who is addicted to drugs.

In the meantime, the point is to be sensitive to the audience and aware of the power of language, while at the same time representing issues and events accurately and observing conventions of written English as closely as possible.

Selected Answers

In keeping with the spirit of successful critical thinking, we acknowledge that considerable variation will emerge as you address the exercises in the text. Where we think it will help you, we do offer a limited selection of sample responses.

Chapter 2
EXERCISE 2B

Distinguishing Between Facts, Inferences, and Judgments

1. This is an inference based on a collection of unstated facts and assumptions. It is also a judgment; the term "should" expresses the writer's approval.

Chapter 3
EXERCISE 3A

Reducing Simple Arguments to Standard Form

4. 1. Anything that involves personal rights and the onset of life raises serious moral questions.
   2. Abortion involves a woman's right to privacy and the question of when life begins.
   ∴ Abortion raises important moral questions.

EXERCISE 3D

Identifying Hidden Assumptions

1. a. [Musicians don't understand business.]
   b. Maggie is a musician.
   ∴ She won't understand the business end of the partnership.

Chapter 5

EXERCISE 5B

Distinguishing Inductive from Deductive Reasoning

1. Inductive. The reasoning moves from specifics to a generalization. The conclusion—that Marie is out of town—does not necessarily follow. There are other possible explanations: she may be ill, or worse.

4. Deductive. The conclusion—that Philippe is devoted to his glass of red wine—follows of necessity from the premises. We can reach no other conclusion given the premises, and the reasoning moves from the general to the specific.

Chapter 6

EXERCISE 6A

Identifying Relationships Between Classes

1. Exclusion

EXERCISE 6B

Determining the Validity of Categorical Syllogisms

1. Invalid

2. Valid

EXERCISE 6C

Evaluating Deductive Arguments in Everyday Language

1. The argument reduced to a categorical syllogism:

    a. Plagiarism is wrong.
    b. Paraphrasing the words of others without proper acknowledgment is the same as plagiarism.
    ∴ Paraphrasing the words of others without proper acknowledgment is wrong.

Circle diagrams to determine validity:

The argument is valid.

The first premise—plagiarism is wrong—is a judgment, one that is part of our culture's shared belief system and therefore acceptable.

The second premise—paraphrasing the words of others without proper acknowledgment is the same as plagiarism—is also a judgment shared by the community, especially the academic community, and is therefore acceptable.

Final evaluation of the argument:
Because it is valid and the premises acceptable, the argument is sound.

EXERCISE 6D

Determining the Validity of Hypothetical Arguments

1. If *a* (through window), then *b* (window unlocked).
    b (window unlocked).

∴ *a* (through window).

The consequent is affirmed so the argument is invalid. An unlocked window is not the only way for a burglar to enter a house.

5. If *a* (respect opinion), then *b* (seek advice).

not *b* (don't seek advice).

∴ not *a* (don't respect opinion).

The consequent is denied so the argument is valid.

EXERCISE 6G

Editing the Illogical Series

1. This sentence suggests that "extra hours" and "[working] through many lunch hours" are separate classes when in fact one class is a member of the other. One possible revision:

> In their attempt to excel, these people will work extra hours, often giving up their lunch hour.

EXERCISE 6H

Supplying Parallel Structure

2. She // rushed home, threw her assorted debris into a closet and prepared dinner for her guests.

6. There are two misfits—"economic" and "social"—adjectives in a list of nouns. The sentence can be corrected by replacing them with "economics" and "social status."

Chapter 7

EXERCISE 7A

Evaluating Inductive Arguments

1. The conclusion: all the containers of Sweet and Sour Yogurt filled that day are safe for consumption.

> The target population: all the containers of Sweet and Sour Yogurt filled that day.
> The projected property: safe for consumption.
> The sample: one out of every thousand containers (about one every 15 minutes) filled that day.
> Evaluation: the conclusion is justified because the method—random selection—and the frequency—one container every 15 minutes—lead to a representative sample.

Chapter 8

EXERCISE 8A

Identifying Fallacies

2. Slippery slope: This argument suggests a chain reaction that begins with allowing students to turn in papers after the due date and ends with all of America becoming "more ignorant," too large a consequence to result from a teacher's lenience.

9. Poisoning the well: Such an assertion puts the listener or reader on the defensive, forcing him to defend his patriotism and relieving the speaker or writer of the need to supply substantive premises in support of his conclusion that Americans should vote for Republicans.

16. False cause: Superstition is often based on false cause reasoning. In this example, walking under the ladder occurred before he lost his wallet and received a speeding ticket, so he assumes on the basis of the sequence of events that the first event caused the other two.

27. Hasty generalization: He can't conclude on the basis of one incident that all hospitals care only about money, not about people. The sample is too small for such a conclusion.

33. Begging the question: This advertising slogan restates the conclusion—"that S & W vegetables are the best"—as a premise—"they use only premium quality." The two statements make essentially the same claim.

Chapter 9

EXERCISE 9B

Recognizing Appositives

1. Appositive 1: "one they will soon recognize on the streets of Ibarra and in towns and cities beyond." The modified noun: "peculiarity"
Appositives 2 and 3: "a disregard for danger, a companionship with death."
The modified noun: "something"
Appositives 4, 5, 6, and 7: "the antic bravado, the fatal games, the coffin shop beside the cantina, the sugar skulls on the frosted cake." The modified noun (or pronoun): "it"

EXERCISE 9C

Creating Appositives

1. New York, *a city of danger and opportunity,* has long been the destination of America's adventurous young.

3. People have very different ideas about the meaning of poverty, a *condition that to some suggests insufficient income, to others laziness, and to still others a state of unwarranted discomfort.*

EXERCISE 9D

Revising Dangling Modifiers

1. The dangling modifier: While writing today's piece (the subject, "column," can't write).
One possible revision: While writing today's piece, Gerald Nachman lost his column in the computer.

EXERCISE 9E

Sharpening Sentence Focus for Clear Expression and Fluent Style

1. Many prostitutes fear brutality from customers.

Credits

PHOTO CREDITS

Frontispiece
Page ii, Drawing by Weber; Copyright (c) 1987 *The New Yorker Magazine, Inc.*

Chapter 1
Page 2, Reprinted with permission from *Detroit Free Press* and Richard Guindon.

Page 5, DOONSBURY Copyright (c) G.B. Trudeau. Reprinted with permission of UNIVERSAL PRESS SYNDICATE. All rights reserved.

Page 12, Drawing by Leo Cullum; Copyright (c) 1995 *The New Yorker Magazine, Inc.*

Page 15, Drawing by Bernard Schoenbaum; Copyright (c) 1991 *The New Yorker Magazine, Inc.*

Chapter 2
Page 17, The Far Side cartoon by Gary Larson is reprinted by permission of Chronicle Features, San Francisco, CA.

Page 22, The Far Side cartoon by Gary Larson is reprinted by permission of Chronicle Features, San Francisco, CA.

Page 23, Taken from the MONEY LIST column by Brendan Boyd. Copyright (c) UNIVERSAL PRESS SYNDICATE. Reprinted with permission. All rights reserved.

Chapter 3
Page 36, Henrik Drescher

Page 41, Graphic by Dan Hubig; Copyright (c) SAN FRANCISCO CHRONICLE Reprinted by permission.

Page 42, Copyright (c) 1991 by The New York Times Company. Reprinted by permission.

Page 59, DOONSBURY Copyright (c) G.B. Trudeau. Reprinted with permission of UNIVERSAL PRESS SYNDICATE. All rights reserved.

Chapter 4
Page 71, The "Quality Time" cartoon by Gail Machlis is reprinted courtesy of Chronicle Features, San Francisco, CA.

Page 72, Drawing by Koren; Copyright (c) 1988 *The New Yorker Magazine, Inc.*

Chapter 6
Page 112, Drawing by Frascino; Copyright (c) 1993 *The New Yorker Magazine, Inc.*

Chapter 7

Page 125, Drawing by R. Chast; Copyright (c) 1994 *The New Yorker Magazine, Inc.*

Page 129, GARFIELD Copyright (c) 1995 PAWS, INC. Reprinted with permission of UNIVERSAL PRESS SYNDICATE. All rights reserved.

Page 132, Henrik Drescher

Chapter 8

Page 142, The Far Side cartoon by Gary Larson is reprinted by permission of Chronicle Features, San Francisco, CA.

Page 144, DENNIS THE MENACE (R) used by permission of Hank Ketcham and Copyright (c) by North America Syndicate.

Page 146, Robert Gumpertz

Page 148, Drawing by Ed Fisher; Copyright (c) 1991 *The New Yorker Magazine, Inc.*

Page 152, Joseph Farris

Page 158, By permission of Mike Luckovich and Creators Syndicate.

Page 160, The "Quality Time" cartoon by Gail Machlis is reprinted by permission of Chronicle Features, San Francisco, CA.

Chapter 9

Page 170, Reprinted with permission from *Detroit Free Press* and Richard Guindon

Page 174, Drawing by R. Chast; Copyright (c) 1992 *The New Yorker Magazine, Inc.*

Page 176, THE FAR SIDE Copyright (c) 1994 FARWORKS, Inc. Dist. by UNIVERSAL PRESS SYNDICATE. Reprinted with permission. All rights reserved.

Page 177, Copyright (c) King Features Syndicate, Inc. All rights reserved. Reprinted with special permission of King Features Syndicate.

Page 182, Arnie Ten

Page 182, Arnie Ten

Page 184, Drawing by Handlesman; Copyright (c) 1995 *The New Yorker Magazine, Inc.*

Page 188, CALVIN AND HOBBES Copyright (c) 1993 Watterson. Dist. by UNIVERSAL PRESS SYNDICATE. Reprinted with permission. All rights reserved.

Page 190, Copyright © 1990 *The Big Book of Hell* by Matt Groening. All Rights Reserved. Reprinted by permission of Pantheon Books, a division of Random House, NY.

Page 198, Drawing by Koren; Copyright © 1988 *The New Yorker Magazine, Inc.*

TEXT CREDITS

Chapter 1

Pages 10-11, "The Writer" from *The Mind Reader*, copyright © 1971 by Richard Wilbur, reprinted by permission of Harcourt Brace Jovanovich, Inc.

Chapter 2

Page 21, "Commuter" from *Poems and Sketches of E. B. White*. Copyright © 1925 by E. B. White. Reprinted by permission of HarperCollins Publishers, Inc.

Pages 23-24, "Totleigh Riddles" by John Cotton from the *Times Literary Supplement*, July 24, 1981. Reprinted by permission of the author.

Pages 24-25, All lines from "Metaphors" from *Crossing the Water* by Sylvia Plath. Copyright © 1960 by Ted Hughes. Copyright renewed. Reprinted by permission of Harper-Collins Publishers, Inc.

Page 25, All lines from "Mirror" from *Crossing the Water* by Sylvia Plath. Copyright © 1963 by Ted Hughes. Originally appeared in *The New Yorker*. Reprinted by permission of HarperCollins Publishers, Inc.

Page 26, "The Loneliness of Being White," by Bruce Schoenfield, *New York Times*, May 14, 1995. Copyright © 1995 by The New York Times Company. Reprinted with permission.

Pages 33-35, "Hostess" by Donald Magnum. Reprinted by permission; Copyright © 1987 Donald Magnum. Orignally in *The New Yorker*.

Chapter 3

Page 39, "A's Aren't That Easy," by Clifford Adelman, *New York Times*, May 17, 1995. Copyright © 1995 by The New York Times Company. Reprinted with permission.

Pages 44-45, "They're Getting Older on Campus" from *The San Francisco Chronicle*, August 2, 1986. Copyright © 1986 by The San Francisco Chronicle. Reprinted by permission.

Pages 45-46, "Ethnic Restriction At Lowell High" from *The San Francisco Chronicle*, July 24, 1988. Copyright © 1988 by The San Francisco Chronicle. Reprinted by permission.

Pages 48-50, From *The San Francisco Chronicle*, April 19, 1995.

Page 56, Reprinted by permission of United Press International.

Chapter 4

Pages 81-83, "Free Needles Would Be a Help in S.F." by Randy Shilts from *The San Francisco Chronicle*, March 20, 1989. Copyright © 1989 by The San Francisco Chornicle. Reprinted by permission.

Chapter 5

Pages 92-94, Thomas Henry Huxley, *Autobiography and Selected Essays*. Boston, MA: Houghton Mifflin Company, 1909, pages 85-94.

Pages 94-97, From *Zen and the Art of Motorcycle Maintenance* by Robert M. Pirsig. By permission of William Morrow & Company, Inc.

Chapter 6

Pages 115-116, Alexander W. Allison et al., *The Norton Anthology of Poetry*. New York, NY: W. W. Norton & Company, Inc., 1970, page 370-371.

Pages 116-117, "Dulce et Decorum Est" by Wilfred Owen: *The Collected Poems of Wilfred Owen*. Copyright © 1963 by Chatto & Windus, Ltd. Reprinted by permission of New Directions Publishing Corporation.

Chapter 7

Page 130, From Roger Rasmussen, "SAT Slippage Is an Illusion," *Los Angeles Times*, September 19, 1991. Reprinted by permission of the author.

Page 131, "Sexism Rampant" by Dominick Amarante from *The Nation*, June 18, 1990. This article is reprinted from *The Nation* magazine/The Nation Company, Inc., Copyright © 1990.

Pages 131-133, "Schulman Replies" by Grace Schulman from *The Nation*, June 18, 1990. This article is reprinted from *The Nation* magazine/The Nation Company, Inc., Copyright © 1990.

Pages 134-135, "Dispute Over Claims of Ibuprofen Dangers." Copyright © 1990 by United Press International. Reprinted by permission of United Press International.

Pages 136-137, Arthur Conan Doyle, "A Study in Scarlet."

Chapter 8

Page 147, Taken from the *Dear Abby* column by Abigail Van Buren. Copyright © Universal Press Syndicate. Reprinted with permission. All rights reserved.

Page 147, *Miss Manners* reprinted by permission of United Feature Syndicate, Inc.

Page 150, "Lyle and Erik: Killers, Victims or Both?" by Anna Quindlen, *New York Times*, November 16, 1994. Copyright © 1994 by The New York

Chapter 9

Index